THE CHANGING FACE
OF ENGLAND

The Changing Scene. *The Mediaeval church of Mendham by the banks of the river Waveney is seen through the metal lattice of a modern bridge.*

THE CHANGING FACE OF
ENGLAND

THE STORY OF THE LANDSCAPE
THROUGH THE AGES

by

CHRISTOPHER
TRENT

*

WITH SIXTY-TWO PLATES
(INCLUDING FORTY
BY THE AUTHOR)
ENGRAVINGS & MAPS

W. W. NORTON & COMPANY, INC.

NEW YORK

CONTENTS

List of Illustrations, 6

Foreword, 9

I. The Building of the Landscape   13

II. Nature's Mantle   28

III. The Peopled Landscape   43

IV. Roman Outposts   58

V. Saxon Settlement   78

VI. The Mediaeval Landscape   94

VII. The Age of Transition, 1485–1603   108

VIII. The Age of Progress, 1603–1760   132

IX. Industrial Revolution, 1760–1900   152

X. Our Own Times   171

XI. A Glimpse of the Future   196

XII. Exploring Your Own District   205

Bibliography, 216

Index, 220

ILLUSTRATIONS

PLATES

The mediaeval church of Mendham seen through the metal lattice of
a modern bridge   *frontispiece*

The headwaters of the Dee   *facing page* 16

Ladram Bay, South Devon   17

The estuary of the Dee from the Wirral peninsula   32

The North York Moors and the valley of the Seph   32

Milldale and the river Dove   33

Avebury from the Air (*Aerofilms*)   48

Stonehenge from the Air (*Aerofilms*)   48

British Camp, Malvern Hills   49

The Giant of Cerne Abbas   49

Celtic or earlier field pattern seen from the air (*Aerofilms*)   64

Characteristic lynchets in chalk country (*Aerofilms*)   64

Maiden Castle from the Air (*Aerofilms*)   65

The hand of the Roman builders

  Main entrance to the Roman Fort of Anderida (Pevensey)   80

  Earthworks of the amphitheatre near Dorchester   80

The Foss Way near Easton Grey (*Copyright reserved: photo J. K. S.
St Joseph*)   81

Feudal pioneers of the far north

  Field reclaimed from the moorland by the shores of Loch Hope   96

  Crofters' fields like the strip cultivation of Saxon communities   96

A clearing in the Pennine moorlands   97

A modern forest clearing   97

On the hills of Ryedale   *Between pages* 104 *and* 105

Mediaeval bridge, Bradford-on-Avon

Mediaeval bridge, St Ives

The walls and cathedral of York

The West Gate of Canterbury

The Weald from Bexley Hill

Remains of ancient forests

  Sherwood forest   *facing page* 112

  Belvoir Chase

Land won from the sea
Salt marshes of North Norfolk   *facing page* 113
The coastal plain between Chichester and Bognor   113
Cobham Hall, an outstanding example of two styles of architecture
in a harmonious whole   128
Shropshire manor farm   129
Landscape gardening on the grand scale: Blenheim Park   129
Recent man/made landscapes
The new Bedford river   144
The Royal Military Canal, Kent   144
A Midland landscape   145
Knaresborough and the Nidd   145
The Midland Ouse at Newton Blossomville   160
Anemones in partially cleared woodland   161
The changing mountain scene   176
Intrusive pylons   176
An old town lives on: Rye, Sussex   177
The vanishing Broads   192
Under Northumberland Fells   192
More man/made landscapes
A suburb of Bath   193
The new road between Leatherhead and Dorking   193

Unless otherwise stated the photographs are the copyright
of the author.

Map of South-eastern England about 1800 B.C.   *page* 46

Map to show how the Roman roads opened out the English lowlands   60–1

An early mediaeval conception of Britain   84

Working the land in the eleventh century   86

Making an enclosure of wattle in Saxon times   87

Hunting in the forests, eleventh century   89

The shepherd and his flock, eleventh century   91

Harrowing about 1340   100

Sowing broadcast, fourteenth century   101

Reaping in the fourteenth century   102

Harvest time in the fourteenth century   103

The countryside in February, sixteenth century   123

Detail from the title page of *Arcadia*   124

Birmingham in the seventeenth century   133

Uffington Castle about 1800   154

Buckinghamshire early in the nineteenth century   156

Foreword

✦ ✦

THE LANDSCAPES of England show a unique combination o
natural beauty and man-made features. Except in the mountainous regions and the comparatively small areas of heathland and
uncultivated common, man's handiwork is everywhere superimposed on the contours of nature. Most of the south and east can
fairly be described as a garden on a vast scale.

It is almost impossible to imagine a South Devon landscape
without the scattered farmhouses, the tall-towered church in the
distance, the group of cottages on the far hillside, the trim chequerboard pattern made by hedge-girt fields and, above all, the bold
splashes of colour where the red earth has recently been turned.

Throughout the period of recorded history the face of Britain
has been changing rapidly. Within the last two centuries the
change has been accelerated, as science has revolutionized agriculture and the growth of population has made it necessary to cultivate more and more of the countryside.

The first of the cultivators arrived in Britain little more than
four thousand years ago, and carried out the first primitive agriculture on the lower slopes of the downs. The establishment of a
Romano-British government and the abundant prosperity of
Roman Britain produced a great change in the landscape. The
picture of the country as it was then can be reconstructed from
the work of Roman authors and from the results of recent archae-
ological research.

The next stage is represented by the Saxon settlements and the
establishment of village communities in large numbers, especially
near the rivers and on the coasts. The first clearing of the lowlands
had occurred in the Roman period but it was as Saxon England

9

developed that farming as we understand it today came into existence and a great number of 'leighs', or clearings, in the primeval
forest land began to open out the countryside of the weald and of
midland England.

From that time onwards the picture becomes clearer and clearer.
The influence of the Norman forest laws, the continuance of the
Saxon open field system, its gradual modification by enclosure in
the later Middle Ages, and the development of the farming estates,
are all important parts of the story.

The woollen boom which lasted from the thirteenth to the sixteenth century brought major changes to the face of the land. In
this period some areas, such as East Anglia, now consisting almost
entirely of arable land were given over largely to grassland for sheep
pasture. The growth and enrichment of the villages and the rebuilding of farmhouses were direct consequences of the national
prosperity. New materials were introduced for building, for
example, brick, and decorative effects were sought in half-timbered
houses and plaster façades.

With a rapidly growing population the accent in the eighteenth
and nineteenth centuries changes to the provision of additional
areas for cultivation. The effective draining of the fens produced
new and foreign-looking landscapes. New farming methods
made it possible to cultivate many areas which had been neglected
because of their poor soil. Even the second world war effected
major changes in the landscape as the high ground all over the
south came under the plough and the characteristic aspect of the
downs was changed.

The growth of urban communities during the last two hundred
years has brought in its train many other obvious changes, including the disappearance under bricks and mortar of whole rural
districts. It has also produced modifications not so easily recognized, by the development of the railway system, the widening of
roads and, still more recently, the establishment of the grid on a
nation-wide basis.

The whole story is one of human adaptation to changing circumstances reflected in the story of the landscape. It ends with the

very recent acceptance at government level of the need to conserve
the landscape—with the new ideas of town and country planning,
the creation of national parks, and the control of development. In
spite of this there are still important changes in progress and it is
possible to forecast how present economic conditions are likely to
influence the scenery of the country during the next half century.

In this book I have attempted to reconstruct the story from beginning to end in word and picture. The field is a vast one and I
hope readers will overlook the many sins of omission, of which I
am intensely conscious. If reading the book stimulates a fresh
interest in some of the many variations on the theme of England's
Changing Landscape I shall feel that I have not worked in vain.

I can say in all sincerity that I have visited every place mentioned, that every description of scene and building is from personal observation and that I have attempted the near-impossible
task of cross-checking the thousands of facts quoted. I am in-
debted, probably to a far greater extent than I realize, to the published work of scholars in many fields and more especially to the
authors of the books listed in the Bibliography, from every one of
which I have learned something new, and a few of which have
shone the bright light of certain knowledge on phases of the story
previously obscure or only partly illuminated in my mind.

I acknowledge with gratitude the help given by the individual
members of the British Museum staff who helped me to identify
many of the line illustrations in the text and am grateful, too, for
the permission granted by Macmillan & Co. to reproduce the
exquisite drawings on pages 86–91 and 100–3 from Green's *Short
History of the English People.*

Apart from the aerial views all the photographs are my own.
They represent scenes in many widely separated parts of the
countryside which in one way or another recreate in my imagination the picture of things as they were long ago—fragments, as it
were, of England today which either reproduce more or less
exactly or evoke the spirit of the England of yesteryear.

CHAPTER I

The Building of the Landscape

* *

IN THE BEGINNING, I like to imagine, there was a whirling gaseous incandescent mass, a sun in miniature trailing fiery streamers as it sped at incredible speed on its orbit round the parent sun. From this fiery planet our earth finally emerged after count⁄less ages. There are several more modern, perhaps more reliable, theories of the origin of the earth, but none which so strongly cap⁄tures the imagination.

My mind is terrestrial, firmly anchored to the vivid objects among which I live. I find it hard to give reality, even in my mind's eye, to the length of time that has elapsed since that violent cataclysm of nature. Yet against the times and distances which are the commonplaces of astronomy, the age of the earth is finite enough. I just cannot conceive what a million light years means. I know it can be defined as the distance travelled by light in a mil⁄lion years, but my mind is too restricted for the concept to register anything but mild wonder. It is too difficult to accept, as it were, the proposition that the twinkling of the star I saw last night was the light emitted by it hundreds of years ago, that the star I was looking at might not even exist at the moment I was observing it.

But when I am told that our earth began to be recognizable as an earth three thousand or even four thousand million years ago, that is something I can just grasp. I know what a million means, I know if I write fifteen books the length of this one I shall have written more than a million words. Although as a student I used to think that a thousand paces sounded a very long way, when I learnt that it was merely the Roman equivalent for approximately a mile, it did not sound nearly as far. I might even cover a thou⁄sand times a thousand paces in a year and then I would have taken a million paces. Multiply all that by four thousand and for paces or words read years and I have at least something that I can examine dispassionately and contemplate without the impotence of mind to which light years and millions of millions reduce me.

Another fact strikes me as very wonderful. In the primeval, unstable world there were all the elements that have gone to make up the world in which we live. What has happened has been the translation of molten and gaseous substances into solid ones. Wonderful as that transformation appears, it is at least something that we can comprehend, even though neither science nor contemplation can recreate the stages by which it has happened, nor name even a tithe of the causative factors which have been at work. Yet by now we hardly question the awful forces which nature can unleash, when atomic explosions are produced artificially. We take it for granted that radio-activity is something quite different from any other activity that we know.

With our own eyes as well as through the eyes of others in laboratories, we see solid things changing their very nature. We see something that looks and feels very much like a rock, and which, indeed, some geologists regard as a kind of rock, turn into entirely different substances when it is burnt in our household grates. We see the dead leaves and decaying vegetable matter of our woodlands, left undisturbed for a few years, turn into a kind of humus which bears very little relation to the things from which we know it is formed.

How life began on this planet of the sun on which we live we cannot demonstrate with the help of science, but science at least has done a great deal to school our minds to such vast improbabilities that most of us find little difficulty in accepting something that we cannot fully understand. So, the reflective and the unreflective join hands on common ground. Moreover, however obscure the origin and early development of our earth, the nearer in time we come to the present, the more certainty we have in pinpointing the stages which have produced our English landscapes, even though we are still talking of time measured in hundreds of millions of years.

This, then, is our starting-point—a molten mass which gradually cooled until the outer edge began to solidify and the planet began to form a stable crust. The first outer crust was composed of igneous rocks, that is to say, rocks which have solidified from fiery material. No one knows what it looked like, because no trace of the original rock surface has been found in any part of the world.

The present atmosphere is the product of vegetation, for originally there was no oxygen, which is 'breathed' out by all trees and plants. The circulation of an atmosphere containing water vapour created the agents which have done more than any others to mould the face of the land and which are still at work re-fashioning the landscapes we know so well. As Tennyson has it in *In Memoriam*,

> The hills are shadows and they flow
> From form to form and nothing stands.

The sea, the rivers, the rain, the winds, and even the destructive power of frost—all these spring from the atmosphere and are as active in sculpturing fresh vistas as they have ever been.

But thousands of millions of years had yet to pass before these chisels and abrazers of nature could work upon the face of an earth which we might recognize as the ancestor of our own motherland. As the earth cooled further, immense forces of disruption were unleashed inside it. Explosive masses of gaseous material sought to escape from their newly-made prison. They found the weak spots in the still brittle crust, burst through it, and cooled rapidly into the granites and basalts and the other igneous rocks which we can see today. As the crust thickened, many of these eruptions lacked the power to burst through all the layers above them and cooled more slowly underneath the outermost crust, so forming another type of granite rock.

The wayfarer in Britain can see for himself the difference in the colouring and composition of granites in different parts of the country; the glittering crystalline grey of the stone from which the city of Aberdeen is built is quite different from the darker hues of the stone-built cottages of Bodmin Moor, yet both are granites but of different composition, differently cooled, under different pressures. Those few (and how few they are) who have completed the arduous journey to Cape Wrath, are rewarded with a sight which no other part of Britain can offer. The rocks of the Cape Wrath promontory are of a kind of granite, but they are so pigmented that even on a dull day they have a pinkish hue. On a fine day as the sun sets over the Atlantic they glow with an ever more vivid red until as the sun touches the horizon they look as if once more they were molten, their colour enhanced and reflected back by the rays of the setting sun.

Some of the igneous rocks, the granites and the basalts, are the oldest rocks exposed at the surface of our modern landscapes, but igneous rocks are not necessarily the oldest. The columns of Fingal's Cave and the Giant's Causeway are relatively young in geological time. It seems as though the earth's crust becomes unstable periodically and new igneous eruptions break forth on each occasion. The existence of still active volcanoes is evidence enough that complete stability has not yet been reached. The last active volcano in England was in Derbyshire, where comparatively recent lava rocks are found.

The most ancient part of Great Britain is the north-west of Scotland, which is a worn-down plateau—all that remains of a mountain massif which raised its peaks tens of thousands of feet at a time when the far more recent hills of southern England were still under the sea. The oldest rocks in England are in Leicestershire's Charnwood Forest, rocks of extreme hardness which have resisted the weathering of century after century better than any other rocks in the kingdom. The granites of Cumberland are very old. So, too, are the rocks of south-western England, of Dartmoor, Bodmin Moor, and Land's End. Granite also occurs in widely separated areas. It is quarried at Rowley Regis near Birmingham and forms part of the structure of the Wrekin in Shropshire and of the Malvern Hills, to name only three typical examples.

We are on firm ground therefore, if we say that the granite rocks of Devon and Cornwall are older than those which underlie the rolling vistas of Salisbury Plain or the Weald of Sussex. It is

The headwaters of the Dee. *The Dee emerges as a swiftly-flowing stream from springs in the Arenig group of mountains. Already, though so near its source, it is carrying small boulders towards the valley, while its erosive action is sculpturing miniature cliffs.*

Ladram Bay, South Devon. *Here sea and weather have combined to throw back the strata which formed the cliff face into a semicircular bay, while especially resistant portions of the old cliff face are left as isolated stacks.*

wrong, though, to imagine that a thousand million years ago the heights of Dartmoor and Bodmin Moor, or the incomparable peaks of the Lake District, presented an appearance even remotely similar to the landscapes of today. In that great period of time nature, the sculptor, has been at work without remission, constantly modifying and changing the face of the land while, as we shall see later, the subsequent rise and fall of sections of the earth's crust has elevated some areas and depressed others.

The earth's atmosphere is heavily charged with water vapour. Mist or cloud is precipitated as it cools in the form of water. This water deposited over the crust of the earth to form oceans and seas and rivers, set up a physical cycle which continues today. The seas evaporate into the atmosphere, the atmosphere returns the evaporated moisture without fail, not necessarily over the seas from which it was taken but as often as not on the land masses adjoining, where the hills and mountains force up the air currents and by doing so cool the water vapour that they carry. In brief, the effect of water on the face of the primeval land masses was to break them up and to lay the foundations of new, more varied and more interesting scenes.

Water acts in many ways. The waves of the sea break up the rocks along its margin, undermine the cliffs, and for ever eat further and further into the substance of the land. Within the last thousand years whole English villages have gone down cliff through the action of sea and rainwater. Dunwich was a flourishing and busy port in the Middle Ages. Today nothing at all survives save a name and some coastguard cottages on the Suffolk coast. The church is buried half a mile out to sea. The Moot Hall of Aldeburgh which was once the centre of another flourishing seaport, stands forlornly on the promenade. The mediaeval church of Pakefield by Lowestoft is set precariously on the edge of the cliff, its existence still threatened in spite of all that man can do by protective works to avert the peril of the sea. Admittedly these East Anglian rocks are soft, by comparison with the igneous rocks. Because they are soft they are more friable, more prone to yield before the savage attacks of the sea. But all this has

B

happened in a mere thousand years. When we speak of the tools which nature has used to fashion the landscape, we are thinking of thousands of thousands of years.

All along the south coast where the rocks are harder than those of East Anglia, though still not as hard as granite, we can see the effects of sea erosion most vividly in the detached rocks, the stacks and pinnacles of the Needles, or of the Dorset coast. Scarcely a year goes by without mention in the newspapers of a major cliff fall at Beachy Head. Each fall widens the Channel, if only by a few inches. Within living memory the whole contour of the coast from Splash Point by Seaford to Beachy Head has changed out of recognition. What was formerly a well-marked and much used cliffway down to the promenade at Seaford, has disappeared. What is more, the process is continuing in spite of substantial concrete works designed to prevent the sea from eroding away the base of the cliffs.

It is an axiom that what nature takes away in one place it re-places in another. Some of the rock substance which is eroded away or pounded to fragments by the waves, becomes the sand and pebbles of the typical sea shore, and is sometimes carried by strong coastal currents hundreds of miles from its point of origin. The smaller the particles into which the rocks are broken, the fur-ther may these particles travel before they are deposited. The same is true of the rock fragments and other debris carried into the sea by rivers.

'Constant dripping wears away a stone.' That is a proverb the truth of which anyone can judge for himself who has seen a mere trickle of water near the source of a mountain stream scoop out a cup-shaped hollow or pool in the solid rock on which it falls. Lower downstream swift-flowing rivers cut deeper and deeper into the bedrock and make waterfalls where two different kinds of rock are being attacked and one proves more resistant than the other. The harder rock stands firm while the softer rock below it is eaten away and the water cascades from the upper layer to the lower. Yet the upper layer, too, is being worn away all the time, so that the edge of the waterfall gradually moves back.

Frost is a great destructive agent, solely and simply because water at freezing point, when it turns to ice, expands. We all know what happens when pipes freeze up. The water inside them turns to ice and, expanding, bursts the pipe. We may not notice this until the ice melts, when the water begins to flow out through the cracks that have been made, but the damage was done at the moment of freezing. So it is with the crust of the earth. Water seeps into the upper layers of the soil and into minute fissures in sheer rock faces. When it freezes it expands, breaks up the soil and cracks the rocks, so that they are more liable to direct erosion by rain water or by river water flowing over them. Every motorist on the lesser roads of Britain's hilly districts can see this process in action. On level stretches the surface may be reasonably good, but as soon as a gradient is reached, the road is scarred with potholes and fissures, where rain water has flowed down hills already undermined by frost. Here is erosion unleashed upon a specially vulnerable medium.

If so much can be achieved by so little, there is no difficulty in understanding the terrific sculptural effects achieved by the great glaciers which until comparatively recent time covered all Northern and Central districts of what is now England. They scoured out ever deeper valleys as they moved down from the mountain tops, the rocks crumbling before them. They carried boulders and rock fragments with them and deposited them many miles away. Still evident signs of their progress can be seen in Lake District valleys, in the 'spires and pinnacles' of Dovedale and other deepcut gorges, and in the now grasscovered piles of rock and stone which the casual tourist accepts without question as hills just like any others in the landscape. In fact, many of these unexpected hillocks on valley floors, including several in Wensleydale, contain all the debris deposited by a glacier when it was melting, thereafter being covered by soil and finally in recent times by trees.

If anyone doubts how quickly piles of rock debris can be covered by grass and other vegetation, he need only look at the older slag heaps in the coalmining districts and the few remaining undeveloped bombed sites in our cities. The slag heaps will be entirely grass-covered within fifty years and often in a much shorter time, while on the bombed sites there are windborne rosebay willow-herb and many other plants, and even a few young trees, all sown there by nature and apparently flourishing as vigorously as in the prepared soil of nearby gardens.

It has been calculated that if England with all its cities and roads and factories were left deserted for a thousand years, virtually all sign of man's handiwork would have disappeared. Some of the more massive steel and concrete buildings might still be standing, though already beginning to crumble away. Of the roads there would be no sign under the tangled mass of undergrowth, while almost all the brick-built homes of the people would be a mass of ruins covered by plants, if not entirely obliterated. The power of vegetation over millions of years, therefore, quite apart from the colour and variety it produces, is itself a factor in re-moulding the basic structure of the scene. It alters the nature of the soil and breaks up the underlying rocks. At the same time, vegetation brings a greater stability to some changing landscapes by binding together the particles of thin sandy soils with its roots and decaying foliage.

That is the essence of nature's part in landscape building—consolidating in one place, disintegrating in another, destroying land here, building it up afresh elsewhere. Just as we can see the destructive power of the sea along the east and south coasts of England we can also observe the compensating addition of new land within historic times.

So the gradual wearing down of the early continents, continents which by now have been submerged by the sea, was accompanied by the building up of new land from the very beginning. This new land was built up mainly under the sea while the sedimentary rocks were being formed—rocks which are the basis of the majority of our southern landscapes. They include the clays, the sandstones, the limestones, and the chalks—the clays of the Weald of Sussex; the sandstones of Ashdown Forest, of Hindhead, and of the red-tinted landscapes of South Devon; the limestones of the Cotswold hills and of the Pennine Chain; the chalks of the downland ridges which dominate the character of Dorset and Wiltshire.

Each of these rocks was formed under the sea at a different time in our earth's history and under vastly varying conditions of climate. The clays and the sandstones belong to one group, the chalks and the limestones to another. The former are composed mainly of particles detached from the rocks of the ancient land masses, from the granites and the basalts, and carried in suspension down rivers and out into the seas. The larger particles are deposited as grains of sand; the smaller particles form the ooze which we call mud and this in turn is converted into clay.

We can see the first stage of rock formation at almost any point around our sea coast. Above high-water mark the sand is soft and blows about in a strong wind, while lower down the beach where it is washed by the sea these particles have been compressed sufficiently by the tide for us to be able to walk over them and scarcely leave a footprint. The horses galloping along the fine stretch of sands between Bognor and Littlehampton leave hoof-marks so slight that they have disappeared before the next tide moves in. That illustrates the essential difference between sand and sandstone, between mud and clay rocks. When layers of sand or mud are deposited on the bed of the ocean the vast weight of water above them compresses them until they form masses almost, but not quite, as hard as the rocks from which their particles were derived.

The limestones are quite different in origin. Many types con-sist mainly of lime once dissolved in water and precipitated in favourable conditions; others contain the shells of myriads of tiny sea animals which, like the particles of sand and clay, have been deposited on the bed of the ocean and there compressed into solid rock. Generally the shells are broken into thousands of fragments but here and there one has miraculously escaped destruction and can be seen with the help of a microscope in the fabric of the rock face exposed in a quarry or in the cliffs by the seaside.

One form of limestone is built up by a little animal called a polyp which proliferates very like a plant by the formation of buds which gradually build up into a solid platform. These platforms form the basis of the coral reefs of the South Seas and can only exist in waters far warmer than those of our own North Sea or Atlantic Ocean. Yet some of the limestones of Derbyshire and Devonshire are coral formations—further evidence, if any were needed, that the seas round Britain were once tropical—and that in a comparatively recent era of the earth's history.

It is likely, then, that the changing climate of the world deter-mined the order in which the strata, or layers, of rock were laid down in any given region. When conditions were favourable for the formation of more than one kind of rock, two or more were laid down together to form a composite substance. Whatever the precise reason, layer on layer was laid down through the ages, each layer further compressing and hardening the layers beneath it until they aggregated thousands of feet in thickness.

Then these rocks were lifted up until they stood clear of the water surface, often rising many thousands of feet above the sea, far higher for certain than the highest of them stands today. How did it happen? I cannot give a precise answer nor, I believe, can any-one. It is a matter of choosing between several theories, each of which has much to be said for it. One theory is that as the earth cooled still further its crust contracted and while contracting crinkled so that one part of it was depressed, another elevated. That at least explains why it is that the present strata of rock are seldom horizontal but rather bent into folds—a series of synclines and anticlines, as they are called. Most people have seen the con-torted strata exposed in the cliff face, at Lulworth Cove for in-stance, or at Hartland Point in North Devon.

One thing only is certain. The sedimentary rocks which form the substance of most of England were not formed at one and the same time. The farther west one travels in England, the older are the rock formations. The old red sandstones of South Devon and other parts of the West Country, the most colourful and exciting of all England's rocks, were formed long before the sandstones of Crockham Hill or Hindhead and before the chalks of Salisbury Plain or the southern downs. Whatever the natural phenomenon which caused it, the fact remains that these layers of rock were thrown up during a period spread over hundreds of millions of years from the beds of seas and deep lakes. Generally they were planed off by the sea as they were being raised and appeared finally as high plateaux. Then nature went to work on them with water and ice and atmospheric acids in just the same way as it had done on the igneous rocks thousands of millions of years before. Whole layers of rock were worn away while underlying (and therefore older) ones were exposed, the process going on fastest in the chan-nels cut by the rain water flowing down from the peaks towards the seashore—the channels which have become the river valleys of today.

A dome of chalk once linked the South Downs of Sussex with the North Downs of Surrey and Kent. It was the 'anticline' corresponding with the 'syncline', or trough, where the chalk dips under the Thames Valley. The whole of the dome has been eroded away until the sandstones and the clays beneath it have been exposed, and they too have been partly eroded away. If one travels southward from, say, Westerham Hill to Lewes, one passes successively over the escarpment of the chalk, a clay valley at Westerham, a sandstone ridge at Crockham Hill, another clay valley at Edenbridge, another sandstone ridge in Ashdown Forest, yet another clay valley beyond, until one comes again to the other escarpment of chalk which we know as the South Downs. Yet all the rocks between the chalk hills when the landscape was first elevated lay hundreds of feet below the great chalk dome. It is as though our way southward were by a tunnel cut horizontally through the primeval substance of the earth to reveal the succes-sive layers in their orderly sequence.

Today chalk ridges radiate like spokes of a wheel from the cen-tral plateau which we call Salisbury Plain and the Marlborough Downs. Two point south-westward to form the downs of Dorset, one points north-eastward as the Berkshire Downs and the Chil-tern Hills. Others extend eastward and south-eastward to form respectively the North Downs of Surrey and Kent and the South Downs of Sussex. In the central area, especially on Salisbury Plain, the dome is still more or less intact, though even here the river valleys are eating deeply into it. On Salisbury Plain and on the Marlborough Downs we can see for ourselves that when the land was first elevated the chalk was not the uppermost layer. A layer of sandstone which has all but totally disappeared was super-imposed on it. The only signs of this earlier rock covering are the greywethers which are so easily mistaken at a distance for sheep grazing. Mankind has used this sandstone rock extensively for building purposes—has done so since the downs were first in-habited. The mighty rocks which form the uprights and lintels of the trilithons of Stonehenge built four thousand years ago—the sarsen stones, as they are often called—are specially large fragments of the original rock covering, while thousands of the greywethers were broken up in the Middle Ages to build roads or village homes.

Even when the rock layers of the Pennine Chain and of the south country had been elevated, it was still not an England which we should recognize; it was not, in fact, in the least degree simi-lar, especially without the vegetation which forms such a vivid part of our impression of the countryside today. And there were still several stages of evolution before the shape of the hills, of the intervening valleys, and of the coastline approximated to their modern outlines.

The English Channel was a noble river flowing down from the watershed of the chalk where a broad ridge linked the cliffs of Dover with the cliffs of France at Cap Gris Nez. The North Sea was another river, the progenitor of the Rhine, flowing northward towards the Arctic Ocean. The gravel beds of Blackheath were deposited by the progenitor of the Thames as it washed against the chalk hills that fell away from the ridge of the North Downs. The building up of fresh land surface was still going on side by side with its gradual attrition. The whole of the London basin became dry land long after the last of the chalk hills had been lifted up from the ocean floor. So did the Essex flats, that wide expanse of level land which now borders the shallow waters of the North Sea and is criss-crossed by dykes and streams and penetrated by many slow-flowing rivers such as the Stour, the Colne, and the

Orwell. These same rivers flowing through a wide expanse of marshy ground were destined to prove the avenues by which Saxon and Viking invaders sailed into the fertile country of the eastern counties in the first millennium A.D. But in that distant past the whole coastal landscape of Essex was in course of formation, chiefly from the silt and rock fragments carried along in the stream of the North Sea river. The country to the south of Chichester where Bognor and Littlehampton sprawl over the level landscape was under water. It was still being built up like the London basin long after the massive ranges of the chalk had assumed something like their present shape.

So it is with all the coastal plains of England, including the Fylde of Lancashire. The process of building up coastal plains still continues with comparative rapidity, especially along the north coast of Norfolk, where places like Cley and Blakeney, which were flourishing ports in the Middle Ages, have been left virtually high and dry, with a mile or more of salt marshes, partly washed by the sea, separating them from the navigable waters of the North Sea and the Wash.

Precisely the same has happened to ports like Sandwich and Winchelsea on the borders of Sussex and Kent. If one stands by the Ypres tower of Rye, on that naturally defensible cliff predestined to be the site of a mediaeval town, one looks over an expanse of green country where cattle and sheep find rich pasture. Only a thousand years ago from this same vantage point one would have looked over a seascape just beginning to turn into salt marshes but still predominantly sea, with a broad river estuary leading to a fine harbour immediately beneath the cliff. In the present century only determined dredging operations have kept a narrow channel open to Rye—and that navigable only by small vessels.

If such a change can take place in a thousand years, it needs no great imagination to visualize what can have happened in hundreds of millions of years. Still the rivers are carrying down their silt from the hills, still they are building up deltas which ultimately turn into dry land, though now the process is retarded when the river channels are used for shipping by the constant use of modern dredging machinery. But, as the history of Britain's coastal defences has proved, all the preventive measures which man can take are temporary.

In many parts of the world these alluvial lands have become the centres of most intensive human activity. The economy of the whole valley of the lower Nile, for instance, which supports a teeming population, depends on the fertile mud and silt carried down from the hills of the south by the Nile in flood and deposited on the fields within the wide flood plain. So fresh vigour is given each year to a land which is so deficient in rainfall that agriculture on a large scale would not be practicable without it.

Abundant evidence shows that the alluvial coastal plains of England have at different times in the history of the landscape been alternately covered by the sea and standing clear of it. This fact reflects something quite distinct from the convulsions of nature which earlier lifted the hills thousands of feet above the sea. It is something that can be attributed to the varying depth of the sea itself and this, in turn, depends on the amount of water stored in the form of ice in polar regions. There has been no constancy in the gradual cooling of the earth's crust. As we have seen earlier, major differences of climate and of sea temperature can be inferred from the different kinds of rocks that at different times have been laid down on the bed of the sea round our coast and, more certainly, from the fossils found in many strata of rocks.

When the corals that appear in the hills of Derbyshire were being formed, the seas round Britain were semi-tropical and it is likely that the ice caps at the Poles were either non-existent or very much smaller than they are today. It is quite likely that the Poles themselves were in different positions. It has been suggested that if all the ice that even now covers Greenland and the land masses of Arctic and Antarctic regions were to melt, the level of the sea would be raised by about one hundred feet. So most of London would lie under the sea, the whole of the Sussex coastal plain, nearly half of Lancashire, a great part of the Vale of York, and nearly half of Essex. Yet in the period intermediate between the time of the warm seas and of the present temperate climate in our latitudes, an ice age has intervened, when the volume of ice covering sea and land alike must have been ten or twenty times as great as it is today—when, for instance, a sheet of ice linked the highlands of Norway with the mountains of Scotland, and glaciers reached out long fingers from the Pennines towards the Thames Valley and East Anglia.

At the present time we are recovering from the effects of an ice age which ended, so far as Scotland was concerned, about ten thousand years ago. Before the ice cap melted the level of the sea must have been much lower than in historic times. That helps to explain (quite apart from inferred changes in the level of the land itself) how it was that in a comparatively recent era, England was linked to the Continent not only by the chalk bridge between Dover and Cap Gris Nez, but by a broad plain of alluvial land in place of the shallow waters of the North Sea between the East Anglian coast and that of Holland. The sandbanks of those treacherous waters are a stillpresent reminder of that episode from our recent past.

As the Arctic ice cap is still diminishing and the climate of Greenland is slowly improving, while the limit of winter ice also recedes a measurable average distance computed over a number of years, it follows that the level of the sea is still rising. No man can foretell when, if ever, the process will be reversed but it is as certain as anything in nature can be that if the polar climate continues to grow warmer, another great change in the English landscape will occur within a few hundred thousand years.

CHAPTER II
Nature's Mantle

* *

WITH THE PLATEAU of the Cumbrian mountains gradually being worn away into peaks and valleys and scree-covered slopes, with the Pennine Chain uplifted and forming the backbone of the new England, with the chalk and sandstone hills of the south raised far above sea level, and with the new alluvial land being built up on the coastal fringe, the stage was indeed well and truly set for the drama of landscape building that was to follow.

It needed one thing and one thing only to transform this gloomy world into the world we know. It needed the miracle of life to quicken it into the vibrant pulsating organism it is, with its constant change in detail from year to year, from season to season, almost from day to day. Life in the little world that was to become England, as in the greater world of the continents, cannot be measured in terms of mankind's existence. Man, in fact, is one of the latest forms of life, though the one which has had greatest influence on the changing scene during the last brief four thousand years. But man most certainly did not make his appearance until a million years ago, not, at least, in a recognizable form. It may well be that his span so far has been no more than half that time, a short span indeed relative to the age of the earth. Moreover, for at least ninety-nine per cent of that brief period man was no more than one of many kinds of mammals, gifted with a mind (hence his name Homo sapiens) but otherwise ill-equipped to struggle with the larger and more numerous creatures among whom he lived.

Until the time of his cultural development—until the time, that is, of the New Stone Age in the Near East—his contribution to the changing face of the land was negligible. He lived in caves or in rock shelters—in Kent's Cavern near Torquay, in the Creswell caves of Derbyshire, in the Paviland caves of Gower; when the climate allowed he lay down to sleep under the stars wherever his perpetual hunt for food, his constant struggle for existence, had brought him. He was neither a cultivator nor a herdsman, but must have seemed, if one of our own generation could be trans⁄ ported miraculously to view the scene in those times, just one of many species of mammal taking part in the struggle for survival.

Millions of years before the time of Homo sapiens—hundreds of millions of years, if mere multiplication of numbers helps the understanding—mammals of other kinds were wandering over the land that was to become England. Before the mammals there were other creatures of whom many of the earliest were amphibian. Before that again life was measured in terms of primitive plants and tree ferns, taking us back to nearly four hundred million years ago, well before the south Devon sandstones or the chalk hills had been raised from the sea.

A prerequisite for plant life on earth was the formation of soil. For many millions of years after life had appeared and living plants had taken root in the soil the history of the changing landscape is as much the province of ecology, the scientific study of living things in relation to their environment, as it is of geology, which is concerned with the modifications brought about by erosion and the pent⁄up vigour of the earth's convulsions. Though soils are modified by the myriads of living things which make their home in them, in their essential nature they do not differ much from the rocks from which they are formed. In the mountains of Cumber⁄ land or even on the high ground of Dartmoor, we can see for our⁄ selves the point at which the exposed rocks end and the soil begins. We shall see that wherever soil is overlaid on the rocks there is vegetation, even if it is only clumps of rank unpalatable grass. That is the essential difference which makes such a startling con⁄ trast between the bare rock face or the ragged screes, and the smooth grass⁄covered slopes which run down to the highly⁄ cultivated valleys.

Some soils were formed where they lie today from fragments of the rock which still underlies them. If we dug down on a plateau, that is, a fairly level expanse of elevated land, we should find under the fine top soil a subsoil in which the rock fragments were much larger, and beneath that again the bedrock. If the bedrock was sandstone, then the soil would consist mainly of sand modified by whatever vegetation grew in it. At a depth of a foot or so the sand would be mixed with larger sandstone 'pebbles'. Below that again we should reach solid sandstone. If we were to dig down through the soil on a chalk plateau we should find a mixture of chalk fragments and flints until the native rock was reached.

Flints, which occur in most layers of the chalk (as can be seen where the chalk cliffs are broken off at Beer Head or Beachy Head in the south or Flamborough Head in Yorkshire) resist erosion far better than the rest of the substances which make up the chalk. They were found by prehistoric man on the surface of the ground and fashioned by him into primitive weapons and implements. On the surface they are usually broken into fragments. That is why prehistoric man at a later stage in his development dug shal-low mines to recover them intact from undisturbed layers of chalk. A field newly turned by the plough on the Marlborough Downs or the hills of Dorset will take colour from the broken flints which have been thrown up by the plough-share from the subsoil. Often it will look as though there is more flint than soil. It comes as a revelation to see how well the sturdy corn crops overcome these hazards of nature, taking firm root in the calcareous land and ultimately disguising its myriads of flints with their green covering.

Relatively few soils, however, remain in the places in which they were formed. Once the soil particles are small they are at the mercy of wind and water, which carry them sometimes for hun-dreds of miles. We have already seen how sandstones and clays were laid down on the sea bed from particles carried down by the rivers from earlier hill ranges. Many of the particles held in sus-pension by the streams never reach the sea but are deposited on land surfaces when the rivers overflow. So soil which was formed on the Cotswold Hills may find its way into the London basin or

soil formed on the slopes of Plynlimon may be carried by some
tributary of the Wye or Severn all the way down through the
Welsh hills into the English border land, there to be superimposed on and ultimately mingled with the top soil already lying
there. Again water seeping down a hillside after heavy rain tends
to carry with it masses of soil from higher to lower levels. After
a long dry spell a strong wind may carry away the topsoil from one
area and deposit it again in a sheltered valley where the strong air
currents subside. This in turn is mixed ultimately with the pre-
existing soil.

So far as the English lowlands are concerned, most of the fertile
soils are formed of such a mixture. The marls of the central lowlands are a mixture of clay and limestone in various proportions;
the wonderfully fertile lowlands of the Weald and many other
parts of the south are a similar mixture of clay and sandstone. But
many soils are predominantly clay, especially in the river valleys.

Hundreds of different kinds of soils of varying fertility have been
catalogued but the bulk of them fall in England into the four
categories, chalk, sandstone, limestone, and clay, together with the
marls and loams. They are still, as they have been from time immemorial, the chief factors that determine the wide local differences
in England's vegetation. A large number of our trees, shrubs,
and plants have been introduced within historic times but the
types they represent could not flourish unless they were well
adapted to their environment.

If one says that soil plus climate equals environment in the
world of vegetation, one is not far from the truth. Sandy soils are
very light and porous. They let through the rain water that falls
on them; the more sandy they are, the less they retain. So plants
that require a lot of moisture do not flourish in sandy places unless
the rainfall is exceptionally heavy. It is thus obvious why the
sandstone soils of England include so much barren heathland and
open common. All who know Surrey will recognize the sandstone country round Aldershot and to the south of the Tilling-
bourne valley, the broken hill country on either side of the Hog's
Back and the dominant heights of Hindhead and the Leith Hill

range. The sandy warrens of Breckland on the borders of Suffolk and Norfolk are an outstanding example. Here only a few centuries ago minor sand storms were by no means uncommon in windy dry weather, especially in spring. The planting of trees, particularly the hardy conifers which do not require much moisture, has changed the face of the land and by providing windbreaks has minimized the risk of sandstorms, while the roots of the trees have helped to bind together the soil.

In places where the sandy soil has virtually no other components the planting of marram grass, the least moisture-loving of all plants and the hardiest, has served the same purpose. The movement of the Culbin sand hills, for instance, facing the Moray Firth has been halted by this means. Yet these same sand dunes only a few hundred years ago overwhelmed the whole barony of Culbin and thousands of acres which were so fertile that they were known as the granary of Moray.

If the climate were drier our sandstone hills would be arid desert, as unproductive and featureless as the Sahara or the desert of California. But England's rainfall is nowhere at present below about twenty inches a year and that only in the driest corner of south-east Essex. Moreover the rainfall is well distributed throughout the year so that even in the sandiest of countrysides plants do not have to go for many weeks without receiving moisture. So we find that the sandy warrens are generally covered in bracken and heather, while the brilliant blooms of the rhododendron add colour to the scene in gardens and parks, and many varieties of pine will grow to maturity in all but the thinnest soils.

Ashdown Forest in Sussex and the commons which lie on the fringe of the New Forest are all predominantly sandy country, all show the same types of vegetation. In a few places on the sandstone ridges where the proportion of clay is somewhat higher, as around Toy's Hill and Chartwell, Sir Winston Churchill's country residence in Kent, the scenery is as varied and attractive as in any of the hill country of the south. The rhododendron plantations are at their finest, pine trees are mingled with the hardier varieties of deciduous trees, while patches of heather and

he estuary of the Dee from the Wirral peninsula. *The geologically more recent land
bordering the river bears abundant corn crops, while the older land of the peninsula in the foreground has been weathered until the rocks are exposed and only clumps of stunted bracken and
heather can grow. The Welsh hills can be seen in the distance.*

he North York Moors and the valley of the Seph. *The moorlands are cleft by wide sweeping
valleys, fertile and picked out with English forest trees, while the thinner soil on the higher grounds
bears only recent plantations of conifers.*

Milldale and the river Dove. *Erosion past and present is illustrated in this photograph, which shows the exposed rock faces on the steep limestone slopes sculptured by glacial action, while the swiftly-flowing river modifies the landscape as it constantly deepens the gorge, its course marked by a number of shallow waterfalls.*

bracken-covered common alternate with fertile grass fields in the shallow valleys.

By contrast with the porous nature of sandstone soils, the clay is most retentive of moisture. There are more varieties of clay soils than of any other kind, ranging from the light clays which are a feature of many parts of East Anglia to the heavy clays which are found in parts of the Thames Valley, the Vale of York, the Trent Valley, and the valleys of the Severn and the midland Ouse. The clay soils, if we include the marls and the loams, are by far the most productive, and for ever associated with the trim chequer-board pattern of the English valley scene, in which grass fields alternate with corn fields and the whole landscape hums with activity from early spring until the last of the harvest has been gathered.

Where the clays are light and so less retentive of moisture wheat does best, especially if summer sunshine is plentiful and rainfall light. That is why East Anglia has become the true granary of England. In a moister climate, or in slightly heavier clays, oats and other cereals do best, while the heaviest clays are too liable to be waterlogged for corn crops to flourish, though they make admirable pasture land. That is why midland England is a land of mixed farming.

To the west, where the rainfall is heavy and the hillsides exposed to wind and rain and the summer temperatures are generally lower, corn crops grow only in the sheltered valleys above the flood plains of the rivers. Even there the cereal most often grown is oats to serve as winter fodder for the cattle rather than for human consumption. The clay soil, too, is the traditional home of the 'native' English trees, especially the oak and the elm. The great oaken forest of Anderida reached its peak two thousand years ago in the clay soils of the Wealden valleys. As one looks down from some high vantage point the clay lands always appear well wooded, 'the dim blue wooded goodness of the Weald' which Kipling saw from the northern escarpment of the Sussex Downs. The long avenues that point the way down Warwickshire lanes are in the same tradition. So are the scattered woodlands and coppices and generous hedgerow timber of the Vale of York and the Cheshire Plain.

C

The chalk downs have a characteristically thin top soil, while water tends to run off quickly from the chalk ridges. The most characteristic vegetation of the chalk and of the limestone, too, is grass, which makes the wonderfully springy turf of the downs when it is close-cropped by flocks of sheep, which have pastured over it for the last thousand years. Though, as we shall see in later chapters, the downs are capable of producing corn crops as they did in prehistoric times and as they have done again during the last few years, grass is their natural covering, and sheep the natural stock-in-trade of the downland farmer.

Where a covering of clay is overlaid on the chalk the resultant soil is unusually well adapted for the full development of the beech. So thousands of acres of the Chilterns are covered in dense beech woods. These provided the raw material for the rural industry of furniture-making which is centred at High Wycombe. Other deciduous trees, too, grow well where the clay is mixed with the chalk soil, as in the western downs of Sussex and in the Chiltern country during the first millenium A.D. But the wooded slopes around Goodwood or Stokenchurch are not really typical landscapes of the downs. The almost treeless expanse of Salisbury Plain and the sunny open slopes of the Dorset Downs, or for that matter of the Berkshire Downs, represent more truly the natural features of the chalk country.

Because limestone mixed with clay yields one of the most fertile of all soils, the limestone country of the Cotswold Hills is equally suitable for pasture and for arable farming. That is one of the reasons why those much-loved landscapes of Gloucestershire and Oxfordshire, and farther north where the ridge runs into Northamptonshire, are among the loveliest of England today. Only on the highest ground above Winchcombe and Cheltenham, on Broadway Hill and Edge Hill, is the soil so thin and poor that crops will not grow.

Something of the same fertile beauty is apparent in the valleys of the rivers which flow towards the North Sea from the Pennine Chain, where the soil is often a mixture of clay and Pennine limestone. Lower Wharfedale and Lower Wensleydale, the valleys of the Wharfe and Ure respectively, have much in common in their scenic character with the lower slopes of the Cotswold range in Northamptonshire and Leicestershire.

Ecology, then, is the key to the apparel of the English hills and valleys as we know them. It is equally the key to the story of the developing landscape long before man had come to make an impression on the pattern of nature. Modern science in its application to agriculture has done a great deal to modify the natural soils and so has varied the environment in which the plants and crops and trees must grow. But all man's efforts in this direction are puny compared with the massive work of nature in producing the soil that is overlaid on the rock and in determining the climatic conditions of different parts of the country. All man has done is to bind together light soils by planting grass and trees, to reclaim heathland, marshland and fen that was worthless before reclamation and to enrich tired soil by the addition of chemicals or lime so that crops will grow fruitfully where before they gave but a poor return to the husbandman.

All these efforts tell a wonderful story of man's tenacity of purpose, of his successful efforts to harness nature to his special needs. Yet all in all they amount to nothing compared with the effects of natural phenomena such as the last ice age when the glaciers which flowed from the high ground of central England over Yorkshire and across the plain of East Anglia deposited millions of tons of what we call boulder clay, so producing some of the most fertile arable land in the world. Boulder clay is a light fine clay containing a varying number of rocks and boulders. Its composition can be seen in vivid detail where the chalk hills are broken off at the sea by Flamborough Head, for there and in many other places a thick layer of boulder clay is overlaid on the chalk.

The glaciers as they flowed over the landscape, moving inexorably forward often a few feet a day, scoured the valley sides and the hard frozen surface layer of the land, gathering particles of soil and fragments of rock broken off the hillsides as they went. They acted in just the same way as (but far more powerfully than) the rivers flowing down from the limestone or chalk hills which

carry particles of soil in suspension (so thick a suspension sometimes that the waters of a clear stream are turned muddy when it
flows in spate after heavy rain). The glaciers carried along a far
greater weight of material than the rivers and deposited it as they
melted often farther away from its source and always over a much
wider area. The visible result today is that thousands of acres of
the east Yorkshire Wold, which consists of low chalk hills, grow
corn and root crops as well as any part of England, instead of the
springy turf which we find on the South Downs over which no
glacier flowed. It is one of the reasons, too, which underlies the
abundant fertility of the East Anglian Plain.

That magic transformation scene was one of the last acts in the
prehistoric drama of the landscape. If we go back three hundred
million years, there was still a cover of vegetation on parts of England that were above the level of the sea, though the vegetation
bore no resemblance to the natural covering of the land today.
About that time the coal measures were being formed. Coal consists partly of decayed vegetable matter probably laid down in
much the same way as the far more recent peat. It formed in
marshland or river deltas when the climate was wet and the level
of sea or land or both was unstable, so that periods when the land
was relatively dry alternated with periods when it was just covered
by the sea. The evidence suggests that a similar state of instability
existed on the borderland of the fens in Cambridgeshire during
the last two thousand years B.C. and the first thousand years A.D.

The most characteristic form of life in that far distant age was a
tree the nature of which can be reconstructed from individual
leaves or fronds which have been fossilized in the coal measures.
From these fossils we can say for certain that the trees of the coal
age bore no resemblance to our oaks or elms or ashes, or indeed
to any tree that grows now in England. They were more like
gigantic ferns or club-mosses in the form of trees, bearing cones or
spores. A layer of clay is often found under the coal measures. In
this clay are the roots and trunks of the trees whose debris forms
the coal itself. It is the soil, in other words, in which the trees grew.

It is a long long jump from the vegetation that helped to form the coal measures to the time when England was beginning to recover from the final ice age. In no other strata of rock are fossil remains of plants and trees so clearly seen as in the coal measures.

When we come to the last phases of the ice age we are very much on the threshold of our modern world. Trees and plants and shrubs familiar to us today were well established in the world of nature. Then a new act in the drama is unfolded, its scenes dominated by the varying nature of the vegetation as determined by the recession or advance of the glaciers. When the ice covering was at its greatest the whole of northern England was enveloped in a gigantic ice cap. All life had been extinguished. The seas and shores were frozen solid and ice ridges linked the Cheviot and the Yorkshire hills with the Scandinavian glaciers, while on the other side of the Pennines the glaciers flowed down the steep hills to link with Ireland and came to an end in the warm waters of the Atlantic far out to sea. Southward the glaciers extended from the Peak of Derbyshire over the greater part of the Midlands but stopped short of the Thames Valley, though the characteristic indentations in the face of the South Downs where they face north may well have been scooped out by masses of packed snow, each forming a glacier in miniature, which melted perhaps only once in a number of years, when warm winds blew in from the sea for an unusually long period.

Though the countryside to the south of a line drawn from the mouth of the Thames to the mouth of the Severn was unglaciated, life there was restricted, its vegetation practically non-existent. No more than twenty thousand years ago the whole of the south was a tundra, its climate and vegetation rather similar to the tundra of northern Siberia near the Arctic Circle. Primitive man and many other mammals certainly dwelt in England before this last phase of the ice age but equally certainly they must have been driven out in search of warmer climates when the ice advanced for the last time.

Again we may well marvel at the incredible transformation effected in this period of twenty thousand years, so insignificant in comparison with the total age of the earth. The birch was the first of the trees to take root in the south; the hardier varieties of pine followed. These moved northward as the ice retreated, and were followed in the south by the hazel, alder, oak, elm and lime. The pine and the birch, in fact, are still moving northward, though their advance has taken them now far beyond northern England, into the high valleys of Scotland and Norway and into Lapland almost on the shores of the Arctic Ocean, where even a thousand years ago they could not have existed for a single season.

Precisely as our modern vegetation and crops are determined partly by local variations in climate, so the advance and recession of the natural covering of the landscape in these last twenty thou/sand years has been determined by repeated variations in the climate. Our knowledge of the sequence of events, which is far from orderly, derives from modern scientific research by means of microscopic examination of deposits in lakes and bogs. Wind/borne pollen, it seems, from trees in neighbouring woodlands blew over the lakes and bogs. Inevitably some of the pollen settled on the surface of the pond, and ultimately reached the bottom. In such still and enclosed sheets of water the deposits were not greatly disturbed by agitation or currents. As pollen from all the princi/pal trees and flowering plants can be distinguished under the microscope, a vertical section of a lake deposit yields definite evi/dence of the character of the vegetation in sequence.

Such scientific methods are of greatest value in a country like Scotland, where the land has never been disturbed for drainage and where large areas of the Highlands are given over to peat bogs and small lochs. Even in the south, however, the same methods have yielded remarkable results, especially in the marshy land of Somerset and in some of the many high/lying pools and small lakes of the midland counties. Naturally the lowest levels of the lake deposits yield birch and pine exclusively; then there is a layer in which the pollen of alder is conspicuous; then again pine pre/dominates, until rather suddenly in the most recent deposits pine pol/len is rarely found, while the pollen of the 'native' English trees, especially of the oak and elm, increases rapidly at the expense of all others. The lesson drawn from these facts is that as the ice sheet retreated, say about ten to twelve thousand years ago, the tundra/like conditions of the south country gave way gradually to a climatic cycle in which though the winters were still Arctic, the summers became comparatively warm and without excessive rainfall. In these conditions the pine and birch became established and spread gradually northward until the conditions once prevailing only in the south covered the whole of Britain. The greater part of the English landscape was by then covered in gloomy forests of conifers.

After that there was a recession during which the ice sheets advanced again slightly from the north, but soon an improvement set in once more and continued with only temporary setbacks until the present day. In a climate which gradually became rather like our own, though often with rather colder winters and perhaps wetter summers, the deciduous trees spread northward from the continent and established the forerunners of the oak forests which were such a conspicuous feature of the English landscape four to eight thousand years ago and continued to be so until historic times. Only the accident of England's separation, by the formation of the English Channel, from the continent of which it formed a part prevented a larger number of trees and plants establishing themselves in southern England. In the event a number of trees quite common in Europe did not take root in our island until Tudor times or later—and then were imported deliberately to beautify the parks and estates of the newly rich landowners. The climate and soil of the southern clay-lands are still very suitable for the development of forests of oak. Only the continued depredations of Romans and Saxons and Normans in clearing the land for agricultural use, the felling of mature trees to provide timber to build the royal navy in Tudor times, together with the depletion of the wealden forest to supply fuel for the iron furnaces of Sussex finally destroyed the last large natural forests of England.

One other fact stands out from the scientific evidence that has been collated. About the beginning of the first millenium B.C. there was a period of a few hundred years during which the climate was appreciably wetter than it is at present. The mean temperature of the year may not have varied much from that prevailing in the twentieth century. Probably the winters were milder and the summers cooler, with little frost at any time of the year.

The interest of this climatic phase so far as it has had a permanent effect on the landscape is that the greater part, if not all, of England's peat bogs were formed during the period. Though England can show nothing comparable with the vast peat hags of northern and north-western Scotland, or even of the Tweedsmuir Hills in Scotland's southern uplands, they are extensive enough on the plateau of the Pennines and on Dartmoor to form a characteristic feature of present-day scenery. Quite apart from the influence of peat-cutting (a rather negligible factor in England to-day) the area of English peat bogs is gradually decreasing. Strong walkers who have found their way to Cranmere Pool in the loneliest and bleakest part of Dartmoor at intervals of ten years or so will surely have noticed that the area of bog is diminishing. What is so demonstrably true of Cranmere Pool is equally true though less obviously so of the bog lands around the Cheviot and down the Pennine Chain as far as the Peak in Derbyshire. The bogs are all beginning to dry out. No fresh peat is being formed, while in many places where the surface layer of the ground is relatively dry soil one will find a layer of peat a few inches under the surface.

So marked was the climatic change in the first millennium B.C. that many parts of the upland country previously well wooded became bare of trees, while the decaying vegetation helped to build up the beds of peat. The process which had once formed the coal measures was at work again in a different medium.

The story of man and his ultimately successful attempts to colonize what is now England are closely linked with this and similar changes in climate and vegetation. Though there is ample evidence of primitive man in England during the periods of greater warmth that divided the ice age, there is no evidence at all of tribal organization or of cultures approaching those of the warmer climates of southern Europe and the Middle East until about two thousand years B.C. Then, as we shall see in the next chapter, inhabitation was largely confined to the uplands, especially the chalk hills of the south, which stood clear of the prevailing undergrowth and forest covering of the Weald. When the climate of the south country deteriorated in the phase that produced the peat bogs, the area of the downs under cultivation probably declined; when it improved again about the time of the Roman occupation more and more of the upland country came under the plough (see Chapter IV).

The same period that produced the peat bogs on the moorlands must have encouraged the growth of the oak forests of Sussex and Essex and of the midland plain, so that these features of the landscape were probably more prominent at the dawn of the historic period than at any other time. That is a fact which explains the extraordinarily slow progress which was made successively by the people of the Iron Age in the few centuries immediately preceding the Roman occupation, and by the Romans themselves, in clearing the undergrowth so as to make the river valleys habitable and uncover sufficient fertile land to support a growing population. All Roman chroniclers who wrote of Britain were as much impressed by the forests as they were by the fierce demeanour of the people.

The picture we have sketched of the building of the landscape and of its embellishment by nature's mantle of vegetation is one of which even the outlines are in places badly blurred. The detail of the picture may never be filled in, though every generation of scientists reveals new facets of the story and propounds new theories based on the most recent research. Every statement about a time of which there can be of necessity no record other than the mute evidence of rocks and fossils and deposits, whether on the surface of the land or under the sea, is inevitably arrived at by inference from observation. One need not doubt the validity of the observation to question some of the inferences that are made, especially as different scientists of apparently equal calibre often arrive at different inferences from the same observations.

So it requires a certain courage even to build up the outline picture and present it as a sequence of probable fact. It needs a still more intrepid approach to attempt a chronology, since even the basic dates, such as the age of the earth, are still hotly debated. However, the attempt must be made if the picture unfolded is to assume the semblance of reality. We are not likely to be contra-dicted if we state that the early stages in the building up of the landscape were completed more than five hundred million years ago, that by then the older granites that determine the character of Dartmoor and the Malvern Hills had been formed. The oldest of the sedimentary layers to be elevated from the bed of the sea was the old red sandstone, still a powerful factor in the beauty of the countryside not only of South Devon but of many other parts of the West Country and especially of the central districts of Here-fordshire. This great event in the building of the land must have happened rather more than three hundred million years ago, while about the same time the coal measures were being formed in other parts of the country, and the carboniferous limestone of the Pen-nine Chain was laid down. Then followed the limestones of the Cotswold, the sandstones and chalks and clays of the weald and southern downlands.

That phase was completed perhaps a hundred million years ago, while the London clay was laid down much more recently, not much more than fifty million years ago at a time when mammals were becoming common. The most recent land of all is that which makes up England's coastal plains, the plain of Sussex be-tween Worthing and Portsmouth, the Fylde of Lancashire, and the areas which have only been reclaimed in historic times, such as the Somerset plain and the fens of Lincolnshire and Cambridge-shire.

CHAPTER III

The Peopled Landscape

◆ ◆

MANY MILLIONS OF YEARS passed in brief review before us in the preceding chapter. Now time slows down as we come nearer to the present day. This chapter spans a period of little more than two thousand years, which stands in the same kind of relationship to the time taken by nature in making and moulding the land-scape as an inch stands to the distance round the earth.

This is the time when man begins to make an impression on the face of the land as nature fashioned it. In England (but not, of course, to the same extent in Scotland and Wales) this impression of man's handiwork from tiny beginnings reached sensible pro-portions within an incredibly short space of time. Today, about four thousand years after scenery began to be affected by human life, half the country is like a landscape garden on a vast scale in which man-made features and colours are superimposed every-where on the canvas painted by nature.

When this chapter opens Great Britain was already an island. It had probably been separated from the continent of Europe for some thousands of years, although scientists still differ on the ques-tion when the chalk bridge linking the Dover cliffs with Cap Gris Nez finally disappeared. The whole of Britain, too, was free of the influence of the retreating ice. The melting of the ice had raised the level of the seas, so that the low-lying marshes of the Dogger Bank exposed during the ice age were flooded again and only a few islands remained of the great plain which formerly stretched across what is now the North Sea, and formed another link be-tween Britain and the continent. An oceanic climate dominated by moisture-laden winds from the Atlantic Ocean had well and truly set in.

The warmth-loving vegetation of southern England was flourishing, especially the oaks and other trees which we regard as native to our country. The forest of the Weald (the Forest of Anderida, as the Romans called it), the forest of Essex, and the great midland forest, of which Arden and Sherwood are two insignificant survivals, were all impenetrable expanses of dense woodland and scrub in which only wild animals could find a home. So they continued until man mastered the manufacture of metal and produced implements which could clear and drain the land, which was criss-crossed by hundreds of slow-flowing streams clogged by the roots of trees and decaying leaves.

In the south the chalk downlands stood up abruptly from the morasses and forests of the valleys. In the last two thousand years B.C., when the climate was slightly warmer and moister than it is today, these open tablelands inevitably became the centres of man's developing activities. The population was greatest on the chalk plateau which we call Salisbury Plain and the Marlborough Downs. It was relatively dense too along the ridges which radiate like the spokes of a giant wheel—north-eastward over the Berkshire Downs and the Chiltern Hills to East Anglia, eastward across the North Downs to the Shakespeare Cliff by Dover, south-eastward through Sussex to Beachy Head, and south-westward to the Dorset coast. Thus the countrysides which we know as among the loneliest of the south country were the most densely populated four thousand years ago.

As for the north and west, the highland half of England, the natural features of the landscape were more resistant to human influence. The lowland strip of South Devon was unknown forest-covered country but the uplands of Dartmoor and of Bodmin Moor and of Exmoor, too, were open and unobstructed as they are today. So was the expanse of the Pennine Moors, pointing like a finger from the desolate hills of the border into the very heart of midland England. These areas, then, also became peopled by early man, though less soon and less extensively than the downlands of the south. Even the Lake District of Cumberland and Westmorland was colonized early in the second millennium B.C.

Though Britain was indeed an island cut off permanently from the mainland of Europe, the civilizations which directly moulded its history and indirectly its landscapes were derived from the continent. They sprang originally from the early culture of Asia Minor and the Mediterranean world. They came sometimes by peaceful penetration (aided by the primitive trade routes that existed between the Mediterranean world and the far-flung outposts of Europe); they came sometimes by the invasions of nomadic tribes seeking greater living space in the fabulous lands across the sea. Some of the invaders advanced directly across the Strait of Dover, others across the shallow waters of the North Sea, making landfall by the Wash and settling in the gentle hills of Norfolk or Lincolnshire; others again crossed from Brittany to the Cornish coast, or sailed up Southampton Water and the waterway of the Avon. Occasionally influences spread over Britain indirectly from the Mediterranean world by way of Ireland, but most often their impact was strongest on the eastern districts and most usually the south-eastern corner of England.

When archaeology was in its infancy it used to be said that the prehistory of England consisted of a series of migrations, all of which started in northern Europe and spread from east to west across the trackways of the downs. The migrating peoples brought first of all skill in working stone, then a knowledge of craftsmanship in bronze, and finally the greatest of all mankind's blessings and the true secret of his incredible development in the last two thousand years, the secret of iron metallurgy. Thus arose the traditional division into three ages, the Stone Age, the Bronze Age, and the Iron Age. Modern research, though it leaves those three ages in their consecutive order, has proved that the story of the three migrations is over-simplified, and has modified in many important respects the details that fill in the general outline.

The basic fact remains that the earliest advance towards a recognizable civilization was made in the south-east, while later inventions and discoveries that made further progress possible spread only gradually towards the north and west. From this it follows that the first subtle changes that affected the English scene occurred in the south and east. Changes in the north and west were not only later but lacked the drama of those in the south because the highlands have always been, as it were, the home of lost causes, and have tended to absorb fresh influences in their own time. A

Land eroded away
Marsh land
Natural forest
Scrub covered

The Cotswold
The Icknield Way
Chiltern Hills
•AVEBURY
STONEHENGE
The Pilgrims' Way
South Downs
Isle of Thanet

South-eastern England about 1800 B.C.

new way of working the land, for instance, might alter the face of south-eastern landscapes in a generation, but in the north-west was only gradually realized and then perhaps never to the extent that it was in the climatically-favoured open country of the southern downs. The same conservatism, the same adherence to traditional forms, has been a factor in the shaping of the highland half of Britain throughout its history.

Recent estimates place the limits of the New Stone Age at 2250 and 1600 B.C., of the Bronze Age at 1600 and 400 B.C., with the Early Iron Age following and completing the period before the Roman occupation, though itself representing several infusions of separate cultures from the continent. The first of these civiliza-tions, that of the New Stone Age, may well have broken upon England almost overnight, when a fresh and vigorous people of skilled craftsmen carried all before them and then made their settlements at will in the southern downlands. The Bronze Age and the Iron Age, however, had no such distinct beginnings. As trade became established first bronze and then iron weapons made their appearance and exercised an important influence without necessarily involving a conquest by a migratory people armed with weapons of the new material. One fact stands out clearly, that for a thousand years up to the middle of the first millennium B.C. there was a period of peace unparalleled before or since, during which a relatively advanced civilization was built up with marked improvement in agricultural methods and a correspondingly marked change in the typical southern landscape.

Estimates of population are just as difficult to make as estimates of dates. In the middle of the Bronze Age there may have been fifty thousand people living in England, certainly not many more, perhaps a great many fewer. In another thousand years by the time that Roman ideas were making a dynamic impact on the people of Britain, the population may have increased to four or five times that number, but it was still small by comparison with that of mediaeval England.

When once man the cultivator was established the amount of land used to raise crops necessarily increased with the size of the population. While the number of its people remained small, the landscape changes which crop cultivation produces were small in proportion. So when we speak of the downlands of southern England as prehistoric man's granary, we must not think of them as a minor version of modern East Anglia, but as more analogous to the meagre cornlands that exist today in the high valleys of the north and west, as islands of varied colouring in a scene still predominantly monotone.

Farming had begun at least by 2000 B.C., though neolithic man was primarily a stock-raiser and depended for much of his food on wild fruits and berries and on the wild animals which he trapped or shot with his arrows, rather than on the crops of cultivated soil. He had no plough to help him turn the earth, but only a version of the hoe, fabricated from stone and wood. Because of the impermanence of wood the timber-built villages of Stone Age man yield little evidence for the archaeologist to interpret. In the

Dartmoor and Bodmin Moor area, however, where stone was a more convenient material for building than timber, enough has survived to give an outline picture. We can infer that the typical Stone Age village was a small group of hutments on a sheltered slope facing whenever possible southward towards the sun and surrounded by a shallow entrenchment and perhaps a palisade. Each family cultivated a small plot of land on which barley and wheat were grown, or at least recognizable variants of these staple cereal crops. Such villages were not permanent settlements, for the neolithic tribes moved on from place to place as the local pasture was exhausted.

Even so, the downs must have presented a very different picture from that of a few hundred years before when there were no farm settlements and mankind was represented only by a few hundred unco-ordinated groups of people whose life was a perpetual struggle with nature and who knew nothing of the arts of agri- culture or building.

By the time the first bronze implements were making their ap- pearance in Britain, Stone Age settlements were quite thickly dis- tributed over a wide area. An observer on the summit of the Trundle, or on the slopes of Eggar Dun in Dorset, looking over the chalk landscape around him might have seen on a clear even- ing the smoke of a dozen fires curling up from the nearby 'villages' and farms. By then, too, several of the prehistoric trackways had been constructed, with rough fords over many of the rivers. The Icknield Way was a link between all the people who lived among the Chilterns and the East Anglian Heights, the Pilgrim's Way between those who lived in the North Downs country, while a more complex network covered the central chalk plateau and the Sussex hills. Such trackways are traditional, in the sense that they are virtually coeval with organized life, but equally they did not come into full or general use until many centuries had elapsed. They started as local ways linking one community with another, or safe routes for driving cattle without the necessity of climbing to the summit of steep hills, or the risk of being bogged down in the dangerous morasses of the valleys.

vebury from the Air. *The greater part of the modern village was built inside the earth works prehistoric Avebury. A number of the original stones of the great stone circle can be seen, also some of the concrete blocks set up to mark the position of others which have been destroyed.*

onehenge from the Air. *This photograph brings out clearly the earthworks surrounding the monument of Stonehenge, the detached Hele Stone and the barrow some distance away.*

British Camp, Malvern Hills. *The natural contours of the beacon were re-moulded by the builders of the prehistoric settlement, of which the ramparts and ditches can be clearly seen.*

The Giant of Cerne Abbas. *This is one of the oldest of the prehistoric figures cut in the chalk downs of southern England, and possibly dates from the New Stone Age.*

Late in the Bronze Age the plough in the modern sense of the word made its bow. Its use was a turning-point in the story of farming; it proved the most important single invention which has ever modified the British scene. As the early Iron Age progressed oxen-drawn ploughs could have been seen in almost every part of the peopled land. The 'Celtic fields' formed the basis of a genuine rural economy that presupposes some measure of tribal government, fixed homes, and organized labour. The Iron Age plough was fragile by modern standards. That is why the rich heavy soils of the valleys were never ploughed, even though Iron Age man had implements made of the new-fangled metal capable of clearing the worst of the undergrowth. But the new plough was perfectly adequate to turn the light soils of the chalk country.

How extensively this land was cultivated is demonstrated by the lynchets or series of terraces which any wayfarer can see today where the downs slope away from the high ridge and where the land has never been cultivated since prehistoric times. The date of the lynchets is determined by the fragments of metal and other objects discovered in the soil. Without this knowledge it is hard to distinguish the genuinely prehistoric lynchets from those of later date, especially the furrows of Anglo-Saxon fields on the lower slopes of the downland country.

First the turf was removed from the face of the downs, then an oxen-drawn plough turned the underlying soil on the highest slopes first, gradually working downhill. Some subsidence of the soil was inevitable, so that the furrows at the lower end of the field were built up while those at the upper end were denuded. Thus natural terracing was formed, which in the course of time was covered with new turf, but still retains the typical and clearly visible form of the lynchets. (Early observers often confused these cultivation terraces with the horizontal parallel striations left by glaciers in valleys through which they flowed.)

Much of the 'Celtic field' system can be observed at ground level. Much more of it can be seen from above. Aerial photographs taken with the help of the long shadows of the setting sun

D

again and again reveal a complex pattern of fields even in places where the land has been ploughed again.

During the last few centuries B.C., Iron Age man was coming down into the valleys to live, even though he could make little progress with ploughing the valley lands. There were certainly groups of stock-raisers living in thatched timber-built villages and fattening their cattle in the green meadows by the banks of many southern rivers. These Iron Age lowland settlements were made sometimes perhaps when the population of the hill villages over-flowed. The sites that were chosen in many cases became the sites of Roman, mediaeval, and modern cities. The people who built the great earthworks on the Trundle may have been the founders of the first settlement on the site of Chichester. The people of Maiden Castle may have founded the town which is now Dor-chester. By 200 B.C. at the latest there was a settlement on the site of modern Canterbury by the banks of the Stour, and probably one on the site of the city of London where Ludgate Hill rose like an island from the wide area of waterlogged land through which the slow-flowing Thames meandered towards the sea.

The countryside of the Iron Age was beginning to look much more like our idea of a cultivated scene. There were ever in-creasing splashes of colour on the slopes of the green downs where barley and wheat and now oats were cultivated. Since the end of the Bronze Age, flax with its bright blue flowers had made a bril-liant addition to the changing pattern. Man had certainly made no insignificant mark on the natural beauty of the south where only the oaken forests remained unchallenged and the extensive areas of salt marsh and swamp defied man's efforts to advance into nature's preserves.

Even in the less clement climate of the north and west there were enough people earning a living from the soil to show the first signs of a changing landscape. In the highland zone during the Bronze and Early Iron Ages nature herself was modifying the moorland scene at an unusual speed. It was a period of uncom-monly heavy rainfall. In the course of a mere five hundred years or so the greater part of the peat bogs of today were formed—in Scot-

and and Ireland most rapidly, but also on the plateau of England's Pennine Chain and in the mountainous country of the north-west. The heavier rainfall caused the rivers to flow more swiftly and speeded up the natural process of erosion. Nature is for ever modifying the outline of the landscape, today as much as ever, cutting deeper valleys, levelling off the upstanding hills—adding land here, removing it there—but in those five hundred years as much change took place as in any subsequent period of twice that length.

A traveller in the south country at the end of the Iron Age would have noticed other changes in the scene besides the obvious and dramatic effects produced by man the cultivator. He would have been surprised by the number of memorials raised during the preceding two thousand years—memorials that could be seen in almost every part of the inhabited country. He must have marvelled at the burial mounds of various shapes and sizes, at the vast single standing stones, at the stone circles, and still more at complex stone monuments such as Avebury and Stonehenge, which have appealed to the imagination of every age as works of almost unbelievable difficulty for primitive man to achieve.

The great number of barrows (or burial mounds) on Salisbury Plain moved one traveller to describe the whole area as a vast cemetery. Assuredly two thousand years ago, before natural erosion had levelled the earthen banks and filled in the surrounding ditches, the barrows on Salisbury Plain must have been a far more striking feature of the landscape than they are today.

The vast majority of barrows are roughly circular in shape, though within this group six or seven distinct types have been classified. A few only are described as long barrows, because they were oval in shape. Generally only the stonework of the burial chamber which it covered has survived. Wayland's Smithy beside the trackway which leads over the Berkshire Downs and Kit's Coty near the Pilgrim's Way in Kent are two good examples of burial chambers which were once covered by long barrows. One or two, such as Belas Knapp in Gloucestershire, have been reconstructed.

The distinction between the round barrows and the long is that the former belong mainly to the Bronze Age, while the latter were all the burial places of Stone Age man, generally designed to be opened again and again when fresh corpses were placed in the burial chamber. It seems likely, to say the least of it, that such elaborate burial was reserved for very special families in the community, perhaps for members of the priesthood, as some have suggested, or for the 'royal' house of the larger communities.

Some of the round barrows of the Bronze Age also covered a small stone cist or burial chamber. Others were piled up over the simply buried bodies of the dead. Many are in groups, more numerous than at first glance appears, as once again aerial photographs reveal. The group of barrows in Berkshire traditionally known as the Seven Barrows of Lambourn probably numbers a dozen. In the latter part of the early Iron Age the modern idea of ordinary inhumation had been accepted. Large cemeteries have been discovered in Kent, Surrey, and elsewhere and have proved beyond any doubt to be earlier than the Roman occupation.

Standing stones occur, singly or in groups. They are often of enormous weight and size, and are set up in various parts of the country, but especially, of course, where an abundance of local stone made quarrying them relatively easy. Many of the boulders which were once thought to be prehistoric monuments, in the Pennines and in the Lake District particularly, have proved to be natural features of the landscape—the eroded remains of rocks fashioned by the last surge of Britain's glaciation. Yet many mighty stones remain which the evidence shows conclusively to have been set up by human agency. The Devil's Arrows in Yorkshire near Boroughbridge are among the most striking of these, three vast stones averaging twenty feet in height with another five feet buried in the ground. The stones must have been quarried fully eight miles away and, literally, dragged to their present position. That was a task which demanded scores of strong men, working under skilled direction and moved by some greater than normal compulsion—whether to do honour to a dead chieftain or to carry out a religious rite of tribal significance is something which can never be known.

Stone circles, that is numbers of standing stones arranged more or less exactly round the circumference of a circle, are not by any means confined to the stone country of the mountainous west and north, though Arbor Low in Derbyshire and the Keswick stone circle are very fine examples. The complex circles at Stanton Drew in Somerset and the Rollright Stones on the northern face of the Cotswolds in Oxfordshire are two in the 'lowland' countryside which are no less impressive. These and the many others which have been listed fade into insignificance when they are compared with the two great stone monuments of the chalk downlands, Avebury and Stonehenge.

Stonehenge is the better known of the two and presents the more inscrutable riddle. Its alignment is such that four thousand years ago to an observer at the centre of the monument the sun would have appeared to rise on Midsummer's Day immediately behind the detached stone known as the Hele Stone. The most startling thing about this discovery is that it is not precisely true today. That is to say, the hundreds of people who make the pilgrimage on Midsummer's Day to see the sun rise behind the Hele Stone (even if they have the good fortune of a clear morning) are inevitably disappointed because it no longer rises precisely in that position. What has been proved by astronomical calculation is that it did do so about four thousand years ago.

When one has said that, one has said almost all that is known for certain about the purpose and history of Stonehenge. One is left with a sense of wonder at the fantastic amount of manual labour that was expended in its construction. The stone uprights and the lintels they support and the stones of the free standing circle were found locally. They are part of the sandstone covering which millions of years ago was overlaid on the chalk. Granted that the stones were lying conveniently to hand, there was still the work of dragging them to their present position (each weighing many tons) setting them upright and finally placing the horizontal slabs with their primitive toggle joints above the uprights. That was a task which must have involved a great gathering of the clans, the labour of hundreds of men operating in welltrained and welldrilled gangs and working with skill and persistence over a long period.

A still more remarkable fact is that the circle of 'blue' stones, the smaller stones of the ruined monument as it is today, were anything but local. Geologists have shown that the nearest point where they could have been quarried was the Prescelly Hills of Pembrokeshire. Here is another marvel—the means by which these smaller but still heavy stones were conveyed across hundreds of miles of only partially cleared country without benefit of roads and without mechanical traction of any kind. Most probably they were brought by sea round Land's End and up the river Avon to within a relatively short distance of Stonehenge but that, too, is a marvel, for it involves either the existence of welltried trade routes or a quite remarkable feat of experimental seamanship.

This fascinating monument, undoubtedly religious in origin, helps to bring to life the picture of England as it was in prehistoric times. We can understand it better if we assume that it is not of one period. The big stones were probably erected at the dawn of the Bronze Age about 1800 B.C. The site was a specially sacred one and additions were made hundreds of years later as the population increased and the primitive rites grew more complex. There may even be truth in the legend long discredited that Stonehenge was a temple of the Druids. The Druids belong to a period immediately before the Roman occupation. There is no reason at all why the site should not have preserved its sanctity and should not have been in full use right up to the time that the Romans came to Britain. It is certain, though, that the Druids had nothing to do with its building, which was undoubtedly complete a thousand years or more before Druidism had spread from Gaul.

Avebury in its own time must have looked even more impressive than Stonehenge. It is all the more remarkable because it was complete in its final form by the time Stonehenge began to be built. It was the supreme monument of the New Stone Age, finished about 1900 B.C. It consisted of an earthen bank and ditch surrounding a double circle of stones, with a stone avenue leading away towards the Sanctuary, which was a comparatively small stone circle of a more conventional pattern.

That the earthworks of Avebury have no defensive significance is shown by the fact that the bank is on the outer side of the ditch, so that it would have been quite useless in defence (the entrenchments of the hill forts have the bank on the inner side of the ditch so that bank and ditch together double the height of the obstacle to be overcome). Only a few of the original stones of Avebury survive intact, though excavation has revealed the sites of many others, which are now shown by concrete blocks. Unfortunately the mediaeval village was built largely inside the monument. Inevitably most of the giant stones were broken up and used to build the mediaeval homes of Avebury people, while others were carted away and used to repair the roads. But there is still enough of Avebury to fire the imagination and to bring home to the wayfarer what a striking difference its building wrought in nature's landscape.

Nearby Silbury Hill, 125 feet high, is just as striking an addition to nature. That it is prehistoric is known because a Roman road was diverted so as to encircle the base of the hill. Shafts have been sunk from top to bottom. Other shafts have been driven through its base, but no one either by excavation or analogy has been able to demonstrate its purpose. One supposition is that it is an outsize in burial mounds, but all we really know is that it is artificial, the largest hill of its kind in Europe, a striking enough landmark for travellers of today along the Great West Road beyond Marlborough. How much greater must have been the impact it made on prehistoric people, how much more dramatically it must have demonstrated the power of man to modify nature's contours.

Silbury Hill is unique in size but is only one of several artificial additions made to the landscape in prehistoric times. The Dane John just inside the walls of Canterbury is another artificial hill which many believe was built before the Roman occupation. It is now thought more likely, however, that the Dane John like the

'Bartlow Hills' was a burial mound of Roman origin. Originally it was one of a group of three, of which the other two were
levelled when the railway station was being built. If these were
levelled, how many others may not have been destroyed in the
passage of two thousand years or more?

During the last five hundred years of the pre-Christian era,
there were wars and rumours of wars, and Iron Age man began to
construct fortified strongholds to defend himself against fresh waves
of invaders. His defensive earthworks added yet one more spectacular modification to the pattern of hill and dale. In neolithic
times, settlements had been surrounded by primitive earthen banks
and ditches with wooden stockades for greater protection. Many
of these have been excavated, though none has survived intact
enough to be a recognizable feature of the scene. 'Camps' such
as Whitehawk on the downs behind Brighton, Windmill Hill
near Avebury, and the vestigial entrenchments which were dis-
covered inside the Iron Age entrenchments of the Trundle and
Maiden Castle are typical of the group. They were puny defences
compared with the terrific earthworks that were thrown up to
defend the Trundle and Maiden Castle in the Iron Age and other
fortified villages of similar date such as Cissbury in Sussex and
Chalbury or Rawlsbury in Dorset. Here are works greater even
than an Avebury or a Stonehenge. They are numerous in the uplands of the south, though they do not all date from precisely the
same period, nor is it likely that they were inhabited, as many historians supposed until recently, by whole tribes for any considerable length of time. Rather they were built as defences against a
specific threat of aggression and occupied by the people of surrounding villages for only a short time until the threat had passed
or until the defences had been breached and the people sheltering
within them done to death. In one or two places abundant evidence has been found of mass slaughter, which suggests that then,
as now, an apparently impregnable fortress proved inadequate to
its task.

With these mighty defences prehistoric man altered the contours of existing hills rather than, as at Silbury, adding fresh hills

to the landscape. The so-called 'British Camp' on the summit of the Malvern Hills, Eggar Dun in Dorset, the Trundle, and many others when seen from a distance, present a man-made silhouette against the sky; though time and weather have half-levelled the banks and ditches the circular or oval entrenchments can still be seen from miles away, evidence of the unbelievable energy and purposeful work of prehistoric man.

Not all the forts are on hill tops, though every one is in a commanding position relative to the surrounding country. Maiden Castle, the greatest of them all, commands the plain of Dorchester, though there is much higher ground near at hand. Caburn commands the valley of the Ouse in just the same way, and so on without end. Iron Age man had a wonderfully keen eye for a suitable defensive site. This fact is illustrated nowhere better than at Butser Hill at the western end of the South Downs, where nature's steeply pitched contours on three sides made it necessary to construct the usual banks and ditches only on the fourth and naturally undefended side.

The hill forts of the chalk country are the most spectacular today, and must have been even more so when the ramparts were gleaming white and perpendicular. But there are many prehistoric defences in the stone country of the west, also, as for instance at Worle Head overlooking Weston-super-Mare. There, however, though the stone walls of the hill camp can be distinguished quite easily, time has been less kind than in the chalk country. The stones of the original walls are widely scattered, while more recently planted trees have obscured the view from a distance.

One indisputable fact stands out from the speculation which these mighty works of man have provoked—that whether invasion threatened from the continent, or attack was expected by neighbouring tribes, the people of Britain were well enough organized and numerous enough to build defences which would not have put a modern military power to shame. In so doing they varied to an appreciable degree the sculpture of many hills in southern and western England.

CHAPTER IV

Roman Outposts

• •

WITH THE COMING of the Roman legions to Britain we arrive quite suddenly at a period in the story of the landscape when the impact of civilized life in the fullest sense of the term is felt for the first time. The Romans were a civilized people, not only in the sense of being literary and artistic and political beings, but in that other more accurate though seldom used meaning, that their culture was based on city life.

Roman culture flowed from the city of Rome into the cities of the outlying provinces. These cities, small though they were by modern standards, were yet the focal points from which sprang knowledge of Roman institutions, of Roman law and art, of agriculture, of engineering, and of every other science which revolutionized European life. Every Roman province was a microcosm of Italy; every town in a province was moulded, however vaguely, on the pattern of Rome itself. To obtain Roman citizenship was the ambition of all who dwelt under the protection of the 'Roman Peace', the peace that was guaranteed, paradoxically, by the strength of Roman arms. 'I am a Roman citizen' was as proud a boast of the British townsman in Roman times as 'I am a British subject' was of the free colonists in the early days of the Empire.

Probably the Roman Empire meant more in the ancient world than the British Empire in the nineteenth century. In the eyes of its subjects it stood for peace against the forces of barbarism, for a bulwark of stability against disintegration, for organization against anarchy. One was either a Roman citizen or one was completely beyond the pale.

Those facts are vitally important in assessing the changes that took place in the landscape during the period of Roman influence. It was not only a case of the handiwork of man being superim/ posed on the pattern of nature but of the pattern of Roman life being superimposed on native institutions. Nature still bulked large in the landscape at the end of the Roman occupation as it did in the beginning, but the work of the cultivator and the builder had modified it by then in a hundred details. So, too, the native institutions of Celtic Britain, of the Belgic people who were in occupation of south/east England immediately before Britain be/ came a province of Rome, flourished side by side with those of the Roman invaders, though greatly and progressively modified by them. This was as true of agriculture as of any other phase of human activity.

The story of Britain as a Roman province differs also from the story of earlier periods in another important particular. Our whole knowledge of life among prehistoric peoples is based on the work of the 'pick and shovel historians', the archaeologists whose re/ search has made possible the reconstruction we have attempted. Now, from the first century onwards, we are in a stage of transi/ tion. The evidence of archaeology is still of vital importance but its purpose is not so much to draw a picture in broad outline as to fill in the detail. The broad outline is sketched in for us by written records, by the writings of contemporary and near/con/ temporary historians. Though there was no native historian of England until the time of St Bede the Venerable, Julius Caesar himself and, more reliably, the Roman historian Tacitus, are authorities for the events which happened in the early stages of the occupation. Many of the events in the later period are vouched for by a number of Roman writers as well as by inscriptions in Latin and other positive records.

It is a sad commentary on the dark age following the decline and fall of the Roman Empire that ninety per cent at least of what was written has been lost and that we are still dependent on in/ ference for constructing a progressive picture of social life. We can reconstruct the picture in general terms without any great difficulty. It is when we come to put the changes that took place

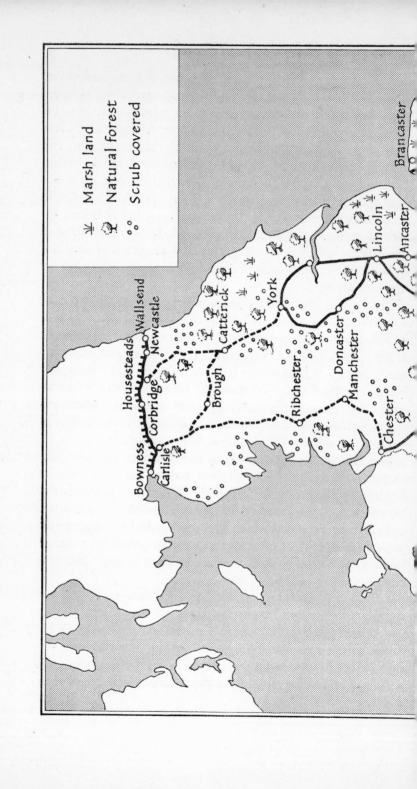

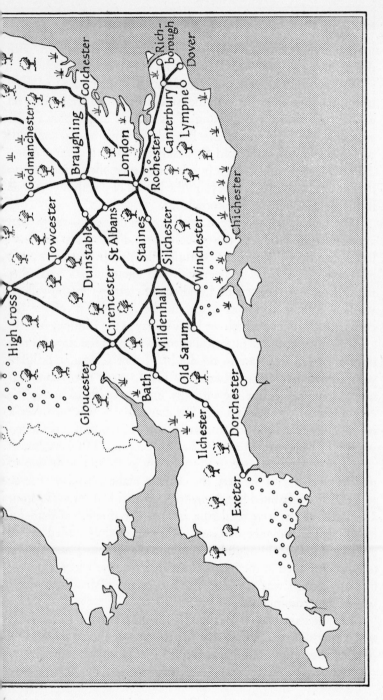

How the Roman roads opened out the English lowlands

in chronological order that we find ourselves confronted with difficulties.

We can say with certainty that during the three hundred years of comparative peace between the establishment of the province on a firm basis and the beginning of its decline major blows were struck in the war against the English swamps and woodlands which previously had defied the best efforts of man to tame them. To say precisely when, even in what sequence, the various blows in that war were struck is beyond the bound of possibility, at least in the light of our present knowledge.

That war, however, waged with conspicuous success by man against nature, produced the greatest single difference in the deve/loping landscape during the centuries that Britain was a province of Rome. The dense undergrowth and forests of oak and other native trees were broken by hundreds of clearings in the valleys, while a definite start was made on the reclamation of the fen country and the area which we know today as the Romney Marsh.

The sequence of the historical events which set the stage for this transformation scene are in no doubt. Julius Caesar, a brilliant young governor of the province of Gaul, made two reconnais/sances in force against the virtually unknown island across the North Sea in 55 and 54 B.C. His avowed aim was to survey a country of which little was known, though by repute it was judged worthy of being added to the Roman Empire. His expeditions served two purposes, one to give his troops field exercise and to test the efficiency of the fleet, the other to make a display of force in a country inhabited largely by tribes which had migrated from Gaul and which were rendering assistance to disaffected elements in the settled province of Gaul. Caesar certainly added to his prestige at Rome, although his reports on the promised land appear to have been filed in the imperial archives for nearly a century be/fore any action was taken to implement the plan for conquest which he recommended.

Thus the stage was set for the Claudian invasion in A.D. 43. It was a very different Britain that the Romans found in the middle of the first century from that described by Caesar a hundred years

before. Not even Caesar with his gift for verbal embroidery could
have described the British people who opposed the Romans under
Aulus Plautius in A.D. 43 as woad-painted savages. For three or
four generations the group of tribes whose capital was at Colchester had been exporting corn to the Roman Empire and im-
porting many Roman manufactured goods and, still more
important, Roman ideas. Already some change might have been
discerned by a perceptive eye in the general aspect of the landscape.
A beginning had been made in clearing the lowlands when the
Britons founded settlements in the valleys such as those on the sites
of Roman Dorchester and Chichester. The real work of attack-
ing the heavy clay lands was yet to come but the lighter soils in
parts of Essex and especially the gravelly country near the course
of some of the rivers had been brought under the influence of the
cultivator. Moreover, as the Romans were to find to their cost,
the tribal organization was by no means incompetent.

So although Aulus Plautius was able to land his troops from
his flotilla, which lay off the coast of Kent, and march by the
Stour crossing at Canterbury as far as the ford over the Medway,
with only the lightest of skirmishes, much more serious fighting
was to come before the conquest could be said to be complete.
Inevitably, however, when battle was finally joined the Romans
triumphed by sheer force of superior numbers and equipment.
Plautius was able to invite the Emperor Claudius to journey
from Rome to take command of the army. The Thames was
crossed at London and the way to Colchester was open.

The British chieftain there, Cunobelinus, Shakespeare's
Cymbeline, duly made his obeisance to the Emperor. The or-
ganization of yet one more Roman province could begin. Other
British chieftains, whose realms were centred on St Albans and
Chichester, sent formal tokens of their welcome to the Roman in-
vaders, while no opposition was expected from the Iceni of East
Anglia.

Claudius was probably genuine in imagining that the end of
British resistance had been reached and that he was justified in
returning to Rome to enjoy a well-earned triumph. The Roman

engineers who travelled with the legions and were, in fact, dual-purpose troops, went to work immediately on reconstructing this strange and unknown country which had so swiftly been added to the Empire. And their work made a conspicuous addition to the man-made features of the landscape. Within a very few years they had developed the small trading settlement by the banks of the Thames on Ludgate Hill into a compact town, though one necessarily mainly built of timber. A new and larger version of Cunobelinus's capital of Colchester, too, had been built, while by the banks of the Ver the new Verulamium was taking shape. The day of the town planners had begun. The first scars on the landscape that we might ourselves recognize as towns were being built.

To serve these towns and to enable the Roman legions to travel speedily to the western and northern marches of the province, completely new roads on fresh sites were being engineered. These were another new factor in the English scene. The Roman roads were arterial roads. They became, literally, arteries of commerce, through which was pumped the blood that gave life to the growing number of Roman-founded settlements in the midlands and north country. They were channels along which could be ferried the supplies, the arms, and the men to defend the far-flung outposts of empire.

Soon ports were established on the Kentish coast, sheltered harbours into which the ever-growing number of vessels from the continent could put in without let or hindrance. These were at Reculver, Richborough, Lympne, and Dover, though Richborough was by far the most important as it was the most sheltered and adequate roadstead. Roads straight as the flight of the proverbial crow were engineered across the Kentish countryside from these points to the ford over the Stour, where Canterbury now stands and where, too, a Roman town was beginning to take shape. The several roads united there, and went forward as one in a straight line from the crossing of the Stour to the crossing of the Medway at Rochester and thence to the crossing of the Thames at London.

as of Cultivation. *These aerial photographs show, above, the evident signs of a Celtic or er field pattern at Whitchurch and, below, characteristic lynchets in the chalk country near Chippenham in Wiltshire.*

Maiden Castle from the Air. *The triple banks and the complex defences of one of the* entrances *are clearly shown in this aerial photograph, which also underlines the oval shape* Britain's largest and most strongly protected Iron Age settlement.

London thus became a place through which passed a large proportion of all supplies from the continent. The ford over the Thames was very near the site of modern London Bridge. The road approached it by a course almost identical with that of the Old Kent Road from New Cross Gate, passing what was later to be the Tabard Inn, where Chaucer's pilgrims assembled for their leisurely journey to the shrine of St Thomas at Canterbury. This road which later came to be known as Watling Street (its contemporary name is not known) divided in London, one branch turning north-east to Colchester, another, the main branch, identified today as the continuation of Watling Street, proceeding in a north-westerly direction along the line of the Edgware Road to St Albans (Verulamium) and thence, still wonderfully straight, by the course of today's arterial road (A5) almost as far as Shrewsbury. Another road led directly north from London to the ford over the Ouse at Godmanchester and so to Lincoln, Doncaster, and York—the Great North Road of Roman times.

Here was a permanent contribution to the shape of the modern landscape. The alignments of the roads engineered by the Romans remained for all time the best suited for English trunk roads. For three hundred years they were busy with the multifarious traffic of Roman Britain. For a thousand years after that they were in grievous disrepair and superseded in most cases by rough tracks designed to link together the Saxon settlements by river and sea shore. These mediaeval tracks were the forerunners of the coaching highways of the seventeenth and eighteenth centuries, but modern road engineers have often reverted to the line of the Roman road. The comparatively new Rochester Way which by-passes Gravesend and Dartford is in part on the exact course of Watling Street, whereas the coaching road followed the valley of the Thames and linked Rochester with the Thames-side towns founded long after the Roman occupation. When relief was sought for the congested parts of Telford's highway to Holyhead (the mediaeval road reconstructed by Telford which leads through Coventry, Birmingham, and Wolverhampton), it was by-passed

E

by reverting to the line of the Roman road which still runs on mile after mile through thinly-peopled country, avoiding all large towns. The motorist bound for Shrewsbury and beyond has every reason to be grateful to the Roman road builders, who were not faced by the obstacles which confront modern planners—the vested interests, the developed land, the towns, and the factories.

All these roads and many that were to come later, including the Foss Way from Lincoln south-westward through Leicester and Bath to Exeter (probably in origin a boundary line between the embryo province and the military no-man's-land which separated it from Celtic Britain) were new roads—new, that is, in every sense of the term, newly conceived, newly surveyed, newly built and metalled. They were, in fact, the first metalled roads in England. Previously the main lines of communication had been the broad amorphous trackways, half a mile wide in places, which provided through routes over ground not commonly flooded, forest-covered, or boggy.

Some of the earlier British trackways were redesigned by the Romans. Others were left as they were and continued to serve the needs of the local population. The Icknield Way, the longest and most famous of the prehistoric tracks, reaching from Salisbury Plain to the Wash, formed the basis of a Roman road which was re-aligned, straightened, and improved at its many fords. Other prehistoric trackways, such as the Pilgrims' Way, were not, it appears, even considered by the Roman engineers to serve anything but purely local needs. The Celtic people of Roman Britain continued to drive their cattle along it as their ancestors had done before them, and used it as a means of communication between one settlement and another. But the Romans themselves, if they used it at all, did so only for transport to the settlements established near it and not normally for through traffic.

What a scene the building of one of the new Roman roads must have presented to the incredulous eyes of the British people. Anyone who has seen a remote Scottish highway in course of reconstruction may have some idea of what was entailed. Gangs of workmen must have been encamped or slept rough in close proximity to the roadworks. Deep excavations were going on in one place and the excavated material was being carted to another to form a causeway over swampy ground. Stone for surfacing the road was being brought up from the rear in heavy wagons, while from the speed with which the first survey was implemented we can only assume that hundreds of the British people were pressed into service to assist the Roman legionaries and their skilled en-gineers. To build a highway from Canterbury to Wroxeter (near Shrewsbury) was a task which can fairly be compared with the building of the Burma-Siam railway during the second world war.

The supply of food and necessities for the workpeople must have presented almost as great difficulties as the supply of materials for the road. However much the so-called morass of the English clay lands has been exaggerated, the fact remains that valley settlements except on the gravelly slopes near rivers were virtually unknown a century before these roads were being driven straight across the lowlands. In the first and second centuries, therefore, the roads were being built in practically virgin country, trackless and previously unsurveyed, still less surveyed with the elegant skill which the Romans showed. The new ways were driven straight over hills and through forests. They seldom turned aside from their apparently pre-determined course except to avoid sections of definitely marshy ground such as the edge of the East Anglian fens or a 'natural' obstacle such as Silbury Hill. The Chute Causeway avoids the Hippenscombe Valley apparently for con-venience rather than to by-pass marshlands, but such exceptions to the general rule are few. The Romans showed their determination in Britain as in other countries of the empire to impose their will on nature's pattern, however intricate that pattern might be. In the event they succeeded magnificently, completing a task at which the imagination boggles in any assessment of the manual work or the organization involved.

In Chapter III the extraordinary feat of transporting stone from the Prescelly Hills in Pembrokeshire to the site of Stonehenge was quoted as an example of human achievement two thousand years earlier. The building of the roads in Roman Britain represented no less a conquest of natural difficulties, having regard to the times and the increased scientific knowledge of the period. The chief difference is that one can still only guess at how Stonehenge was built, whereas how and when and in what circumstances the Roman road system was completed is known more or less precisely.

One problem still defies historians—a subtle one but a very difficult one. How did the Romans survey their roads so well? How did they contrive a road alignment straight from one ford to the next through forest-covered country? The traditional answer is that a team of surveyors went to work on a given stretch of the proposed road, treating each hillock or rise in the ground as a key point in the survey between river and river and lighting bonfires on each high point as a guide to the alignment. Having thus got fires burning on each elevated spot, between, say, Canterbury and Rochester, another team would walk in a straight line from one bonfire to the next guided by the plume of smoke rising from it and laying down an easily recognizable trail, a pilot road, as it were, for the roadmakers to follow.

Many other theories have been suggested in recent years. Surveying instruments were certainly available when required, but there still seems to be a great deal to be said for the traditional explanation which has the virtue of demonstrating why it is that when the roads did change direction they usually did so on the summit of a hill.

During the first few decades of the Roman province the towns that were being planned were without strong fortifications and mainly of timber construction. They were townships which definitely changed the face of the land in many parts of the country but would inevitably have disappeared completely in the course of two thousand years, leaving no trace except perhaps the indestructible evidence of refuse pits from which so much of the daily life of the people has been reconstructed. An unexpected sequence of events changed these early plans. The Roman government must have felt secure in the loyalty of the British people, for it left the southern and eastern districts virtually unprotected, while the legions marched to the north and west to strengthen the frontiers. Then, without warning, a powerful group of East Anglian tribes, the Iceni, revolted under their Queen Boadicea, or Boudicca as she is more correctly named.

The old enemy of the Romans, Caratacus or Caractacus (Caradoc), had been defeated in the west and taken to Rome as a prisoner. The people of the south and east had been disarmed. Yet Boudicca, enraged by Nero's refusal to recognize the land of the Iceni as an independent client kingdom as Claudius had done, contrived against all probability to raise an army strong enough to overrun a large part of what now is Essex, Suffolk, and Norfolk. In A.D. 61 the Iceni columns took the Romanized Colchester by storm and marched on to London. The two towns which had been built with pride under Roman supervision were razed to the ground. Verulamium (St Albans) suffered the same fate, and many thousands of the inhabitants, the traders and administrators who lived in the three towns, perished at the hands of the attackers or in the flames.

Once the Roman commanders had marshalled their forces the revolt was not difficult to quell, but it came so near to success and caused so much material damage that the Romans learnt a lesson that they never forgot. Henceforth they built walled towns and encouraged the magistrates of the towns to enforce the building of the people's homes in stone, at least on the lower floor. The walled towns were given strong gates which would be proof against sudden attack along the roads. The walls themselves were defended by turrets at intervals and by a moat running around the perimeter. Henceforward, too, a space was left free of buildings just inside the walls, so that the citizens could patrol the walls constantly in times of peace and soldiers could be deployed to defend them if attack threatened.

The whole nature of urban Britain was revolutionized by this change of policy. It took many decades, more than a century in all, before every important Roman settlement was walled and guarded, but it was a policy which once initiated was maintained

as long as towns were being built. In that, as in the building of
the roads, the Romans laid the foundations of the modern urban
landscape. The sites which they chose for their towns proved the
sites most suitable for the development of urban life. That is why
so many modern towns are on the sites of Roman ones and why the
mediaeval town in scores of instances was the direct descendant of
the Roman walled town, incorporating very often all or part of the
Roman walls. The walls of Canterbury were practically co-
extensive with the walls of the Roman Durovernum. The rebuilding of London again and again brings to light additional
evidence of the Roman town and fresh parts of the Roman walls
that defended it in the third century.

What, then, did these new-fangled Roman towns look like,
these communities so utterly foreign to the traditional way of
British life? The answer is that they were as nearly Romano-
British as any facet of the Roman province, Roman, that is, in
conception and general plan but British in the development of the
plan. Normally in the Roman way the skeleton outline of the plan
included two roads meeting at right angles, the two roads that
linked the north gate with the south, the east with the west.
Chichester's handsome market cross stands at the very spot where
the two main streets of the Roman town of Regnum met at its
centre. The course of the original Roman roads is less well preserved in other towns. At Canterbury, for instance, the Roman
thoroughfares were superseded in the course of successive rebuilding of the town during the Middle Ages. Even at Canterbury,
however, the mediaeval West Gate still stands near the point
where the Roman Watling Street started on its way to London
and the Midlands.

The idea of two main roads meeting at right angles was entirely
a Roman one. Excavation of the pre-Roman Celtic settlements of
England gives no hint of such a plan. The rest of the area within
the walls was also divided in the Roman style into a series of rect-
angles or squares. Roman, too, was the idea of a forum or civic
centre, a square in which the chief administrative offices and social
centres were grouped. The forum was also the market-place and

as such the parent of thousands of market squares which formed the nucleus of mediaeval towns.

There the Roman pattern ended. Whereas Rome itself and most of the Italian cities must have presented a very regular appearance, with dwelling-places aligned in rows, the homes of the people in Romano-British towns were set higgledy-piggledy within the framework of the Roman roads. Excavations on the site of Silchester suggest that this higgledy-piggledy arrangement may have been a deliberate concession to British tradition as opposed to Roman town-planning. The hutments which were the homes of the people who dwelt in the Celtic towns, many of which like Colchester were superseded by Roman ones, certainly had no orderly plan. The rectangular design was so essentially a part of classical architecture and planning that Roman governors of Britain, whose word was law to the local administrators, may have thought it wise to allow the people to maintain their own traditions insofar as they were not prejudicial to defence or likely to prevent the full development of urban culture.

We can trace the same tendency in many phases of life in Roman Britain. Though the Roman religion in the early centuries was, as it were, the official one, it was never enforced on the British people, who continued to worship their own Celtic gods until they were able to identify these with corresponding Roman divinities. Even when the Christian religion was recognized by the Roman government, there was still no compulsion. The early Christian fathers wisely adopted the sacred days of the pre-existing religious calendar and identified them with the saints' days of the Christian Church.

When we come to look at the countryside in the second and third centuries A.D. the dual influence is even more apparent. We see a picture which can be compared quite fairly with that of Tanganyika today, where vast government-inspired farming schemes go on side by side with the relatively small-scale operations of colonial farmers and the primitive agriculture of the native tribesmen. In Roman Britain there was just as striking a contrast between the husbandry of the Roman villas and of the Celtic hill villages, inhabited now, as they had been for hundreds of years, by the tribesmen who had come to Britain when the Belgic invasions took place long before the Roman occupation.

The villa, like the town, was a Roman innovation. It consisted of a house, often large and pretentious, generally stone-built on the ground floor and half-timbered above. It was the permanent home of the farmer, often a Roman immigrant but probably still more often a native of Britain who had grown wealthy in the commercial life of the province, and had chosen to leave his hometown and found an estate in the country. Numerous workpeople lived in wings attached to the house or in adjacent hutments and helped the farmer to cultivate the surrounding fields.

Agriculture was the main preoccupation of the villa folk, sheep their principal stock-in-trade. But several of the villas had workshops attached; one at Chedworth, which was buried for hundreds of years by a landslide in the heart of the Cotswold Hills and when excavated proved unusually easy to reconstruct, had a large fulling shop, a fact which gives added emphasis to the importance of sheep farming in the third century A.D.

The vast majority of the Roman villas were situated on rising ground near the foot of the downs. Chedworth itself is below the high ground of the Cotswolds, which was one of the centres of Celtic hill-farming. Bignor in Sussex is similarly placed in relation to the high ridge of the South Downs, Darenth in relation to the North Downs. Here is constructive evidence of the progress which was made in these few hundreds of years in cultivating the lowlands and in clearing the undergrowth from the vicinity of the river valleys.

Throughout the period, on the nearby downs tribesmen were continuing to cultivate their strips of land on the sunny, southward-facing slopes of the hills, just as their ancestors had done nearly five hundred years before. They were growing more prosperous, their settlements were larger, the area of the downs under cultivation was greater, but the methods were the same, the villages looked much as they always had done. Though the people used Roman pottery and exchanged their corn or their fleeces in the town markets for Roman luxuries, their life was conservative in the extreme. Even the primitive Celtic plough was still being used on the hill fields when the new deeper ploughing machinery of the Romans was converting thousands of acres into productive fields which yielded a far greater weight of corn per acre than the calcareous uplands ever could.

If one had looked down from the summit of Bignor Hill in the third century A.D. one would have seen at least the first semblance of a modern landscape. The Roman villa far below must have appeared uncommonly like a mediaeval village except that it lacked the spire or tower of a mediaeval church. In some ways it would have looked a more modern landscape than it did a thou-sand years later. The Romans as they cleared the land planted it all over with corn, so that in its limited way the land round about the villa must have resembled the corn 'prairies' into which so many English parklands were converted during the second world war—an unbroken sea of gold as the corn ripened under the warm summer sun.

Harvest may have been a little earlier then than it is today. Though an element of doubt remains, it is almost certain that the climate of the south in Roman times was more clement than at any time since. Spring came earlier and the summer was a little warmer, though rainfall throughout the year was certainly no less than it is now. It is unlikely that even the hardy Britons could have achieved their own meagre standard of living in their hill-top communities if the summer weather had been no more reliable than it is in the twentieth century. In the notably cool and cloudy summer of 1954 the slopes of the Sussex Downs bearing corn (since the second world war) for the first time for sixteen hundred years, could not produce a crop ripe enough by early October to be threshed by people with the slender resources of the Britons. Modern scientific farming and deep ploughing, improved strains of wheat and combine harvesters to seize upon the right moment for harvesting and complete the job within a few days—all these were impotent to wrest a good yield from the unwilling soil. Such a year would inevitably have meant starvation for the British settlements and death for their stocks of cattle. But of such calamities archaeologists have found no evidence.

One thing that modern archaeology, with the help of aerial photography, has done is to reveal the previously unsuspected extent to which the downs were cultivated. Photography from the air, especially in the light of the setting sun, reveals the pattern of squarish or rectangular fields, though it may be completely in- visible to the naked eye at ground level. The fields were mainly small, divided by low banks and ditches, but extremely numerous, covering a fair proportion of Salisbury Plain and the Marlborough Downs and other parts of the chalk plateau. It was one of the times of greatest activity in the downlands, a period in which the Roman towns and Romanized villas in the richer valleys were oases in the desert of primeval forest, outposts of civilization in a land still predominantly Celtic, and organized in the Celtic way.

If the forest land of the Weald and the marshy country inun- dated by the sluggish rivers of the south were yielding gradually before the Roman plough, no change, however slight, was per- ceptible in the intractable moorlands of the north country; no change, that is, except the infinitely slow progress that Nature her- self was making in the deepening and widening of the Pennine valleys, in the wearing down of the high plateaux and in the searing out of deep gorges by the swift-flowing rivers. There were permanent garrisons of the Roman legions at York and at Chester. Everything northward of these two flourishing townships was a no-man's-land in which only scattered communities of Britons lived on much as they had always done, though under the protec- tion of Roman arms they now had a better chance of tilling their land undisturbed and of living at peace with their neighbours.

The border country was a military zone. Roads were built, soldiers tramped along them to relieve their fellows at the frontier posts, wagons rattled over them carrying supplies, but these were negligible symbols of civilization. The Romans founded settle- ments at strategic points such as Newcastle, where there was a bridge of boats. Small civilian townships grew up in association

with the military camps but that was all. For the rest the sole pur/
pose of life in these still nearly barren wastes was to ward off the
attacks of the Picts and the Scots from the north and to prevent
the scattered communities of Britons from banding together to
make an attack on the fertile country of the south.

The landscape was changed in only one way but that an
exciting and wellnigh incredible one. A boundary ditch was dug
from Tyne to Eden. Then in the reign of the Emperor Hadrian a
defensive wall was thrown across the narrow waist of Britain from
Wallsend on the Tyne to the Solway Firth. Enough of the wall
still stands in reconstructed form, winding like a snake over the
Northumbrian fells to give the modern traveller some impression
of this achievement of Roman engineers assisted by an army which
was composed partly of Roman legionaries and partly of con/
scripted Britons. Permanent camps were set up at intervals along
the wall, with small forts at distances of about a Roman mile,
while intervening turrets gave added protection. A road was built
parallel with and to the south of the wall, so that men and mate/
rials could be transferred at will to fill a breach whenever an attack
was made on the strong defences. The wall proved impregnable
during the centuries that it was manned. Only when the
legionaries were withdrawn was it possible for the Pictish tribes
to make forays to the south with impunity, or indeed with any
hope of returning to their homelands alive.

What an incredibly lonely life those Roman troops, who knew
so well the pleasures of town life, must have led in these inhospit/
able moorlands. What a day of rejoicing it must have been when
they were relieved and could return to the urban pleasures of York
or Chester, or even to their own home town or village.

One of the reasons why the Romans made no effort to extend
cultivation into the heart of the moors was that the population
was not expanding rapidly enough to supply the manpower
necessary to clear and work the land. The most generous esti/
mates place the population of Roman Britain in its heyday at be/
tween a million and two million. It may possibly have been no
more than three/quarters of a million. There was no economic

pressure to seek a wider horizon for human activity while so much
of the south remained uncultivated. In the south itself, however,
great efforts were made to bring the fen as well as the forest under
cultivation. In particular the fen lands on the border of Cambridgeshire were better drained and more productive than at any
time for more than a thousand years afterwards.

It is possible that inundation of the area bordering the Wash
was not so great when the Romans came to Britain as it was a
thousand years later. A fall in the level of the land or a rise in the
level of the sea, if only by a few inches, would have made a vast
difference. Certainly the Roman engineers did not feel that it was
beyond their power to reclaim much of this potentially fertile
countryside. Probably a start was made on building a sea wall
along the shores of the Wash. One great work indisputably
Roman is the Car Dyke, which runs along the western edge of
the fens and was built as a canal linking the Cambridge area with
Lincoln. It served incidentally to drain thousands of acres of land,
which in the Middle Ages reverted to swamp. But the Roman
works were sufficiently well designed to preserve the area for cultivation well into the Saxon period. The same is true of the Romney Marsh, where a sea wall was built which was the forerunner of
the vast system of coastal defence and marsh drainage which has
added so many thousands of acres to the productive area of
Kent.

The coastline of east Kent has changed out of all recognition
since Roman times. Then the shingle promontory of Dungeness
had not been built up by the tides. The river Rother flowed into
a wide delta in which there were a number of islands now a full
five miles from the nearest sea. The port of Richborough was an
open roadstead just inside the mouth of the Wensum channel
which divided the mainland from the Isle of Thanet by a broad
belt of water at high tide. The Isle of Sheppey, or rather the only
part of it which was dry land, stood several miles out to sea from
the Kentish coast, while the course of Watling Street came close
to numerous bays and inlets at various points between what are
now Faversham and Sittingbourne. Many other changes have

taken place round the coast of Britain but none more dramatic than these.

That, then, is the Roman heritage, the contribution made to the shape of the modern landscape during the centuries that Britain was a Roman province. Perhaps its most important part was the laying down of what have become in so many cases the main roads of England and the siting for all time of some of England's largest and most famous towns—London, York, Chester, Winchester, Chichester, Gloucester, Newcastle, Leicester, Cirencester, Bath, Colchester, Dorchester, Canterbury, and dozens of others. That alone was a major contribution.

To this must be added the progress made in clearing the land and reshaping the lowland country. And there was one small but significant contribution which historians most often omit to mention: the brilliant white flowers of the cherry brought to Britain for the first time by the Romans pointed the way on Kentish hillsides to the design of the 'Garden of England', even though nearly a thousand years were to intervene before any further progress was made towards its fulfilment. It is possible too that the Romans were responsible for the addition of the sweet chestnut, the sycamore, and perhaps even the beech to the short list of earlier British trees. If so, they assuredly contributed more than their fair share to the beauty that is England today.

CHAPTER V

Saxon Settlement

✦ ✦

THE BEACON of the Roman lighthouse on the cliff above Dover was still guiding ships along the trade routes from the Continent when the first piratical bands from across the North Sea descended on the English coast. Lighthouses were regarded then as the last word in man's inventive genius. There was only one other in the Roman world, and that at Alexandria at the other end of the Roman seas. To many it seemed as though that lighthouse by Dover was the very emblem of Roman civilization. It still stands on its cliff top as one of the most interesting monuments to the days of peace and plenty when Britain was a Roman province. Ships from Gaul and much farther afield sailed up the channel in frequent succession, helped by its light past the dangerous rocks at the foot of the chalk cliffs into the safe anchorage of Richborough and the sheltered passage through the Wensum into the Thames estuary.

However settled the scene might appear, clouds were rolling up from the horizon. Only the ignorant and the wishful thinkers refused to see them. The Saxon raids were increasing in violence. Britain had already been divided into several administrative provinces. The old system of communications was beginning to break down. The estates of the villa land-owners were decaying and, greatest tragedy of all, the civic life of the towns was slowly coming to an end. Even then, long before the Roman world collapsed, the landscape was changing perceptibly as it began to revert to nature under the stress of economic depression.

The Roman grip on the whole empire was lessening as armies of barbarians from outside the Roman world pressed southward and westward towards the nerve centres of the outlying provinces and towards Rome itself. A last but fruitless effort was made to maintain the province of Britain. A fleet was manned with bases at Boulogne and Richborough to sweep the sea clear of pirates. Unfortunately the British fleet, so well conceived, could not achieve its mission. All too often its admirals rebelled against their Roman masters and joined the piratical forays on the coasts of England and France. As any modern strategist could have told the Roman government, a naval force of sailing ships could never hope to intercept small boats such as the Saxon warriors used. Moreover, it was open to the Saxons to cross the sea by any route they chose, starting from no known base and landing on the shores of any of the estuaries of East Anglia.

A military commander with the title 'Count of the Saxon Shore' was appointed to protect the coast and supplement the abortive efforts of the fleet. At enormous cost and incredible hardship a series of strong fortresses was constructed in a wide arc round the coast from the Wash to Southampton Water. The Forts of the Saxon Shore were yet one more spectacular addition to the landscape of south-eastern England. The ruins of Richborough and Pevensey (Anderida) give a vivid impression of their size and strength. Large numbers of troops could make them their base and protect at least the natural harbours which the castles overlooked. Richborough and Anderida, both rising on the shore of sheltered lagoons high above the level of the marshes which flanked them, must have seemed as monstrous to the British people of the time as a Hampton Court Palace or a Hardwick Hall looked to generations more than a thousand years later.

Unfortunately, the massiveness of the forts' construction did not make them the more effective. They might have proved a valuable protection against an organized invasion if the invaders had needed the use of harbours. In fact the Saxons had no need to take them by storm. They could always by-pass them and did in fact repeatedly do so, for there was no defence in depth.

That the Forts of the Saxon Shore were well sited and durable is proved beyond doubt. Two of them at least, Anderida and Portchester, were adopted by the Normans, who built castles within their strong walls, while the walls of several others, in-cluding Burgh Castle in Norfolk, have survived the attacks of nature's weapons and the depredations of mediaeval road builders to the present day.

The Saxons were not the only threat to Britain's security. Picts and Scots were beginning to infiltrate through the defences of Hadrian's Wall in the north. Pirates from Ireland were sailing across the Irish Sea to devastate the West Country. The squeeze was well and truly on. When the Roman legions left Britain to defend the frontiers of their empire nearer home cracks in the fabric of Roman Britain very soon appeared. The dissolution was a gradual one, but it might just as well have taken place in a single attack had there been an enemy well enough organized to make it. A dark age was at hand in which for a time the forces of barbarism were all-powerful, as witness the sack of Rome by the Visigoths. The light when it came was to appear not from any resurgence of the old order, but through the growing strength of Christianity and the cultural influence of conquered peoples on their conquerors.

The civilized 'new look' of the landscape which had reached its peak in the third century A.D. was very fragile. In the fourth century the position was that settlements, whether towns or villas, had been made in many parts of what is now England, but by no means the whole of the country was even sparsely inhabited. If one looks at a map of the Roman roads one might suppose that England then was not so very different from what it is today. Nothing could be farther from the truth. Roman roads went through the forests and scrub land for mile after mile without coming to a habitation or settlement. The villas were centred in the recently cleared and fertile country near the foot of the hills which were the traditional home of the Celtic people. Towns, as we have seen, were sited along the roads, often coming into exis-tence at a road junction, but on either side of the road, especially in the Midlands and West Country, there were thousands of square miles of virgin untouched scrub land in which the alder and the oak, the hazel and the elm, disputed with each other for

e hand of the Roman builders. *Roman builders have left a permanent mark on the lish countryside, as in the main entrance to the Fort of Anderida (Pevensey), shown above, and in the still prominent earthworks of the amphitheatre near Dorchester, below.*

The Foss Way near Easton Grey. *In this long and unbroken length of the Foss Way*
exact course of the original Roman road is more clearly apparent from the air than from
viewpoint at ground level. In places its site is occupied by a metalled road, in others by a track
but its most interesting feature is that it has survived as a clearly marked 'through' way as tho
superimposed, like a modern arterial road, on the natural pattern of field and hedge.

living space, grew to maturity, then succumbed to storm or decay, with no one to fell them or clear away the fallen branches. The tangled undergrowth of the forest was still well-nigh impenetrable. This applied particularly to the heavy clay lands such as those of the East Midlands and the Trent valley, and to the large expanse of untouched country which filled the bowl of which the North and South Downs form the rims.

An early chronicler tells of Saxon invaders burning the Romano-British cities, so that flames extended from one coast to the other. Doubtless many of the Roman towns were burnt because the Saxons regarded them as places of ambush and possible retreat for their enemies. They had no experience of town life and regarded stone buildings as foreign to their way of living. But recent research has suggested that by the time the Roman soldiers were recalled at the end of the fourth century, many of the smaller Roman towns were already mouldering in decay with only a small fraction of their once prosperous population living on among the ruins of their gracious homes.

Excavation on the site of Roman Canterbury, carried out so painstakingly in the years since German bombers laid waste a large part of the city, demonstrates that time and neglect rather than invasion were the factors which destroyed the Roman town of Durovernum. Undoubtedly the departure of the Romans put the finishing touches to the scene of desolation, for with the legions went what few wealthy Romano-British people were left. Long before that, however, a fall in the birth rate or perhaps an increase in pestilence had decimated the population, so that many of the ploughed fields surrounding the country villas had ceased to be tilled, their place taken by the natural vegetation which so quickly moves in when man, the cultivator, moves out.

Let us not deceive ourselves. We are proud of being an Anglo-Saxon people, while the England that we know undoubtedly springs from the Anglo-Saxon tradition. The familiar landscapes of today are the direct descendants of the landscapes which the Anglo-Saxon tribes created, but the age into which the English countryside was thrown after the decline of Roman

F

Britain was a dark age in every sense of the term. It was not only an age of which there is little or no authentic record but one in which culture and science and sensibility were thrown out utterly from the scheme of things. The south country did not again reach the stage of civilized life which it enjoyed in the third century until at least fourteen hundred years later, even though in the meantime the population was increasing and the actual day-to-day course of history becomes a matter of known fact instead of inference.

The truth of this is most apparent in the story of travel and transport. The people of Roman Britain could travel from London to York in a couple of days if need arose, so well made were the roads and so well organized the means of transport. In an emergency an army and all its baggage could be moved with remarkable speed, as was seen even in the early days of the province during the revolt of Queen Boudicca. That was a facet of life which disappeared when Roman Britain declined and was never re-established until the Turnpike Acts and the era of mail coaches once more produced order out of the chaotic condition of English roads. What is so demonstrably true of the roads was true less obviously in many other walks of life. The key to this strange paradox is that from the fourth century onwards there was never real peace in the land for a thousand years, nor a central government so strong as the Roman.

Inevitably the landscape reflected the changed fortunes of the country. The stone-built and half-timbered homes of the Roman villa people were not replaced for seven hundred years or more; until the eleventh century there were few, if any, permanent buildings in stone. There was none of the ordered activity, the trade convoys, the comings and goings of merchants, the gathering of the rural people at the amphitheatres of the towns that had characterized Roman Britain. There were not even the fields of waving corn surrounding the villa homesteads. For a time at least the Celtic settlements in many parts of the downs which had continued to flourish all through the Roman occupation were left deserted like the Roman villa estates on the lower slopes. The fields which the Celtic cultivators had ploughed, and their fathers and forefathers before them, were left to nature to replant with grass and weeds.

In central England however the native settlements survived until they were absorbed by the new settlers, but Kent and Sussex and the Chiltern country must have presented a scene of utter desolation and abandonment as the fifth century began. In the far north-west, in the Lake District fells and valleys, in the still predominantly Celtic lands of Devon and Cornwall and the far western marches of England, life went on much as before, untouched by the Saxon invasions as it had been four hundred years before by the coming of the Romans. But these people of the Celtic west and south-west were backward, their ploughs and their agricultural methods three hundred years out of date. Their settlements of thatched dry-stone walled huts in the granite country of Devonshire and Cornwall still broke up the monotony of the grey country on the fringe of the moorlands. Yet though they survived, no evidence suggests that these Celtic settlements multiplied during the period that Anglo-Saxon England was being colonized. Their standard of living may well have been so poor, the area of land which they could cultivate so meagre, that there was no room for an increase in the population. Hemmed in by the forests of Somerset, by the scrub land of Devonshire's South Hams and by the Bristol Channel, these people who had preserved their identity so strangely from a bygone age had neither the opportunity nor the initiative to extend their dominions or to seek fresh fields across the seas.

In view of this, it need surprise no one that the bright torch of Christianity was kept alight through the centuries here if indeed anywhere in Britain, its flame kindled no doubt by Christian refugees from the Roman province in the fifth century. The Saxons were heathens but not savages. They were members of tribes which had lived just outside the sphere of Roman influence but had progressed a long way in the science of agriculture, especially in the use of a deep-cutting ploughshare, which is the key to early improvement in tilling the land. They were agriculturists, then, these Angles, Saxons, and Jutes, who arrived in increasing

An early mediaeval conception of Britain and the adjoining parts of Western
Europe. (Hibernia = Ireland: Cantia = Kent: Ispania = Spain.)

numbers after the fall of Rome. Their inherited experience, won
in the hard way amid the inhospitable countryside of northern
Europe, stood them in good stead when they came as plunderers
and stayed as settlers. Britain may well have seemed to them a
promised land with its already considerable clearings and its fertile, easily worked soils.

The Anglo-Saxon settlement of the country has two distinct
phases. The first lasted until a truly Anglo-Saxon regime was
established and England was divided into seven petty kingdoms.
This was a period of settlement by the easy way, of settlement, in
fact, in country which needed no hard work to render it suitable
for cultivation, in the countryside of the lighter lowland soils and

on the sheltered slopes under the downland ridges, where so many of the Roman villas had earlier been established.

The Angles settled in what is now East Anglia, in Norfolk, the country of the 'north folk', and Suffolk, that of the 'south folk'. The Saxons settled in Essex and Middlesex and Sussex, while a few penetrated even in that early phase to the traditional Wessex, coming probably from the Wash along the line of the Icknield Way rather than, as some have supposed, up Southampton Water.

Another group of tribes, called the Jutes, a more advanced and cultured people than the others, made their first settlements in Kent, south Hampshire, and the Isle of Wight.

It is possible to build up pictures of Saxon England at different times in its history merely by the study of modern place names. These early settlers came in small groups, a single family perhaps, or a community of two or three families. Many of the places they founded retain the termination 'ing' or 'ingham' added to a personal name. Hastings, Reading, Wokingham (and Woking), and Dorking are examples which spring to mind. An interesting commentary on this fact is that a map of early Saxon burial places shows much the same distribution as a map showing the situation of places which have these terminations.

It is perfectly clear that this early settlement was 'by river and seashore', mainly in east Kent, along the coast of Sussex, on the lighter soils of East Anglia and Lincolnshire, and to a lesser extent in the area of the middle Thames. The question is sometimes asked how Saxon settlers reached the middle Thames when the way was probably still barred by a township on the site of London held by the remnants of the Romano-British people. The answer may be that the London people were so decimated and enfeebled that they had no means of stopping the Saxon boats. Alternatively, the river was so wide then, with mud banks covered at high water on the south bank towards Southwark, that the Saxon boats were able effectively to by-pass the mouldering fortifications of London town.

Another significant fact is that the Sussex coastal plain has few, if any, of these early settlements west of Lancing, which itself is in the foothills of the downs. The answer to this riddle is two-fold and helps us to build up a more precise picture of the landscape in Saxon times. On the one hand, the coastal plain was still marshy,

Clearing scrub and working the land in the eleventh century [Ms. Harl. 603].

undrained and therefore an unlikely place in which to found settlements; on the other hand, settlements may well have been founded on the very edge of the sea on 'islands', as it were, rising from the marsh on its seaward side. In the intervening fifteen hundred years the sea has been constantly eating back into the marsh, while the marsh itself has been drained and made fertile, so that these settlements, like many on the East Anglian coast, were overwhelmed by the advancing sea. That is especially true of the Selsey peninsula, which has shrunk perceptibly within the last two or three centuries and may well have been the site of many of the manors mentioned in Domesday of which today there is no trace.

Yet another fact which shows how alien the picture of Saxon England was to that of Roman Britain can be deduced from the complete absence of early settlements on or near the line of the Roman roads, with the sole exception of the Icknield Way. The latter was the only effective road from the Wash to central England because all the Chiltern country was then densely covered in forest and quite impenetrable, while the country to the north of the Icknield Way was mainly still boggy and untrodden as well as partly forest-covered. So the Icknield Way remained a line of communication because it was the only possible one. For the rest, the Saxons had no more use for Roman roads than they had for Roman towns or Roman villas, or anything else that was part of a civilization which they abhorred.

But a new picture of the landscape was being drawn in the

Making an enclosure of wattle in Saxon times [Ms. Harl. 603].

south, as the Saxon family groups built their little clusters of wooden or mud-walled huts with thatched roofs rather like those of the pre-Roman Celts. As their numbers began to multiply they encouraged their sons to found new settlements and bring a few more acres under cultivation. Though there was no semblance of the trim fields of the Celtic cultivators, still less of the Roman villa estates, yet the land was being broken up afresh and a new fertility was beginning to make its appearance.

Yet even by the time that Ethelbert was King of Kent and St Augustine came to Canterbury to preach the word of God to the men of Kent (A.D. 597), this changing scene was confined to the south and east. No real attack had yet been made on the dense forests of the East Midlands and the Weald, on the heavy clays of the broad river valleys, or on the boulder clays which later brought such wealth to farmers in the central areas of East Anglia.

It is possibly a coincidence that the re-introduction of Christianity was followed by a sequence of events which provided the stimulus for the Saxons to extend their domains, thus once more changing the face of England. The fact remains that between A.D. 600 and 650 the second phase began. The iron axes and the deep ox-drawn ploughs of the Saxon people moved purposefully into the heavy lands of the eastern counties and central England. The forests protecting the original Saxon kingdoms diminished in extent. That in turn opened the way to unification through conquest or absorption. When the Forest of Blean and the Forest of the Weald ceased to convert the kingdom of Kent into what was virtually an island, Kent had no defence to offer to its larger and more powerful neighbours. Similarly with the gradual disappearance of the Forest of Essex, at least as a continuous rampart, the settlements of the east Saxons near the coast were quickly absorbed, as was the smaller kingdom of the middle Saxons by the rapidly increasing forces of Wessex. Wessex, in turn, as penetration was made into the forest lands which formed its western border, extended further and further to the south-west and brought Saxon influence into most of Devon although it never reached the still Celtic countryside of Cornwall.

Here again, place names are clues to the various phases in the slow revolution. In Cornwall, for instance, quite apart from the fact that most of the villages have Celtic names, the majority of the churches are dedicated to Celtic saints, while in Devonshire there is a mixture of the two, with Saxon names and Saxon saints predominating in the fertile country of south Devon, which previously had been covered in unpeopled woodland. All the 'hursts' and 'leighs' and the 'dens' belong to this latter phase of Saxon expansion. The termination 'leigh' (usually contracted to 'ley') is especially common in the clay lands of the East Midlands and in the Weald of Sussex and Kent, districts in which primeval nature had never before been touched by the hand of man. Hadleigh, Rayleigh, and even Leigh-on-Sea, were originally clearings in the Forest of Essex. Though 'hurst' itself means a wood, all the 'hursts' of Sussex and Kent, from Paddockhurst to Hawkhurst, began their history as village settlements made by these latter Saxon colonists.

Similarly the 'dens' of Kent—Biddenden, Tenterden, Smarden and many others—were lodgements in the forest where the son of a Saxon thane had hewn a small clearing in the scrub for his family and perhaps the families of his brothers or trusty friends, so

Hunting in the forests into which herds of swine were driven to feed on acorns in the autumn, eleventh century [Ms. Cott. Jul. A VI].

founding a new village community, which in turn despatched sturdy husbandmen in the next generation to found new 'dens' or 'leighs' still nearer the heart of the forest country.

These southern forests, which were mainly of oak, had a further advantage in the eyes of the Saxon cultivators, since they were able to drive their swine into the woods in the autumn to feed on acorns and so turn the harvest of the 'bad lands' to good account. In the beech wood country beech masts served equally well for fodder. Some scholars have even suggested that it was not the village people so much as their livestock which were responsible for clearing the less tractable parts of the forest of their covering of scrub and undergrowth. Young shoots and self-sown saplings were tempting morsels; after they were eaten there were no young trees to replace the giants of the forest when they fell.

This second phase of development was slow in reaching the Lake District and the far west. Celtic names still predominate in Cumberland and Westmorland, not quite to the same extent as in Wales or in Cornwall but sufficiently to mark down the fells and dales of Lakeland as predominantly Celtic-held territory until the eighth or ninth centuries. Even in Worcester and Hereford the map shows a mixture of names which suggests a very late Saxon penetration.

An interesting fact that emerges is that when the Celtic territories ceased to be protected by their forest shields, the native peoples and the Saxon colonizers appear to have lived peacefully together in the same area, one absorbing the culture of the other until they were united in fighting against the common enemies of England—the Vikings and the Danes. This was true even in the late-maturing kingdom of Wessex, where a number of Celtic settlements had continued to exist far into what is normally regarded as the Anglo-Saxon period.

It is usual to speak of the Anglo-Saxon kingdoms as primitive. No doubt they were by comparison with Roman Britain or with the united England that developed in the eleventh century. But, just as the elaborate defences of Iron Age fortress-villages increase our respect for the organization of the British tribes before the Roman occupation, so the massive earthworks which probably served to divide one Anglo-Saxon kingdom from another must impel us to revise the traditional view of these early kingdoms.

All the earthworks, commonly called dykes, which are attributed to the Saxon period consist of a single bank and trench, now partly filled in but still suggesting the wonderfully impressive achievement they represented when they were built, with their perpendicular sides thirty feet high in places, as formidable a defensive line as could be achieved with limited manpower and inadequate implements. Offa's Dyke, which was the line of demarcation between Mercia and the 'free' country of Wales, can be traced from the Bristol Channel to the estuary of the Dee. Grim's Dyke runs athwart the Chiltern Hills from the Thames gap to Berkhamsted and beyond. Most likely it divided the East Anglian kingdom from the group of Saxon settlements along the Icknield Way. Two other complex systems include the parallel lines of the so-called Roman Way, the Fleam Dyke, and the Devil's Dyke in Cambridgeshire, and the Wansdyke, which extends from Inkpen Beacon westward into Somerset, and is supported for a few miles of its course in Wiltshire by the Bokerly Dyke.

So England was born, not as yet a land flowing in milk and honey but at least a land which increasingly showed the changes

The shepherd and his flock, eleventh century [Ms. Cott. Jul. A VI].

that follow intensive cultivation. By the ninth century its crops and other man-sown vegetation burgeoned more prolifically than in the heyday of the Roman province. An observer in an aero-plane flying over southern England would have seen a landscape which in part was rather similar to that of the wooded country of Africa or South America today. In the clay lands the forest-covered areas still exceeded the clearings, while each individual clearing was small and the village settlement no larger than a modern hamlet. Elsewhere the area of the cultivated clearings was beginning to exceed the forest and waste land. One feature of each village settlement was quite novel. That was the wooden chapel with its nave and chancel like a modern church and some-times with a small squat tower, too. Certainly by the ninth cen-tury the village church looked little different from what it did two hundred years later, except that it was built of timber instead of stone. The walls of the nave might be fashioned from the split trunks of oak trees, like the nave which has miraculously survived in the church of Greensted-juxta-Ongar, in the very heart of the Forest of Essex.

Each forest clearing, each village community, that is, was a farming unit in which sheep, cattle, and pigs were reared, corn crops grown, and bees kept to make the national drink of mead. The home of the head of the community was different from the other homes only in that it was somewhat larger. Even the palaces of the early kings were like timber-built barns. When King Ethelbert gave his 'palace' in Canterbury to St Augustine, he was giving, in effect, only a site on which a church could be built. The buildings which are referred to as his palace were unsubstantial and valueless. An Englishman's home was no more than a place in which to seek shelter from the elements, whether he was king or slave. As yet neither time nor resources were available to embellish it, nor was what we call beauty appreciated for its own sake.

Functional, then, is the word which best describes the Saxon communities. Their method of agriculture was functional too. Each household was responsible for tilling an area of land, but in order that one household should not profit at the expense of another by tilling better soil, each holding was divided into a number of strips in various parts of the common field. That was the essence of feudal tenure and the great difficulty which stood in the way of enclosure hundreds of years later when the time came to consolidate the people's holdings.

The land was worked at first and in most districts on a two-field system. One common field was ploughed this year, a second next year while the first was left fallow. That must have given a very characteristic appearance to the countryside. Where the three-field system was adopted, so that two out of every three plots of land were under cultivation in any single year, the scene grew much nearer to the typical landscapes of today. In the absence of any scientific aid to agriculture the two-field system was an effective one, because it prevented the soil from becoming exhausted. Most likely the three-field system was only successful where the soil was unusually rich.

At harvest time the countryside was as animated as it was fifty years ago, especially when settlements were growing so dense that one often adjoined another and was differentiated from its neighbours by prefixes such as north and south, and suffixes such as end or west end, many of which still appear frequently on the ordnance map. Every available man and woman went to work with their scythes and then bound the cut corn into stooks, just as every countryman did in the England of yesteryear until machinery revolutionized the scene. A very pleasant land, one would say, except that in winter the settlements were virtually cut off from their neighbours. The only means of communication was still by rough unmade tracks through undrained land which became impassable as soon as the first autumn rains fell.

It was a great achievement to have turned so much scrubby forest land into smiling fields. It was an age of transition but one full of promise, even though might was equated with right and there was no likelihood of peace between the states that made up Saxon England. Now, just as at the end of the Roman period, new clouds were building up on the horizon; pagan warrior tribes from Denmark and Scandinavia were threatening the fragile security of English life. Their inroads were destined once more to change the course of English history.

CHAPTER VI

The Mediaeval Landscape

◆ ◆

THE PATTERN of the Anglo-Saxon settlements set the style for the future development of the English scene. It is an exaggeration to say that the pattern was set for all time, but certainly our lowland landscapes owe more to the Anglo-Saxon tradition than to any other factor. By the time that the Anglo-Saxon kingdoms were well and truly founded much of lowland England was showing without any possibility of its being overlooked the influence of man on the natural scene. Yet the country was still far less civilized than in the heyday of the Roman province. The essential difference was that the people of the Roman province had been concentrated in the neighbourhood of the Romano-British towns and in close proximity to the network of Roman roads. In Saxon England the Roman roads had fallen into disuse, while the population was much more scattered. There had been a marked shift of agriculture from the uplands to the lowlands, while the positions of the new villages were already determining the casual winding course of the tracks which were the foundation on which England's road system was built.

The modifications superimposed on the Anglo-Saxon countryside have been largely those springing from successive economic changes, especially by the subsequent growth of population, by the enclosure of the fields (the agricultural revolution), and the development of industry (the industrial revolution). The historian of the countryside, therefore, has relatively little to chronicle in the Middle Ages except a gradual extension of the man-made landscape at the expense of the natural one.

The process was so very gradual and suffered so many setbacks that there is no period of, say, fifty years in which one can point to dramatic changes such as those which overtook the rural scene from Tudor times onwards. A man might be born in a village community, work there all his life, and die without ever going further afield than his own parish. The chances were that how' ever perceptive he might have been, he would have noticed little, if any, change within his horizon in the whole of his lifetime. How different from today when gnarled and bent gaffers fore' gather in the 'local' and regale their unwilling victims with stories of the country as they knew it fifty years ago, infusing their stories with something of the unreality of travellers' tales.

Between the ninth and eleventh centuries large parts of eastern England suffered major incursions of alien elements when pagan invaders from Norway and Denmark wrought havoc among the Saxon husbandmen. Later the Normans, the cultured descen' dants of the selfsame Norse people as had invaded England two hundred years before, established themselves as overlords of the Saxon realm. One might have thought that these events which bulk so large in the nation's formal history might have had a pro' found influence on the face of the country. As we shall see, their influence on social development may have been considerable but their power to vary the landscape pattern was negligible, so firmly entrenched in the land was the Anglo'Saxon tradition.

Raids by tribes deriving from Norway and Denmark were commonplace in the eighth century but serious settlement did not begin until the ninth century. Even then it is uncertain how far the Norsemen established new village settlements in the eastern half of England and how far they took over those already estab' lished by the Angles and Saxons. The evidence suggests that in many places the two peoples lived side by side in amity. In others it is probable that the Saxon settlers were left to work the land while the Norse overlord took command of the village settlement and treated the Saxons as serfs. In others, of course, the Saxons were driven from their homes and the Norsemen took over.

Whatever the actual course of events the results were roughly the same. The common fields of the Saxons continued to be ploughed and sown and reaped, while the coming of more

mouths to be fed prompted the bringing of more land into cultiva⁄
tion, so that the common fields spread higher up the hillsides and
further along the valleys. Thus Lincolnshire and Yorkshire and
parts of East Anglia, as well as the east midland counties, deve⁄
loped the cultivated look more rapidly than other parts of the
country. New clearings were made in the natural forest, more vil⁄
lages were founded, and additional hamlets were thrown out by
existing villages as advance outposts of cultivation.

The Danelaw, that part of England ceded to the Viking in⁄
vaders in the reign of King Alfred, seems to have had no definite
boundaries. In general the Norsemen were given undisputed
rights in all the country to the north and east of Watling Street,
though it is doubtful if they ever settled in Northumberland or
Cheshire. Within the Danelaw and also in the Lake District,
where Viking invaders landed from earlier settlements in Ireland,
the alien people had paramount influence in determining the place
names which appear on the maps of today, among them the 'bys'
and 'thorpes', and in the north⁄west the 'becks' and the
'thwaites'. Nevertheless the countryside itself shows no trace of
Scandinavian influence, not even in the Lakeland fells, where the
invaders helped in the early stages of agricultural development.

When the Saxons, united, or partially united, under the leader⁄
ship of Wessex, reconquered the Danelaw they took over naturally
where the Norsemen had left off. As the Norsemen had left the
Saxons to work the land, so the Saxons in their turn absorbed the
Norse population. One factor in the changing scene which is
due to the Norse influence was the rebirth of the idea of nucleated
townships. Norse domination over the Midlands was based on
their five boroughs—Derby, Stamford, Nottingham, Lincoln,
and Leicester. At the same time King Alfred's capital at Win⁄
chester began to take on the appearance of a town in our sense of
the term, while London continued to develop as a flourishing
centre of trade and commerce.

Saxon life was based on custom rather than law. In a country⁄
side in which every expedient was required to encourage pioneer
clearing of the land, it became customary for younger sons of free

dal pioneers of the far north. *The crofting communities of Scotland's far north have much ommon with the feudal communities of mediaeval England. The single field reclaimed from the rland by the shores of Loch Hope, above, must be typical of the pioneer efforts of the Saxons. e view below, looking from Farr to Bettyhill, shows cultivation rather like the strip cultivation of Saxon communities.*

A clearing in the Pennine moorlands. *In this valley under the slopes of Pen-y-ghent past farming is carried on successfully on the narrow strip of level pasture between the river's brink the rock-strewn hillside.*

A modern forest clearing. *This forest clearing in the dense woodlands of Westmorland rec the clearings made in the primeval forest of the Weald by the Saxon cultivators. Here a fine har of grass has been cut on rising, relatively dry, land near the course of the river.*

men to found their own offshoots of the village community and
for these new settlements to be regarded in time as their property
which they could bequeath to their sons and their sons' sons—
individual holdings in which the founder and his family had
special rights. Thus arose the numerous Saxon thanes whose
privileges and duties became merged after the Norman conquest
in those of the lord of the manor. The custom was by no means
universal but probably influenced the development of several
counties including Kent, where a great number of 'dens' in the
forest were most likely enclosed from very early times.

One major variation was introduced into the country theme in
the century before the Norman conquest. Long before this every
parish had its church but the vast majority were still of timber in
the tenth century. Exceptions to this rule there certainly were, such
as the abbey church of St Augustine's in Canterbury, which was
of masonry largely taken from the ruins of the Roman city, but
building in stone was an art developed in Normandy and introduced into Saxon England by Norman craftsmen and master
masons, before as well as after the occupation.

The early stone-built churches were of simple design and construction but they were the prototypes of the great Norman and
Gothic churches which became the landmarks of the later
mediaeval countryside. Benedictine abbeys had been founded in
many places, too, and here the monks joined with the master
masons to build ever more beautiful structures to the greater glory
of God. Edward the Confessor just lived to see the completion
of his dream, the new Abbey of Westminster, built on an island
in the marshlands which bordered the Thames about a mile from
the outskirts of London. That must have seemed to the people of
the time a wonderful achievement, the very consummation of the
ideals of man the builder.

Then came the Norman conquest, which in terms of the
countryside was merely the superimposition of a foreign ruling
class on the existing pattern of country life. The Normans did not
initiate the feudal system. They merely adapted something that
was already in existence to their own purpose and systematized by

G

law what was already a matter of custom. So once again the
variation wrought in the landscape was small. William parcelled
out the kingdom among his 'barons' and they in turn, with the
king's approval, parcelled out their portions among the lesser
orders of Norman nobility, granting to them a varying number of
manors. The Saxon thanes were degraded, but generally continued with their work as farmers by grace of the lord of the manor
though in an inferior position.

It may well be that the two-field system, which had been common in many parts of England during the Saxon regime, gave
way to the three-field system generally, but there is no agreement
on that point. Most probably the two systems with their strikingly
different appearance still continued side by side. The richer the
land, the more likely was the three-field system to be adopted,
especially when the community possessed adequate stock to graze
over the stubble and by manuring the land to revivify it for more
intensive cultivation.

The Domesday Survey, initiated by the king in Council at
Gloucester in 1085, is the chief source of information about the
appearance of the countryside in the eleventh century. Interpretation of that massive inventory of land and work on the land is
difficult but one thing stands out clearly, that the occupation of
the country by Norman William and his barons had not been
achieved without sad wastage of the country's assets. Again and
again the value of manors is shown as lower in 1086 than it had
been in the days of Edward the Confessor. Armies on the march
had desolated whole tracts of country. The rebellion of the north
country in 1069 and the terrible reprisals which William ordered
had reduced north and east Yorkshire to a shadow of their former
selves. A fair inference from Domesday is that the two Ridings
were producing no more than a quarter of what they had been
producing a generation before. Recovery, however, was swift, so
that in every part of England ploughlands temporarily turned to
waste were soon brought back into cultivation and the gradual
advance of the human landscape continued.

As the first great era of building in stone, the eleventh and twelfth centuries left an indelible mark on the face of the land. A number of artificial mounds and enclosures scarcely worth the name of castle had been constructed by the Saxons, but it remained for the Normans and their successors to build the chain of magnifi/ cent fortresses of which the ruins, in many cases, remain a perma/ nent feature of the landscape. The purpose of the castles was strategic. They guarded important fords over rivers, as at London and Rochester; they guarded the gaps in the chalk downs, as at Bramber and Arundel; they were placed at convenient points to dominate likely trouble spots, as at Norwich and Hedingham. Often they were built in the precincts of the embryonic towns which had begun to increase in size during the last decades of Saxon rule. The houses, or as we should probably call them, the hovels in which the people lived were ruthlessly demolished, more than one hundred and fifty of them, for instance, in Lincoln alone to make way for the new fortress. The castles rose high above the huddled roofs and must have seemed awe/inspiring structures to the simple/minded common people of the time. Fifty castles are listed in Domesday. The number was multiplied several times in the hundred years that followed.

The Norman barons ensconced in their strongholds led forays of their men on the surrounding countryside and literally lived off it, burning and pillaging as they went to give the people an idea of the retribution which would await them if they were unruly. So more waste was added to that produced by the occupation itself. In the twelfth and thirteenth centuries relative peace re/ turned to the land and towns began to grow up round the castles, secure in their protection and dependent on them for the trade which made the economics of town life possible.

Side by side with the building of castles the construction of cathedrals, greater in size and in cost than the castles themselves, proceeded apace. What must a Durham or a Chichester have looked like to the people of the eleventh and twelfth centuries? Many of these beautiful buildings are landmarks for miles around in the twentieth century and dominate the cities in which they are set. Chichester Cathedral is far/seen over the Sussex plain. Ely

on its island in the fens can be discerned on a clear day from thirty
miles away. Durham, 'half church half fortress 'gainst the Scot'
is still one of the most impressive features of the north country.

This phase of building in stone and the growth of towns that

Harrowing about 1340 [Luttrell Psalter].

followed closely on its heels was a far more important change in
the appearance of the countryside than any due to the efforts of
man the cultivator during the twelfth century. Often, however,
the building of magnificent churches and the development of the
land went hand in hand. After the beginning of the twelfth century the Cistercian Order founded numerous monasteries, especially in the north country. The abbots became great land holders
and by the efforts of the monks and the countrymen they employed
transformed much of Yorkshire and many areas on the borderland
of Wales from unused moorlands to valuable sheep pastures. The
ruins of Rievaulx in Yorkshire's Ryedale give some idea of the
beauty of the mediaeval abbeys in their heyday. But here, as elsewhere, imagination is necessary to reconstruct the landscape as the
monks knew it. The dense woodlands which today cloak the
surrounding hills are all of later origin than the time of the abbey's
greatness; so are the expanses of wild garlic, which transform the
ground beneath the trees into a pure white carpet in early summer.
To crown all, the bluff under which the abbey lies is decorated
with artificial temples and gazebos modelled incongruously on the
styles of ancient Greece.

Much has been written about the Norman forests and especially about the New Forest, which was first dedicated to the sport

of kings in the reign of William I. In fact the forests were nothing new to England, nor were they what many understand by the term. The forests were areas *foris*, that is to say outside (the ordinary law)—areas to which the special forest laws applied. They

Sowing broadcast, fourteenth century [Luttrell Psalter].

were not necessarily dense woodland which, if unbroken by open country, would not have been suitable for hunting over. They mostly included wooded areas—after all, the greater part of the midlands and south was still well-wooded—but a few of them, like the Forest of the High Peak, could not boast a single tree. The majority, like Sherwood Forest, included parts of the ageless oak forests of the clay lands but also large areas of sandy waste and common.

There is not enough evidence to estimate with any degree of accuracy the total area occupied by forests in twelfth-century England. One theory puts it as high as a third of the whole kingdom, but it must be remembered that even if this is true, the greater part was moorland or waste. It was no part of Norman policy to kill the goose that laid the golden egg, to dispossess the Saxon labourers from the land which they had reclaimed, and which they were working for the benefit of their Norman overlords. Even the New Forest was mainly waste land, as it is today. No man could grow crops on the Stoney Cross plateau or on Beaulieu Heath. The truth seems to be that only a very few clearings had been made on the fringe of the arid sandstone country which forms the nucleus of the Forest and that these village communities were transplanted wholesale to areas outside the forest land. This may have seemed a great hardship to the people, but it can scarcely have represented a major social injustice. At the same time, whole counties were subject to forest law, including Devon, Cornwall, and Essex. That does not mean that the whole of these counties

Reaping in the fourteenth century [Luttrell Psalter].

was maintained as uncultivated land but rather that so much of it was hunting country that the forest laws were extended to cover the village settlements outside it, including the many 'leighs' and 'fields' that had made their appearance on the fringes of the Forest of Essex, over which Castle Hedingham stood guard.

There may have been a political reason for treating the three counties in this way. Norman authority was weak in the south-west, perhaps negligible in Cornwall, where Launceston marked the most westerly outpost of their influence, and comparatively slight in Devonshire west of the Exe. The Forest of Essex, though well within the most effective region of Norman rule, might have been designed by nature as the hiding-place of resistance forces as difficult to subdue effectively as the Isle of Ely, where Hereward the Wake carried on prolonged guerrilla warfare against the new regime.

Wild deer were the most prized objects of the chase in Norman times, though wild boar were also hunted and other animals which survived in the sparsely inhabited forest areas. It is a striking commentary on the inter-relation of landscape changes and the gradual disappearance in Britain of wild animal life that wild boar did not long survive the break-up of the mediaeval forests while wild deer have become isolated in only a few remote districts of England such as Exmoor, where nowadays they seldom move abroad in the hours of daylight. There are still wild deer, it is said, in the Home counties, but they must be relatively few in number and probably spring from groups of deer which have escaped from 'domesticated' parkland herds and have then 'gone

Harvest time in the fourteenth century: tying up the sheaves [Luttrell Psalter].

native'. Brian Vesey-Fitzgerald has recorded that an open pond in the garden of his house in south-east England is often frequented by deer during the night, though few who live in the neighbourhood have ever seen a deer, or even imagine that one could survive outside the sheltered sanctuary of a deer park.

Although little, if any, of the original vegetation of the mediaeval forests has survived, many of the areas then formally set aside for the chase have retained a great deal of their character. The Forest of Dartmoor and the High Peak probably look today much as they did then. The New Forest and Sherwood Forest have the same mixture of open heath land and densely wooded covert that they had in Norman times, while in Sherwood there is at least one tree, the Queen Oak, which may have been a vigorous young sapling in the eleventh century, and very many others that were flourishing five hundred years or more ago but are now 'like mouldering towers noble and picturesque in their decay', as Washington Irving described them. Epping Forest and Hainault Forest, both fragments of the Forest of Essex, are probably better wooded now than they were at that time. Near Loughton the still visible bank and ditch of an Iron Age camp (Ambersbury Banks) are evidence enough that the land was relatively unwooded at the time of the Roman occupation, though on the lower ground and especially in what is now central Essex, where the soil is mostly of clay, oak wood must have predominated as it did in the wealden forest of Sussex and Surrey between the North and the South Downs.

Other mediaeval forests are only names on the map today, though many of those, too, show the same strange conservatism, the same tendency to be especially well wooded, to be, in brief, forests in the modern sense of the term. Among them are the Forest of Bere in Sussex, the Forest of Blean in Kent, Rockingham Forest in the Midlands, and, of course, the Forest of Dean in the western marches of Gloucestershire. As a contrast, Rothbury Forest in Northumberland is bare and open moorland or rock-strewn common. It is only within comparatively recent years that the last trees of the mediaeval oak forests have disappeared from our landscapes (apart from a few debatable cases like the Queen Oak). Books written before the turn of the century refer to a number of oak trees probably a thousand years old in the Weald of Kent round Headcorn. The latest edition of the ordnance map strangely still shows the position of the Doodle Oak in Hatfield Forest near that well-named village, Hatfield Broad Oak, but if one goes in search of it one will be disappointed; since the ordnance map was drawn it has decayed and fallen and left no trace.

We have nothing in England to compare in age with the giant sequoias of California, many of which date back to before the Christian era. Even the churchyard yew trees, some of which like that at Selborne are admittedly of great age, are rarely as old as their champions would have us believe. It is exceedingly doubt-ful if any of them are contemporary with the building of the mediaeval churches, as the romantic antiquaries of the last century stated with such confidence.

The mediaeval forests, judged as a factor in the changing face of England, have less significance than the phase of development represented by the idea of enclosure which from the twelfth cen-tury onwards began, subtly at first and then more obviously, to modify the landscape. It has well been said that a twentieth-century traveller transported back through time into twelfth-

On the hills of Ryedale. *A carpet of wild garlic and mature trees has transformed the once bare slopes of the hills near Rievaulx Abbey.*

Two mediaeval bridges. *Most mediaeval bridges were equipped with a chapel at whi* *travellers might offer thanks for the safe crossing of the river. At Bradford-on-Avon, abo* *and St Ives, below, the bridge chapels have been restored and remain a permanent mediae* *feature of the modern scene.*

The walls and cathedral of York.

The West Gate of Canterbury. *The Church of Holy Cross, on the right, superseded a church of the same name which formed the upper storey of the West Gate, rebuilt in the fourteenth century through the good offices of Archbishop Sudbury.*

The Weald from Bexley Hill. *This view from Bexley Hill looking towards Blackdown wit its isolated farm-houses, its generous woodland cover and its occasional strips of arable land an pasture must be very similar to what it was in the sixteenth century.*

century England would have had difficulty in identifying even well-known districts without their roads and buildings and, above all, without their fields and hedges. Far more land, of course, was uncultivated then, but mere quantity of cultivation is not really the key to the nature of the scene. That resides in the quality of the landscape which, for us, means the chequerboard pattern of hedged fields which we have come to regard as traditional, though in fact it is one of the more recent additions to the English scene. It is probably true that Kent and parts of East Anglia were never cultivated on the open-field system to any large extent. It is much more certainly true that the pattern of banked or stone-walled fields in the south-western counties was set from the earliest age of culti-vation, but in the greater part of lowland England the Saxon open-field system was universal.

The first large-scale enclosures were those effected by the lords of the manor soon after the Norman conquest. The lord of the manor enclosed the demesne and so established his personal estate as something apart from the communal holding of the village settlement. No one complained, no one was in a position to com-plain. This enclosure proved a precedent which was followed quite soon by lower orders in the feudal system. As more of the uncultivated land was brought under the plough the communal system was not applied to the new clearings. The enclosure of waste was a measure generally approved because it added to the bounty of the rural economy. As we have seen earlier, from the reign of King Alfred onwards the idea that a man could make a clearing in waste land and call it his own, to be bequeathed to his sons, had been gaining ground. In the later Middle Ages the idea had firmly taken root.

So long as it was a matter of the enclosure of waste no one was the poorer, but the lords of the manor, who were in the main descendants of Norman families with little regard for Saxon prece-dent, were for ever enlarging the area of their personal demesne, often at the expense of the common pasture. Such action im-perilled the village economy. Nevertheless, by the Statute of Merton in 1235 the principle of enclosure was given legal recognition providing only that enough pasture was left for the village. But who should say, in practice, other than the lord of the manor himself, what constituted enough pasture? The law was already being weighted on the side of the man in possession. The descen-dants of the Saxon thanes and village farmers had good ground for the discontent which came to a head in the peasant revolts of later centuries.

So the landscape went on developing along well-tried lines until the middle of the fourteenth century, when the national disaster called the Black Death brought in its train one of the first major changes in the traditional landscape. The Black Death in 1348 and 1349 wiped out entire villages, decimated the monasteries, and reduced the population of many counties by half. Those who suffered most severely were the poorest classes. As might be expected, the lords of the manor had greater resistance to the plague.

The immediate result was an acute shortage of labour to work the land. The manorial system may have been breaking up before the Black Death, but it was the Black Death which completed its collapse. After the fourteenth century it was the rule rather than the exception for small farmers to pay for their land with money rents rather than with part of their time and labour. The era of the hired workers on the land had begun, also that of the small farmer working independently of the lord of the manor.

Many of the landowners, including the abbots of the most powerful monasteries, took the line of least resistance. Finding that there were no longer men to plough as much of the land as previously (and less demand for cereals owing to the lower popula-tion) they turned over a great deal of ploughland to sheep pasture. This, in turn, involved more extensive enclosure of sheep runs. Well before 1400 there were probably as many as eight million sheep in the country and that at a time when the total population was scarcely more than two millions.

The change-over from a rural economy based mainly on cereal production to one dependent on increased pastureland not only produced widespread and very obvious changes in the appearance of the landscape, but heralded in a period of prosperity which has seldom been equalled in our history. The woollen boom of the fourteenth and fifteenth centuries was a very real thing. It enabled many of the small farmers to build pleasant homes for themselves and the bigger landowners to elaborate the design of their houses, such as Ightham Mote and Penshurst Place in Kent, and to embellish them with fine wood carving and stonework. It also enabled village communities under the lead of the local landowner or tenant in chief to rebuild many village churches in the chief wool-producing areas such as the Cotswolds, Kent, and East Anglia in the elegant Perpendicular style of the times. The most striking features of these churches were the tall towers which began to dominate many parts of the country, new landmarks bespeaking a growing wealth and an enhanced appreciation of beauty.

CHAPTER VII

The Age of Transition
1485-1603

• •

IT MIGHT APPEAR an historical absurdity to call an age which produced literature of the calibre of Shakespeare's plays, and a world-wide prestige for English daring and seamanship, a transitional one. Yet in the history of the countryside the period from the accession of King Henry VII to the death of Queen Elizabeth I is essentially one of transition from the feudalism of the Middle Ages to modern conceptions of life on the land. That transitional element was reflected in the appearance of the landscape all over England as new ways of farming the land superseded the old and improved standards of living were reflected in the changing aspect of rural communities.

The accession of King Henry in 1485 ended a long period of civil strife which had culminated in the Wars of the Roses. It held out the promise of a settled government once more. The promise in fact was fulfilled. The peace which settled over the country for many generations was an important factor in permitting a greater use of the potential wealth of the land and a genuine agrarian revolution.

At the beginning of the sixteenth century the rural scene was not so very different from what it had been two or three hundred years before. The population had increased to perhaps four million since the depredations of the Black Death. This reservoir of labour encouraged the lords of the manor to extend the limits of agriculture. Sheep farming on a big scale meant the end of farming for subsistence and the introduction of a commercial element into the working of the land. For the first time the farmer (that is to say, the lord of the manor as farmer in chief of the village community) was beginning to look on the land as an investment and his activities in farming as a money-making venture.

Even so, if one had looked down on any of the fertile valleys of south and central England from the summit of the nearby hills during the reign of Henry VII one would have been struck by the persistence of the traditional type of landscape. There were the same village communities, that in most cases the Saxons had founded, consisting of much the same elements as when Norman overlords came to dispossess the Saxon thanes. There were the church and the manor house, and the rude cottage homes of the village people, either ranged at a discreet distance from each other around a village green or strung out along the dirt track that led from the nearest so-called road to the lord's demesne.

The manor house would most likely be the only sizeable dwelling place in each village; the church adjoined it or at any rate was within the land enclosed by the hedge or wattle fence surrounding the lord's private 'estate'. Beyond the demesne, however, the land was still generally worked on the open-field system, each man in the community still being responsible for working two or three or more narrow strips of land in different parts of the open fields, which by then were usually three in number, two bearing crops in any one year, the other lying fallow. Unploughed baulks of turf divided the individual holdings of the villeins and still acted as rights of way to take the villagers from one of their strips to another.

So far a wayfarer looking down from the Blackdown Hills on to the Vale of Taunton or from the crest of Ivinghoe Beacon across the fertile Vale of Aylesbury would have noticed nothing essentially different from the view of two hundred years before. But there was in fact one important difference, and that one which from 1500 onwards became increasingly apparent. In mediaeval England where the open fields ended there had been the woodlands, the waste, and the common lands which all the members of a community used in common for pasturing their animals, or as the case might be, for cutting wood for their fires. Now an ever-increasing number of small fields surrounded by some kind of rude hedge planted generally on a low artificial ridge were making their appearance. They were creeping gradually further and further up the hillsides.

Sometimes such enclosures provoked disputes which came before the manorial courts. In general, however, the process went on quietly enough, progressing as always in the English countryside by compromise and agreement. The time was yet far away when every prospect in the south showed a chequerboard pattern of field and hedge, but at least a start had been made on the most revolutionary of all the influences which have changed the appearance of the country beyond the recognition of another age.

If one had looked a hundred years later over the same pleasant landscapes—over the Vale of Taunton or the Vale of Aylesbury —one would have seen an incredible transformation, for by then the whole idea of the manor had been revolutionized. The open-field system was disappearing, individual scattered holdings were being consolidated and enclosed; the charming chequerboard pattern now filled much of the valleys and reached towards the middle slopes of the low hills.

In this latter change again compromise and agreement played their part, the individual tenants agreeing among themselves to consolidate their various holdings and so divide up the common fields among them. When one says 'agree among themselves', there is the implication of approval by the lord of the manor, who was still effectively the leader of the community, the patron of the church, the strong arm of authority, the refuge to which the villagers turned in times of distress.

The breeding of sheep for wool was probably the principal factor in hastening the policy of enclosure. But once enclosure started it became apparent that the new method of farming was expedient on other grounds also. The development of sheep farming, however, was almost entirely in the hands of the lord of the manor. The tenants, whether villeins or freeholders, did keep a few head of sheep, pasturing them on the common land and folding them in the fallow field or turning them loose on the stubble of the corn after the harvest. But all the great flocks were the property of the lords of the manor who, as the woollen industry expanded, aimed to produce a better and better quality of fleece for export to foreign centres of manufacture or to the growing number of craft factories in nearby towns. Spinning might still be carried on in the farm-houses but weaving had become centralized in the towns.

The great benefit of enclosure was that it made possible a closer control over individual flocks; it also facilitated breeding from selected sires in a way which was impractical when flocks great and small belonging to the lowliest villein or copyholder and to the lord of the manor were mingled together in the open pastures. That profit could be made from sheep farming had been dis-covered long before. All that the Tudor farmers did was to ex-ploit the lesson which their fathers and grandfathers had learned and to take what steps they could to meet the demand for better quality wool.

The emergence of a commercial farming class was not without its pitfalls. Many contemporary chroniclers complained bitterly at the hardships which enclosure imposed on the rural communities. They complained, too, that sheep were ruining the wealth of the land and destroying the security of village life. The enclosure of wastes and commons took an important part of the livelihood from the villagers. 'Sheepe', as Sir Thomas More says, 'have eate up our meadows and our downes, our corne and our wood, whole villages and townes.'

Discontent was probably exaggerated. There have always been more voices raised in horror at impending change than in praise of innovation. And this has always been particularly true of the English countryside with its wonderfully conservative traditions, its quiet even tenor, and the firm convictions of so many agricul-turalists that change and decay are synonymous terms. The same voices are raised today singing the same song to different words, as we shall see later. That there was occasional hardship is un-deniable. So much power was vested in the lord of the manor that an unscrupulous one here and there could enclose and put to his own use valuable common land without any compensation to his tenants. The big landowners, including the abbots and priors of monastic establishments before the dissolution, were the greatest offenders.

The average lord of the manor in Tudor times, however, was not unlike the traditional squire of the eighteenth and nineteenth centuries. He depended on the co-operation of his village community as surely as they depended on his goodwill. Absentee landlords then as now had no real sympathy with their village folk but absentee landlords were very much the exception.

Much legislation was introduced to check enclosure, framed, one is compelled to conclude, by the very people who were the prime offenders or by those who had little knowledge or experience of the country and its ways. Inevitably such legislation was ineffective. When early in the sixteenth century reports were brought to the king's ministers that whole villages were being abandoned because of enclosure effected by the lord of the manor and even churches were being used as sheep pens, there was a great show of indignation and stringent requirements were laid down for fresh enclosure to be legalized. Yet in 1563 there was need of another Act of Parliament on the naïve pretext that previous legislation had proved unworkable. The problem was not only one of enclosure as such, but of shortage of good arable land after the conversion of so much that had been ploughed to enclosed pasture. This latter Act proposed that land which had been under the plough for four years since the early part of the century should remain arable and that all arable land which had been converted to pasture should be restored to the plough. Such legislation slowed down but did not stop the process of enclosure. When there was a fresh incentive to enclosure the provisions of the Act were conveniently forgotten.

Our interested traveller in the England of 1500, of course, would only have seen the very beginnings of this revolution, though he might have noticed one other change in many landscapes—and that also one for which sheep-rearing was indirectly responsible. If he had been travelling over the hills of Gloucestershire and Somerset, or through the undulating country of northern

mains of the ancient forests. *Sherwood forest and Belvoir Chase retain many oak trees* *which undoubtedly formed part of the forest cover in Elizabethan times. Above are three of what* *Washington Irving described as 'mouldering towers noble and picturesque in their decay' in* *Belvoir Chase; below, the Queen Oak in Sherwood forest.*

Land won from the sea. *The salt marshes of North Norfolk around Cley-next-the-S above, are steadily becoming less subject to inundation. The final stage of evolution of land from the sea is illustrated by the level fields of the coastal plain between Chichester and Bog below, where modern drainage has produced fertile fields from what was boggy and unproduc land four hundred years ago.*

Essex and Suffolk, if he had visited the South Hams of Devon-shire, or the fertile Weald of east Kent, he could not have failed to notice the number and beauty of the lofty pinnacled church towers, mentioned in the previous chapter. Wherever the flocks of sheep had multiplied, wherever wool market towns had arisen, the accumulated wealth of farmers and merchants had been diverted to the enrichment of the parish church. This had meant that in all the most prosperous parts of the country either new churches had been built or old ones had been enlarged with the addition of one of these typical late Gothic towers which are so appropriately called 'Perpendicular' in style. A sixteenth-century writer tells us that thirty church towers could be discerned in a single view, from a vantage point in the hills of Northamptonshire.

Neighbouring communities would vie with each other to see which could build the tallest tower. The tower of Tenterden in Kent is a landmark for many miles around. The pride of Tenter-den folk at the beginning of the sixteenth century was that their tower rose above that of neighbouring Biddenden and was taller than that of Lydd down in the Romney Marshes. Their boast was that it rivalled even the new central tower of Canterbury Cathedral, designed to replace the fallen angel steeple. In vain Latimer preached before Edward VI that Tenterden tower was built at the expense of a much-needed sea wall to keep the sea from inundating the Romney Marsh. Whether Pope or King was head of the Church, the people's pride in their tower was proof against all such 'wicked lies'. In East Anglia the noble towers of Thaxted and Lavenham and Saffron Walden, of Long Melford and many a lesser parish church, dominated the landscape, as those of a Northleach or a Cirencester stood over the rolling Cots-wold countryside like watch towers guarding the shepherds and the workers in the fields. Wherever there are a number of these lofty embattled towers, it is a fair inference that this was a sheep-rearing area in the fifteenth and sixteenth centuries, for the simple reason that wealth followed the flocks.

The hill country of Devon and Cornwall, the north-western moorlands, and the border country were still thinly peopled. They

H

showed no such evidence of prosperity as the pasture lands of the south. The deep valleys of Cumberland were well-tilled; so were the Yorkshire dales where the Wharfe and the Ure and the Aire watered broad valleys approaching the level landscapes of the Vale of York. But higher up the Pennine valleys and in much of the south-west it was just not possible to extract a subsistence standard of living from the unwilling soil in the face of climatic conditions which were little different from those of today and without adequate farming implements or tools. Here the dominant theme of the landscape was waste land, with the moors stretching much farther down into the valleys than they do today and hill farming only just beginning to make some belated progress.

The west country, however, which is now the cattle country of England—especially the hills and dales of Shropshire and Herefordshire—was rich in flocks, and the fleeces from these sheep were highly prized. Even so, all that has been said so far applies with greatest force to the areas south and east of a line drawn from the Severn to the Wash, including the whole of the midland plain, the Cotswold range, the southern counties, and East Anglia. It was in these areas that the open-field system of farming in the Middle Ages had been universal. It was here that the change-over to commercial sheep farming had its most obvious effects and that the consequent changes in the landscape were most noticeable.

The Reformation is perhaps the single event in the sixteenth century which had the most considerable effect on country ways and indirectly on the detail of the landscape. Its most obvious result was to check further church building. Few new churches were built until recent times except to replace a structure that had been burnt out or otherwise destroyed. In the countryside at large, as opposed to the towns, the number of new churches completed since 1550 is quite extraordinarily small if one is thinking only of building under the auspices of the Established Church. General reconstructions in the Perpendicular style of early Tudor times that were not completed were left unfinished.

As the nature of the village communities changed, the church ceased to be the centre of their community life. The simple folk of the Middle Ages had regarded the church as a social centre quite as much as a place of worship. The chancel had belonged by custom to the priests, the nave to the people, who gathered there for recreation on week days as they did for service on Sunday, at a time when the actual words of the service said in Latin were quite meaningless to them. Sixteenth-century villagers, more especially those of the Elizabethan era, began to lose their veneration of the chancel as they did their pleasure in the nave. Their change of heart did no more than reflect a different outlook on the part of the lord of the manor. It was not so much that religion had died as that a greater understanding engendered an entirely different attitude of mind which could visualize many uses of surplus wealth, just as attractive as the building or rebuilding of churches.

That was one side of the coin. The other is represented by the dissolution of the monasteries. The larger monasteries in town and country had stood as independent communities centred upon the abbey or priory church. When the abbot was forced to sign away his office and the monks were ejected, the often beautiful buildings quickly began to decay. Nominally the buildings and the church and the considerable area of land which the religious houses held became the property of the Crown. In practice many town and country communities purchased the monastic church for their own use for a nominal sum from the Crown, as in the town of Romsey. In many other cases the king granted the buildings and the land to royal nominees on varying conditions. The new owner sometimes built a house for his use from the monastic buildings, ruthlessly tearing down the monks' dwelling places and building a new house from the materials so ready to hand, or adapting and extending the abbot's house to suit his own convenience. The abbey church was all too often left to moulder away into ruins, its stonework perhaps being carted off at a penny a load to fill in holes in the nearby roads or to provide material for building other lowlier homes. In one or two cases, as at St Augustine's just outside the walls of Canterbury, the king retained the abbey and converted some of its buildings into a royal palace, though that, too, later passed into private hands and ultimately served as a tavern and brewery storehouse.

In all cases the monastic buildings were degraded. In the course of a generation or two they lost much of their incomparable beauty. By the end of the sixteenth century many were already in ruins, or so transformed that they could not be recognized as the same buildings which had inspired such pride a century earlier.

It might be thought that the Reformation produced only decay in the man-made features of the English landscape, but that is only part of the truth. However much in retrospect the vanishing beauty of the monastic establishments may seem to mark the end of an epoch, it is equally true that it symbolized the beginning of a new one. In the countryside of the times there were many signs of the emergence of this new order. It was an age of high adventure and commercial progress.

Before the death of Queen Elizabeth I a new aristocracy was well established—one that owed its position to its financial standing rather than to its feudal ancestry. Then, as now, families with much new wealth at their disposal were eager to use it in the creation of great houses which might be a proof to the whole world of their success and a pride to themselves and their children. The break-up of the monastic estates accelerated if it did not begin this social change in the countryside. The successors of the abbots and priors as land-holders having acquired their estates from the Crown, either by direct purchase or in consideration of services rendered, quickly proved themselves no more considerate as landlords than their predecessors. Often the undoubted rights of tenants on the monastic estates were ignored and the new owners set about enclosing the land without the slightest regard to the justice of the case. The new estates thus protected by enclosure proved far more profitable to work than they had been under the management of the monastic order. The result was a new class of prosperous farmers on the grand scale added overnight to the more progressive of the feudal landlords, who had gradually adapted themselves to changing economic conditions.

The sixteenth century, therefore, witnessed a change of accent from the religious to the secular, rather than an eclipse of the art of creating beautiful buildings. Before the accession of Henry VIII mansions which could be called by any stretch of the imagination palatial, were few and far between. Some, like Penshurst Place, were undoubtedly homes of outstanding taste and distinction which added a notable feature to the landscape. Others, like Herstmonceux, imitated the style of the mediaeval castle without adding very much that was new. Almost all were dwarfed by the splendour of the nearby church. By contrast, when Eliza-beth's reign was drawing to its close there was scarcely a district in all England where one would not have seen one or more magnifi-cent houses, either recently completed or nearing completion. These were frequently dominant features of the landscape, stand-ing on an exposed hillside or commanding a quiet valley scene with something of the arrogance that before had belonged only to the grim castle buildings of the Normans.

Early in the period Wolsey's palace at Hampton Court was a most striking sign of the times. It is one of the relatively few build-ings of the time of Henry VIII which have survived intact. To an observer on the other bank of the Thames, to one of those, per-haps, who dwelt in the village of Molesey, which was set like a low island in the midst of marshy land, the new palace must have looked large enough to swallow the whole of his village. As it took shape it presented the appearance of a new and strange town with its hundreds of builders camped around it and the constant comings and goings of river craft at the special landing stage built beside it.

If a knowledgeable visitor had crossed the river to inspect the buildings at closer quarters, he would have noticed one thing im-mediately—the new palace was being built of bright red bricks, thus setting a style which was rapidly to become fashionable. Layer Marney Towers in Essex had recently been built in brick; a few other great houses in various parts of the country had been built of the same material during the past century. But this was the first time that brick had really come into its own in the home counties. It was a change destined to modify not only the appearance of many great buildings in the future but also their whole design.

Our visitor would have seen, however, that so far as Hampton Court was concerned there was nothing particularly revolutionary about its design. In fact it combined in almost equal parts the appearance of a mediaeval castle and a mediaeval monastery. There was the suspicion of a moat and drawbridge and gatehouse, all part and parcel of the castle tradition, though by Tudor times no one supposed that any house would be called upon to withstand a siege, nor were the defences provided adequate to repel a single day's attack if the need had arisen. But there was still the feeling, as there had been a hundred years before when Herstmonceux in Sussex was being built, that a gentleman's residence should retain something of the outward semblance of a castle. (The fad for 'Victorian' Gothic in Scotland three hundred years later was another outbreak of the same disease, though it is only fair to say that the baronial style was by no means confined to districts north of the border when once the salutary restraint of Georgian ideals had lost its potency.)

Behind its mock defences Hampton Court was rather like a monastic cloister with a complicated series of buildings surrounding it. Even after the dissolution of the monasteries it was a long time before the tradition they established was entirely forgotten.

The monastic influence on Tudor building would have been even more obvious in Oxford, where through Wolsey's enthusiasm Christ Church College was founded in a prominent position just below the meeting place of the two main roads that passed through Oxford, on a low hill overlooking the broad valley of the Thames or Isis. Here there was the same arrangement of gatehouse (to which Sir Christopher Wren later added Tom Tower), and cloister or quadrangle, with the domestic buildings, the hall and the chapel (in this case an old-established one which became the cathedral of the Oxford diocese) ranged round it. As additions were gradually made to mediaeval Oxford and Cambridge the basic form of quadrangle survived as a pleasant anachronism which even now gives an air of monastic seclusion to many comparatively modern university buildings.

There is something extraordinarily conservative in the story of English architecture. Paradoxically its conservatism has never been more fully demonstrated than in the transitional phase from Gothic to the full flowering of Renaissance building. The Gothic style is said to have been given that name by Sir Christopher Wren, who regarded it as barbarous and named it jocularly after the Goths, who had helped to bring anarchy to mediaeval Europe. Yet it was truly an English style by the beginning of the sixteenth century, having evolved, like most other 'English' styles, from continental ideas. It had been so domesticated that English people came to look on the Gothic churches as peculiarly their own and regarded the new ideas which were spreading from Italy —the revived classicism that sprang from the Renaissance in Europe—as something to be toyed with rather than embraced wholeheartedly. So Gothic strives with Classical in the decoration of the great Tudor homes, locked together in a long struggle which was not completely resolved by the time of Queen Elizabeth's death.

It is said that the Queen herself was conservative in her architectural taste and far preferred the traditional style to the newfangled Renaissance designs. Certainly many of the great houses built in her reign, such as Wakehurst, in Sussex, show remarkably little of the new influence, in spite of the degradation of the gable into a mere ornament and the growing impression of symmetry which all the new houses gave. Burghley House, one of the great show places of the times, was distinctly more classical, a fact which throws some doubt on the Queen's allegedly passionate dislike of classicism. Lord Burghley would scarcely have invested in such an essay in magnificence if the investment carried with it the displeasure of his royal mistress. The core of the matter is probably reached at Hardwick Hall. For Hardwick Hall ('more glass than wall') is essentially a classical exhibition far in advance of its times. Nor is there the slightest doubt that Queen Elizabeth intensely disliked its 'builder', Bess of Hardwick, Countess of

Shrewsbury. On the principle of 'love me, love my dog' perhaps it was the admiration evoked by Hardwick Hall which caused the Queen to vent her indignation on the harmless fabric of the house. By that time, however—the last decade of the sixteenth century—it was fairly obvious which way the struggle would end. Even in conservative Haddon Hall, to which extensive Elizabethan addi-tions were made, including the famous Long Gallery, classical motifs were dominant in the scheme of decoration.

One must dismiss with regret the pleasant fancy that the E shape of so many Elizabethan houses was in honour of the queen. The truth is that this peculiar shape, made up of a long rectangle with a projecting porch and two projecting wings at the ends of the rectangle, was the logical modification of the mediaeval castle or manor house. The latter consisted of a gatehouse giving access to a court surrounded by the main buildings. When the gatehouse disappeared the court necessarily disappeared too, and there were left only a porch in place of the gatehouse and the two wings, which were gradually retracted until only the rectangle was left. That final stage did not occur until the idea of classical symmetry had vanquished the last resistance of the traditional style.

The vast size of so many sixteenth-century houses necessitated another change which in turn reflected changed standards of living. A century before the great hall had still been the essence of the English home. The hall home as such had been very long a-dying. Now towards the end of Elizabeth's reign it was finally dead. All the great mansions had a hall but it was an apology for the mediaeval great hall, no longer the main living-room but rather an apartment reserved for ceremonial occasions. The greater part of the space available was divided into an incredible number of individual apartments—bedrooms, withdrawing rooms, dining-rooms, and so on, many of them almost as big as had been the great hall of a fourteenth-century home.

Not all the new houses that were taking shape were as elaborate as this. Many of the smaller ones achieved their purpose better than the more palatial residences and must have fitted far better into the landscape. The charming ruins of Cowdray Castle by the banks of the Rother in Sussex still give an impression of how beautiful a smaller house of the Elizabethan age could be. Yet Cowdray, for all its unpretentious attractiveness, was built virtually without thought of expense. In its ruins, too, the same struggle between Gothic and Classical is apparent as in the largest mansions. The oriel windows of the dining-hall look back to the traditional English home, but much of the decoration is classical. What distinguishes it from many contemporary homes is that it was not, like Hardwick, a house which dominated and changed the surrounding landscape, but rather one which fitted admirably into its natural setting.

The farther west and north one went in England, the more frequently one would have found new houses that fell into the same category. In the Cotswold country one would have seen almost as many homes being built as in the south-eastern counties, but certainly none that went beyond the canons of good taste. For the most part additions were being made to existing houses to bring them into line with the trend of the times. One would have seen a Compton Wynyates giving added point to its landscape and would have noticed the beginnings, perhaps unconscious, of the landscape gardening on a grand scale that belongs to the much later times of Capability Brown. The fact that Compton Wynyates and its lesser fellows among the Cotswold Hills were still being built of the oolitic limestone—the quickly-mellowing, locally quarried building stone—would have given added pleasure. It would have been a tragedy to import bricks into this warm grey countryside, an error which Elizabethan builders showed no signs of committing.

In the wealthy Marcher counties, there was the same conservatism. The fine new houses, great and small, were mainly in the same half-timbered 'black and white' style that was becoming traditional in a countryside especially rich in timber. The decorative façades of Cheshire houses were approaching their most ornamental phase, popularly called the magpie style.

There was more embellishment and enlargement and all the signs of new wealth everywhere except in the northern hill country.

Here the descendants of the mediaeval warrior farmers continued to live in their grey, gloomy, stone-built homes, castles rather than manor houses, yet quite unlike the castles of the south, grim block-houses designed to defend their occupiers from the raids of the law-less bands of brigands who still ranged over the northern fells. Neither the country scene nor the homes of the people showed very much change in the Cheviot hill landscapes, or in the high valleys that point into the heart of the Pennines.

In the most fertile parts of England—in the champion country of the Midlands, in East Anglia, in many parts of the south country, and in the Severn valley—yet another addition to the rural scene was beginning by now to vary the theme of village and manor house. This was the farmhouse of very moderate size, stone-built in the Cotswold belt, half-timbered in the Severn val-ley and in most of the wealden districts of the south. In East Anglia, too, the smaller farmhouse was often half-timbered, though here the absence of a local stone and the diminishing tim-ber reserves made the supply of building materials for the smaller houses something of a problem. Almost any material was wel-come, with the old-fashioned lath and plaster still holding its own in some quite sizable houses.

The Elizabethan farmhouse is perhaps the most attractive of all the new features of the landscape. It rarely shows much trace of advanced classical design and is always a simple, unpretentious building. Its chief ornament in the west country and in Kent is the pleasant pattern of timber beams; in the eastern counties it may be decorated with elaborate plaster work called parge work or par-getting. In these farmhouses the traditional hall survives though in a novel guise, as a utilitarian combination of kitchen and dining-room. The other rooms are modest in comparison.

In such pleasant houses life at the end of the century was still very much on the early Tudor pattern, especially when the main business of the farm was sheep-rearing and the unmarried women of the household, the spinsters, continued to sit for long hours at their spinning wheels, so that a continuous supply of spun yarn might be available for the weaving shops of the nearest town.

Any modern traveller in Elizabethan England would have been shocked by at least one lamentable difference from the countryside of today, a difference not of sight but smell. More refined travellers from the continent often commented on the sickening stench

The countryside in February (from the *Shepherd's Calendar*, 1597).

which drifted downwind from even the wealthiest homes and could be discerned a full mile away. That was a penalty of over-elaboration in building without the slightest knowledge of drainage and without any real attempt to improve on what had been tolerated so long. In towns the stench was multiplied many times, for only open drains were available, gutters as we should call them, to carry sewage and refuse through the crowded thoroughfares to the nearest river.

All that has been said about the prominence of man's handiwork in the countryside during the sixteenth century is remarkable enough but there is still one more item to add to the list. This eventful century witnessed the development of the first real villages, in the sense in which we visualize a village today—a compact integrated group of cottages around a village green or built side by side along a road facing the village church. It produced, as it were, the first 'terrace homes' that had seen the light of day. It was the first century, too, in which cottages were built strongly enough to withstand the vicissitudes of use and misuse and survive to the present day.

Earlier communities had often, it is true, been grouped round a village green, though more often the cottage homes were spaced along the road leading to the church and manor. What dis-

Detail from the title page of the third edition of Sir Philip Sidney's *Arcadia*, 1598.

tinguished the new kind of village was that the gaps between the cottages were closed, making for something much more picturesque, even though many at the time deplored a change which was thought enough of an abuse to be the subject of restrictive legislation, enacting that no cottage might be built without four acres of land attached. Like so much legislation affecting the countryside, this had no effect. The days of the close-clustered village were at hand. As a result the now free workers became more and more dependent on their masters as the land at their personal disposal grew less, and many thought themselves lucky to own a small garden.

Chiddingstone in Kent is one of the best examples of this new kind of village community. It is the only village in England in which there remains a whole row of early Tudor cottages side by side with others of Elizabethan date. It shows so well the development of village architecture during the century, its contrast with the less beautiful styles of later times is so conspicuous that it might well have been designed as a model for a folk museum. Even the church, half hidden by sombre yew trees, fits perfectly into the artless composition.

One must not be misled by the example of Chiddingstone into thinking that every Tudor or Elizabethan cottage was as pleasant to look at and as well built. Probably the majority of agricultural workers' homes consisted of four walls and a roof and nothing much else, at least until the middle of the century. The old tradi-tion of a fire burning in a central hearth (the wood smoke being left to escape as best it could through the door or window opening) obstinately resisted progress but at least a start had been made on rehousing the rural people, while among the wealthy farmers and landowners there was a genuine feeling that the people on whom they depended for the efficient working of their land deserved a better habitation than the hovels with which the cotters and villeins of the Middle Ages had had to be content.

The new-style farmhouse provided the model for the new-style cottage. Some of the Elizabethan cottages of Chiddingstone are reproductions in miniature of Elizabethan farmhouses in the same county. Once again the midlands and the south showed the way. A journey through the rural districts of England today reveals a relatively large number of Elizabethan cottages in all the home counties and in Bedfordshire, north Buckinghamshire, Northamp-tonshire, and Leicestershire, with a fair sprinkling over the counties of the west near the Welsh border lands. But there are very, very few in the north country or in the extreme south-west.

Towards the end of the sixteenth century when the area under cultivation was rapidly increasing, new crops and new methods of cultivation added to the variety of the scene. The oxen-drawn plough was still a commonplace sight in autumn and spring but on the lighter lands the horse was beginning to come into its own and wonderfully efficient light-weight ploughs were in use, very little different from those commonly employed as late as the end of the nineteenth century.

Wheat was the staple crop of the clay lands, and, as it is today, of the greater part of East Anglia and the East Midlands. The benefits of autumn-sown crops were not lost on the sixteenth-century farmer, so that the inspiring sight of young corn turning the browns and greys of the recently-ploughed fields into bright green before the frosts of winter set in must have encouraged the people of those days with its promise of spring as surely as it does the wayfarer of the twentieth century.

Much land also was under oats, but oats were generally spring-sown, though the farmers made a great effort to plough the land before winter and leave the frost to carry on the work which the plough had begun of breaking up the soil into a fine tilth. On the lighter land there was a mixture of wheat and rye, with perhaps more fields of the two combined than of any other single crop. This mixture, which was called blendcorn, yielded the grain from which the majority of the farmhouse-baked loaves was made. Rye was regarded as the more certain crop; in areas where the land was relatively poor it was cultivated extensively, especially in the 'gardens' of the village people. Here and there fields of barley or hemp provided a variation on the general theme.

Turnips grew in most of the village smallholdings, but no root crops were produced on a commercial scale for animal feeding, a factor which influenced the whole rural economy, since it meant that as autumn drew on a great number of cattle were slaughtered to conserve the meagre ration of winter feed.

The science of improving the soil was out of its infancy. Marl-ing the land was a practice which had begun in the north country but by Elizabethan times had spread to almost every area. Another method of enriching the soil was by spreading the ash of burnt turves over the freshly-ploughed fields. This is a scientifi-cally attested method of manuring, so it is not surprising that a practice which started in Devonshire was also quickly adopted in most other parts of the south. The acrid smoke of burning turf curling up into the air must have been as common a sight in autumn as the smoke of autumn bonfires in the countryside today.

There has been a tendency to exaggerate the gaiety of 'Merrie England', to give it perhaps more movement and colour than it really possessed. The picture of village people competing vigorously to glean the fields after the farmer's harvest had been reaped serves to put the scene into perspective. The standard of living of the people at large, though clearly improving, was still far behind what would be regarded as a tolerable minimum today, while the contrast between the ordinary worker on the land and the prosperous farmer was far greater. Even so, at certain times in the year the spirit of Merrie England did come to life and brought added colour to the village scene. Throughout the Middle Ages many pagan festivals had been given the blessing of the Church and were celebrated on the Church's saints' days. The two festivals which are the natural feast days of a rural people were observed as vigorously as ever. These were the festivals of Mayday and of the harvest. In many parts of Britain traditional observances connected with Mayday celebrations are still carried on, such as the Furry Dance of Helston in Cornwall and the festival of the Padstow Hobby Horse. In Elizabethan England the celebrations were more spontaneous and far more widely spread. There was scarcely a village which did not set up its maypole to welcome in the season of growth and which did not have its Morris dancing and its traditional horseplay.

It was customary for the people of a village to go into the nearest woods on the eve of Mayday to gather green boughs and a straight branch to serve as a maypole. A few generations later the leaders of the Puritan reaction saw in these activities nothing but an excuse for drunkenness and rape under the guise of old custom. A contemporary writer, the normally conservative Stubbes, contributes to the impression. A great number of the village maidens, he says, who went into the woods 'to gather in the may-o' came out no longer maidens. It may well be that the advent of the merry month of May brought together many of the village boys and girls. It may well be, too, that much that the Puritans alleged was true, but there is little evidence that Puritan legislation with its abolition of Mayday festivals really succeeded in imposing a new kind of morality on a country so simply organized as rural England at that time.

Mayday was an event which expressed the essentially primitive instincts, with all the primitive people's respect for strength and virility in man, beauty and nubility in woman. It was the first day of the season of maturity, a high light in the rural calendar which typified the country people's hopes and aspirations for the future. Robin Hood and his Merrie Men and Maid Marian were introduced into the routine of the Morris dance to express the spirit of daring and endeavour which defied the authority of new overlords.

So, too, the quieter festivity on the completion of the harvest, with its attendant banqueting—the harvest supper by tradition given by the farmer or the lord of the manor—was a thanksgiving for the bounty of the land and the realization of some at least of the hopes which had been expressed in the festival 'to welcome in the summer and the may-o'.

We have sketched in outline the general picture of the English scene in the sixteenth century. The primeval configuration of the land still provided the dominant theme but man-made features were increasingly apparent and varying the landscape over a wider and wider area. Here and there in the countryside there were splashes of colour in Elizabethan times which made the scene locally brighter and more varied than in any subsequent period. In northern Essex hundreds of acres were planted with the saffron which gave Saffron Walden its name. In the home farms or gardens of the wealthy the characteristic white flowers of the potato plant were beginning to make their appearance. The brilliant blue of the flax in bloom could be seen, as it can today, in parts of Suffolk and also in small but effective patches in many other counties of the south country. In Somerset's Vale of Taunton the flowering of the orchards was a sight which attracted visitors from abroad in spring, though the present-day brilliance of the other fruit-growing area of the west, the Vale of Evesham, was not dreamt of in the sixteenth century, when that fertile countryside was given over to the mixed agriculture typical of the Marches counties.

Of all the English counties, Kent showed most change in Tudor and Elizabethan times. Before the end of the century it was

obham Hall. *Cobham Hall, built of red brick in the last decades of the sixteenth century l enlarged to the designs of Inigo Jones in the following century, is an outstanding example of a mansion incorporating two styles of architecture in a harmonious whole.*

Shropshire manor farm. *The four-square Georgian façade of the manor farm forms part of traditional park-like landscape of the fine grazing country which lies on either side of the Holyh road near the Welsh border.*

Landscape gardening on the grand scale. *This artificial lake in Blenheim Park forms of the vast landscape gardening scheme carried out by Capability Brown as a setting for Sir J Vanbrugh's Blenheim Palace.*

already earning the name of 'The Garden of England'. Only a few miles from the banks of the Thames near Sittingbourne, where the land rises towards the ridge of the North Downs, there is a village called Teynham, now a place of little beauty but of great historic interest. As early as the reign of Henry III it was granted a charter giving it a market and fair. In the reign of Henry VIII a certain Richard Nains, described as the King's Fruiterer, put over a hundred acres under cherries and apples and converted Teynham overnight into the centre of the Kent fruit and market-gardening industry. The cherries which Nains planted were imported from Flanders—the selfsame strain of cooking cherries which even now comprise nearly half the cherry harvest of Kent.

About the same time the first hops, an indigenous plant in its wild state, were being cultivated in the valley of the Stour and up the sides of the hills by Brabourne. The trailing vines were being trained up long poles from the forest of the Weald. Indeed Reginald Scott's *Parfite Platforme of a Hoppe Garden* has a lot to say that would be valuable to a twentieth-century tyro in hop culture. Many of the earliest methods of cultivation have proved to be the best.

The fertile valley of the Medway, too, was being planted with orchards and hop gardens by the reign of Elizabeth, though here progress was retarded by the extraordinarily bad state of the dirt roads across the clay countryside. When Henry VIII rode to Hever to woo Anne Boleyn it was by no means unusual for him to become stuck fast in the mud and to have to await the arrival of servants from Hever Castle to extricate him from his difficulties. In autumn and winter most of the roads over the valley were impassable for farm carts; the great houses of Kent, among them Hever and Penshurst and Leeds Castle, were virtually isolated for months on end, in spite of their proximity to the metropolis.

If Kent was already the true Garden of England, a man-made garden on a vast scale, the craft of making ornamental gardens was being mastered in many parts of the country. These added yet more splashes of colour to a country scene which was by no means

I

drab. A very nearly perfect Tudor garden is preserved near the riverside in Hampton Court Palace. It shows the influence of Renaissance ideas, which rather surprisingly were adopted freely in the laying out of gardens while they were still regarded with suspicion in the more traditional craft of building. In the reign of Elizabeth the Renaissance garden achieved its finest expression in England. Most of the larger houses were surrounded by a small deer park (the days of the vast pleasure park with its own partly artificial landscapes were yet to come). The ornamental gardens were laid out in a corner of the park close to the house and were often surrounded by high walls.

Even the smaller gardens were elaborate: three hundred individual species of flowers were recorded in the garden of a single rectory. Laburnum and white lilac were introduced into the country for the first time. Sweet-smelling herbs were popular and a small herb garden was an inevitable part of every demesne.

Already in the reign of Henry VIII there were statues and fountains among the flower beds and shrubberies. In Queen Elizabeth's time these were taking on more and more elaborate shapes while many sculptors specialized in the design of garden ornaments, especially sundials. 'Knot gardens', carried out in flowers of contrasting colour and dwarf shrubs trimmed short and planted in geometrical designs, were a charming fancy that has never been surpassed, in its own way as colourful as a twentieth-century herbaceous border.

England would have seemed a very pleasant place to the wayfarer of today, jaded by the din and sickened by the smoke of modern towns. The mediaeval towns had not yet developed the fatal middle-age spread which disfigured so much of England in later centuries. Most of them were still confined within their walls with only discreet satellite villages in place of what we now call suburbs. The few larger towns that existed were almost entirely in the south country, for the north had not started on its insensate course of development; even Sheffield, famous already for its cutlery, was a small town from which it was possible to walk into open country within five or ten minutes. London was the largest of all but its size is placed in proper perspective when it is recalled that Westminster still contrived a separate entity and that east of Aldgate there was little save open marshland and green pasture—apart, that is, from the large number of villages such as Wanstead and Ilford and Romford, which have become the satellites of London's industrial complex.

During the sixteenth century a major change was taking place all too rapidly in the forests of the south and midlands. There were iron-working industries in Sussex round Mayfield and Ashburn-ham. The furnaces that kept the iron forges alive were greedy of timber. There was an ever-increasing demand for timber also to build the ships for the navy which Henry VIII sponsored and Elizabeth made into a powerful striking force. Every year more and more of the old oaks were felled, until by the end of the cen-tury the wealden forest was a shadow of its former self. The same thing was happening all over the country. Sherwood, the forest of Robin Hood, was denuded, the great forest of Waltham or, as it was sometimes still known, the Forest of Essex, was being stripped of its ancient trees as fast as Sherwood or the Weald.

For this rapid denudation of the southern forests there was one compensation in Queen Elizabeth's time. While the timber wealth of the country was being consumed so rapidly a start, though a very insignificant start, was being made on the reclama-tion of marshland and bog, and especially of the salt marshes which fringed the east coast. The engineers of the Low Countries had already shown what could be achieved in winning rich land from virtually impenetrable swamps. Wisely it was to Dutch engineers that the English government applied when there were proposals to start the drainage of the vast area which has become eastern England's fenland. This was yet one more token of the transition from the mediaeval scene to the modern English land-scape.

CHAPTER VIII

The Age of Progress

1603-1760

♦ ♦

IT IS FORTUNATE that from Elizabethan times onwards we can refer to the impressions of foreign visitors as well as contemporary English writers to see ourselves as we really were. The latter, after all, took all they saw for granted and were often concerned only to grind their own particular axe. The visitors from abroad were struck by the differences between the English countryside and their own homelands and generally wrote without conscious prejudice.

An ambassador from Italy made a journey through eastern England from London to the Scottish boundary in 1612. He was terrifically impressed with the vigour of English husbandry and with the comparative wealth of the land. That was indeed a tribute coming from a native of sunny Italy. He says that he was amazed by the fact that there was no unfertile land all the way from London to Scotland. In a century of which we are told by many of our own writers that the waste land was a disgrace to every Englishman, this unqualified admiration stands out with singular unexpectedness.

Our Italian diplomat, too, was a great admirer of our rivers which, he said, watered the land so adequately and, in the case of the Trent and the Ouse at least, were so full of barges and small ships that they were clearly arteries of commerce far more effective than the still rudimentary roads. Above all, this sympathetic visitor was struck by the fact that eastern England had so many townships of such obvious prosperity occurring, as he said, every eight or ten miles. Italy is traditionally a country of urban rather than

The prospect of
BERMINGHAM
from Ravenhurst (neere London road.)
on the South east Part of the towne 1640

Birmingham in the seventeenth century showed no sign of its future development as the centre of the Black Country. (From an engraving of 1640.)

rural economy, so that his comment on the English towns is praise no less striking than his impression of the landscape's fertility.

The towns were, of course, very small by modern standards, including Huntingdon, Stamford, Grantham, Newark, and Doncaster. But they were unequivocally towns, not villages, while many of them had several churches. If one stands near the top of the hill today where the Great North Road passes through Stamford, one can see, in spite of the press of modern buildings, three mediaeval churches still standing. How much more impressive they must have looked three hundred and fifty years ago when their spires and towers dominated the merchants' houses and cottages clustered about them.

Doubtless, too, our visitor was right in thinking of them as thriving communities, especially as much of the country through which he passed—the extension of the Chiltern Hills near Royston and the extension of the Cotswold country between Grantham and Stamford—was famous for its wool-bearing sheep, while the woollen trade was still a dominant factor in English life. If one adds to this the fact that the vast majority of the townsfolk were also part-time farmers cultivating their strips of arable land beyond the limit of the town, there is no ground for disputing the virtue of the balanced rural economy that was England in the early part of the seventeenth century.

Another point that struck the traveller from abroad was the number, size, and beauty of the village churches along the route. Here, again, we are on sure ground because the churches which he saw in the seventeenth century are virtually identical with the churches which we can see today if we follow his route. The Reformation was a thing of the past. The great era of church building was over, but men and women still worshipped as a matter of course; even though the monasteries had been allowed to decay, the churches were kept in repair, at least so long as the land was prosperous. A few of them, especially in towns, have been enlarged since then. Many were grievously restored in the last half of Queen Victoria's reign. But substantially they stand today as they did then. And they must have been all the more remarkable at that time because the other man-made features of the country-side were less numerous and less conspicuous than they are today. Moreover, the road, or rather the wide muddy thoroughfare fringed by green strips which passed for a road, went right through all the villages, for no one had thought of the idea of by-passing a narrow street or a cluster of houses.

From the beginning of the seventeenth century until the middle of the following century, when the industrial revolution was begin-ning to cast a shadow over the green land, it was a time of constant development and gradual change. The change-over from farming for subsistence to farming for profit was not yet complete. The idea of food production for sale in the markets alone was still a thing of the future. The greater part of England's ploughland was still given over in the early part of the seventeenth century to the production of bread corn and other food crops necessary to supply the village communities which were responsible for working the land. The area under the plough was most likely determined by the needs of the people, all the rest being given over to sheep farming. Here and there, however, a few commercial crops were being produced, such as woad and flax, both, it is interesting to note, connected with the textile trade, which was firmly established as the basis of rural industry.

The changes that took place during the hundred and fifty years were largely changes dictated by pressure of the increasing population. There was no food to be bought from the continent; in fact, the bulk of the imports exchanged for textiles were luxury goods destined for the homes of the big landowners and merchants. There was no New World, or at least no production for export as yet in the New World, so England, like every other country, had to depend on its own resources for food. A growing population meant more ploughland. That, in turn, could mean one of two things—less sheep or a further attack on the previously uncultivated areas of scrub and common. In the event there was a mixture of the two and both contributed to the gradual evolution of the countryside.

Just how great this pressure on the resources of the land was becoming is shown by the statistics of increase in the population. Estimates differ widely, but in the middle of the sixteenth century it was probably not much more than four millions. By the middle of the eighteenth century it was nearly six millions. Fifty years later it was over eight and a half millions. The abandonment of so much ploughland after the Black Death, though an economic necessity because of the shortage of labour, and as events proved the principal factor in assuring the mediaeval woollen boom, was only possible because of the smaller number to be fed. Throughout the history of our country, cultivation has never been far ahead of the needs of the people except for a short time in the early part of the nineteenth century, when there was an exportable surplus of wheat. By then methods of cultivation had improved so much that more grain was won from a single acre than two hundred years before could be harvested from three.

So the changing face of the land is linked closely with the nation's economic development, however haphazard the methods that have been used to achieve it may seem in retrospect. At times, the development of the landscape has lagged for no other reasons than the extreme conservatism of country folk and the vested interests which have been inherent in working the land almost from the very beginning of cultivation on a commercial scale. In the last chapter we saw how enclosure not only modified the appearance of large parts of England but showed the way to rapid improvement in agricultural methods. Inevitably though, the poorer classes in the farming community were deprived of a stake in the land and became hired labourers with far less self-respect than they had had before the change took place.

The same kind of thing was going on throughout the seventeenth and eighteenth centuries, even though enclosure was occasionally restricted by Acts of Parliament which people soon forgot and which were rarely enforced. No additional open fields were added to the village communities, not even in the champion country of the midland shires. Expansion now was invariably by enclosed plots on the outer fringe of the common fields, while the younger sons of the farming community were still being encouraged to cultivate new land and build themselves a home near the new fields, which often proved the forerunner of substantial Georgian or Victorian farmhouses. Additional enclosure of the common fields until the middle of the eighteenth century was always by agreement between the parties concerned. It consisted, as before, of the exchange of scattered holdings in the common field for a compact area in one part of it.

Slowly, very slowly, the land was taking on its new look, but it is worth stressing once more that all these changes were confined to the south-eastern half of England. Devon and Cornwall, the highlands of the north-west and the hilly country on the borderland of Wales, had always in the main been enclosed. The Saxon open-field system of farming in those areas had been confined to small fertile oases in the hill country and had never been a dominant feature of the landscape. In those areas, therefore, through the centuries there was little change except for a constant tendency for new hill farms to be established at higher and higher levels. Imperceptibly, far more slowly even than in the fertile lowlands, the hand of man was being superimposed on nature's contours and colouring.

The seventeenth century was the first time in history when the reclamation of new landscapes took place as capitalist ventures. Though it was only a century since farming for profit had begun to influence the landscape, now everyone concerned, from the king downwards, was making a great effort to create completely new landscapes for profit. The visible results of their endeavours include the Romney Marsh, the Fylde of Lancashire, the Somerset Plain near Bridgwater and, above all, the fens of Cambridge, Norfolk, and Lincolnshire. All these in Tudor times had been desolate landscapes flooded for most of the year, supporting either no population at all or, at the most, a few scattered communities as, for instance, in the islands of the Fens which had been occupied throughout the Middle Ages. In the case of all of them except the Fens, nature had already gone a long way towards achieving the reclamation with the help of silt deposited by the rivers which meandered in many ill-defined channels across the swamps. It was chiefly a matter of building or renewing sea walls and of making the drainage of the land more efficient.

In the fenlands the aim was to produce half a million acres of fertile country from desolate waste. The story of man's ultimately successful struggle with nature in this area is a fascinating one. The most amazing thing is that it was prolonged over a period of two hundred years, while the successive victories were in every case due to the vision of a small group of men. They were victories which had to be won not only over the passive force of nature but against the constant niggling opposition of those who imagined they had an interest in the maintenance of the landscape as it was. As a consequence, the whole story is one of inordinate delay, sometimes of a century or more, between the discovery of a means to greater production and its general acceptance. Nothing in our whole narrative is so illustrative of the difficulties which beset the reformer on the land as the story of the fenlands.

During the Middle Ages what little had been done to increase the cultivated area of fen had been the work of the monastic houses established at Ely and Crowland. The first blow in what may be called the modern onslaught was struck by Archbishop Morton in the reign of King Henry VII. Morton's Leam is a still-present memorial to that cleric's vision so far ahead of its time. In spite of this and other smaller works, nature was very much holding her own towards the end of Queen Elizabeth's reign. The silt land bordering the Wash was regularly inundated by the sea. The peat lands further inland, where the midland rivers emptied themselves into the marshes, were still an impenetrable morass which dried out for a month or two in the summer, if at all. The only vegetation was marsh grass and weeds, the only inhabitants thousands on thousands of water fowl and other birds.

Queen Elizabeth had seen that here was an acreage equivalent to a whole English county ready for the taking, if only a concerted effort backed with sufficient capital could be made to reclaim it. An Act passed in 1600 laid the foundation of all future reclama- tion. It recognized that individual communities, living on the fringe of the marshland, had neither the labour nor the capital available to make the determined effort necessary. So it was en- visaged that 'undertakers' should 'undertake' to reclaim a given area of grazing land in return for a share of the land so reclaimed. The Act was resisted to the full by the commoners, who were per- haps unduly backward. Camden speaks of them as living a pre- carious existence, going from settlement to settlement, from dry patch to dry patch on stilts. He thought of them as a race apart, depressed in their standard of living to a degree which would not have been tolerated by the more fortunate uplanders.

In the upshot the Act of 1600 achieved little in the few remain- ing years of Queen Elizabeth's reign, but King James I was per- sonally interested and, however unpopular, strong enough to turn his interest to good account. In 1620 he himself became under- taker-in-chief. He undertook to reclaim the whole of the marsh- land in return for 120 thousand acres to be added to the royal estates. King James died in 1625 before the reclamation was far advanced. Although his successor, Charles I, also expressed interest, he could not afford to flout the opposition of his subjects in view of the grave constitutional difficulties which beset him. So it was left to the fourth Earl of Bedford to deputize for the king as undertaker in 1630.

The name of Cornelius Vermuyden is like a bright thread run-ning through the whole fabric of this strange tale. Vermuyden had wrought miracles in Holland. He had surveyed the ground and drawn up a plan of reclamation for King James I. Now he was re-engaged by the Earl of Bedford, though his appointment pro-voked another storm of unreasoning opposition. It was bad enough, said the commoners, to have their way of living changed. It was like sacrilege for men to defy the will of God as represented by the waves of the sea and the waters of the rivers, but it was add-ing insult to injury to employ a blasted foreigner for the purpose. However, Vermuyden persisted, gathering labour where he could, including a number of skilled workmen from Holland. After less than five years he had done what no man had done before. He had created a new river more than twenty miles long and in the process destroyed an old one. He drove a straight cut from Earith towards the Wash (the channel which is called the Old Bedford river) and made the waters of the Ouse flow into it, leaving the old waterway of the Ouse which meandered round by Ely a mere trickle. Thus the lower reaches of the Midland Ouse ceased to exist and the Cam, which until then had been one of its tribu-taries joining it above Ely, became the parent river. From Ely to Denver the name of Ouse is retained, even on modern maps, but it is the Cam rather than the Ouse which flows there.

Vermuyden's aim was to increase the speed of the river's natural current by shortening its course and, at the same time, to prevent inundation of the land on either side by building high banks. Unfortunately neither the increased speed of the current nor the banks were sufficient to prevent seasonal inundation. None of the principals, one imagines, had ever thought they would be, but the outcry of those who had obtained grazing rights on the new land was sufficient excuse for the king to appear as a *deus ex machina* and take over the work where the Earl of Bedford had left off. Vermuyden was still the engineer-in-chief, working away as diligently in the employment of the king as he had in the employ- ment of the earl.

Then came the civil war and the lapse by default of the king's interest. The civil war, as we shall see later, was the root cause of several changes in the landscape but it had no effect on the pro- gress of work in the fens. The difficulty was resolved by the fifth Earl of Bedford, the son of the pioneer Earl, undertaking the work on behalf of the Commonwealth. Vermuyden was still the creative force, possibly bewildered by his frequent change of em- ployer but persevering with that dogged persistence which seems to be a characteristic of all who work in the great fen levels on either side of the North Sea. He must have been cheered to be able to use Dutch prisoners of war on the work. One can imagine their presence making him feel quite at home.

Within a very few years another artificial cut had been made eastward from Earith, the New Bedford River, parallel with and divided from the Old Bedford River by a narrow strip of land which was deliberately inundated when the river was in spate. A number of other main drainage channels were constructed to flow into the new river. The drainage channels, in turn, were linked with scores of dykes or ditches, known locally by a bewildering variety of names, to drain individual small areas. To all intents and purposes the job was finished, though the great fen of Lin- colnshire was untouched and the commoners there remained in undisputed possession of their watery waste, which had changed little since the days of Hereward the Wake.

Soon there were crops of peas and hemp and flax growing in Cambridgeshire and Norfolk, while sheep and cattle pastured over land which proved unbelievably rich. Before long, however, nature began to reassert herself. Vermuyden was dead, so we can never know what steps he would have taken to avert the threats to his handiwork. The fact was that the accumulation of silt carried down by the rivers was blocking their outflow, while the level of the reclaimed land was dropping with alarming rapidity as the moisture evaporated from it and as the cultivators of the eighteenth century burnt off the top covering of peat to make the land fit for cultivation. Further, as the land dried out, it powdered easily, and the top soil was carried away by easterly gales blowing in from the Wash unchecked by any obstacle such as a range of hills or natural forest or even recently planted woodland. All too soon the minor drains became lower in level than the main discharge streams and the land they were intended to drain was threatened once more with inundation by the surplus water.

The answer was found in the installation of pumping machinery. The introduction of windmills began the second phase in the fenland struggle against nature and changed utterly again the whole nature of the landscape. Windmills were designed to pump thousands of gallons of water a day over the retaining banks of the main streams, and to hurry along the water from the minor drainage canals into the larger dykes. It seemed at one time as though the landscape were covered in windmills. In Whittlesey parish alone it was said fifty windmills were in full work. Any traveller across the fenland ways today can see for himself how far the black peaty soil has fallen, if he compares the height of the banks of the Bedford rivers on the inner and the outer sides. The bulk of England's most fertile country is many feet below sea-level.

We must go outside the period of this chapter to complete the story. That the fenlands are as productive as ever is a by-product of the industrial revolution. By 1820, when the first steam engines were introduced to replace the windmills, the latter had become obsolete, for they lacked the power to do the work that was demanded of them, or to do it continuously enough—day and night through calm and storm alike. But the steam pumping stations achieved what the windmills could no longer do. The only change since then has been the replacement of some of the steam engines by others powered by more modern machinery, and the construction of sluices more efficient by far than the primitive methods of pumping the water from the drains over the banks of the river.

A contributary cause of arresting nature's counter attack was the substitution of deep ploughing for the older practice of burn/ing off the peat. By this means the clay that lay below the peat was brought to the surface and reduced the loss of soil, while at the same time giving it more cohesion and permanence. Barring some unpredicted onslaught one can say now that the Fen land/scapes are an integral part of Britain and secure so long as the pumping stations are manned and constant vigilance is maintained over the retaining banks of the artificial rivers. The disastrous floods of 1953 proved that an unforeseen combination of tide, flood/water, and wind may still call for special measures to pro/tect what has been won with such prolonged effort.

Meanwhile, rather late in the eighteenth century, the Lincoln/shire levels had been drained. As time went on the seasonal floods in the Witham valley had grown progressively worse. The poet Cowper, who spent so much of his life at Olney, complained bit/terly of the flooded plain of the Ouse in winter time. Conditions must have been far, far worse in the broad valley of the Witham between Lincoln and the sea, where sheep and cattle were fre/quently drowned in large numbers and the natural pastures were quite unusable except for a few months in high summer. Here, too, the work was not completed until the early nineteenth cen/tury. My own grandmother frequently recalled the childhood memory of fen people walking on stilts across the flooded land and the wonder with which they saw the land drying out as dykes were constructed, until in time they exchanged their stilts for long poles with which to vault the 'drains'. In winter when the drains were frozen the young people of Lincolnshire found unexpected enjoyment in skating along them from village to village.

Every feature of fenland follows the lines of the dykes, even the roads, the straight, rather unattractive, through ways which are often built on a shelf halfway between the level of the fields and the top of the dyke bank. Though such roads may be dull in them/selves, there is compensation in the magnificent views they com/mand over the dead level of the intensively cultivated landscape. Here and there towards the sea, especially in Lincolnshire, roads run along the top of dykes, pursuing a tortuous course with many a twist and turn. Generally these are much older than the modern draining of the Fens and date back to what one might call the amateur drainage of mediaeval England when the waters of the Wash were constantly receding and a succession of dykes, one in front of the other, was built over the centuries, each advancing, however precariously, the limit of summer grazing land seaward. Inevitably roads developed along the top of the banks, linking settlement with settlement.

One can usually distinguish the more recently reclaimed land from the older by the nature of the farmhouses and cottages. The vast majority in the newly reclaimed land are nineteenth-century in date, rather like railway terraces translated into a strange medium with all the incongruity of Victorian cottage architecture in the midst of an empty landscape. The older farmhouses are most often four-square Georgian structures, while the village settlements on the 'islands' have a core of earlier houses and a mediaeval church, though many Victorian and still later rows of cottages have been added.

To return to the seventeenth century, the appearance of the country at large varied little, though the proportion of ploughland was increasing. As a hundred years before, wheat was still the staple crop of the good lands, rye of the poor lands, with barley, oats, peas, beans, and lentils grown in varying quantities on all the ploughlands of the south and east. Bread corn was the essential need, though the grain from which bread was made varied, of necessity, from one district to another. The bread of Kent, for instance, might be mainly a wheaten loaf, while that of Northumberland was mainly of rye. Rye was often grown with wheat and oats with barley, the immemorial mixture as before. A few new crops became more widespread and added a touch of distinction to the landscape. Hop vines could be seen in almost every county, especially in Essex, instead of being confined in the main to two or three as they are at present. Still, as in Camden's day, Saffron Walden was 'looking merrily with most lovely saffron'. The bright blue flowers of the flax were covering an increasing acreage, too, as the London and Lancashire linen industries expanded, and before the import of raw material from the New World supplanted the home-grown flax.

The grape vines which had been a pleasant feature of Tudor England were fast disappearing, no one knows why. Some have suggested that it was due to a change in climate, but no scientific evidence supports the view. Nor is it really credible when one thinks of the enthusiasts one knows in Kent today who grow wine grapes on the open hillsides near Canterbury without any trouble at all. Herefordshire, however, proudly maintained its vines and claimed to be the vineyard of England. Perhaps the root cause of the change was a delayed action result of the dissolution of the monasteries. Certainly the priors and abbots had been among the most sedulous cultivators of the vine. By way of some small compensation for the disappearing vine, King James I, fired by ambition to establish a silk industry, introduced the picturesque mulberry and saw to it that it was planted far and wide, especially in Devonshire. Alas, the mulberry and the silkworms it nourished proved rather a failure, but there are still mulberry trees planted by James himself at Hatfield House, while other old mulberry trees are alive and vigorous at Charlton Place, at New Place, Stratford-on-Avon, in the gardens of Dulwich Picture Gallery, and probably in thousands of other places where there were Jacobean houses, even though the houses have been pulled down and their grounds turned into residential streets. The tradition has not died out entirely. Lullingstone Castle by the banks of the Darent in Kent has kept the industry alive. Silk produced from worms which fed on Lullingstone's mulberry trees was used in the coronation robes of Queen Elizabeth II.

A new agricultural revolution was impending at the end of the seventeenth century, but it gained no momentum until the beginning of the following century, and later marched hand in hand with the industrial revolution. Once again, it is impossible to read the records of the times without being amazed at the slowness with which progress was made. All through the seventeenth century potatoes were a garden crop, but one that was never taken seriously and certainly not cultivated on a commercial scale. As

ecent man-made landscapes. *The draining of the Fens was one of the greatest achievements* *recent centuries. The Bedford River, seen above near Denver Sluice, is a completely new* *er which supplanted the old waterway of the Ouse. Another and quite different kind of new* *ndscape was created when the Royal Military Canal, below, photographed near Appledore,* *was cut through the Romney Marshes.*

A Midland landscape. *The green-fringed road and the hawthorn hedge derive from the u*
of the Enclosure Commissioners. The railway viaduct is the product of Victorian enterp
No feature of this typical landscape is more than two hundred years old.

Knaresborough and the Nidd. *All the main periods of landscape building are represented*
this view of Knaresborough. The elegance of the site, the fine sweep of the river, are nature
handiwork; the graceful church is mediaeval, the houses clustered round it show the styles
several periods of building; the lofty bridge was built in the nineteenth century; some of the vill
are products of the present century.

the eighteenth century dawned, a few fields appeared in the vicinity of the growing towns, the bushy green plants and the brilliant white flowers adding welcome variety to the rural scene in late summer when most of the colours of nature had dimmed. The Royal Society had investigated the possibilities of a nation-wide potato crop in the 1660s. A hundred years were to elapse before the crop achieved anything like its modern economic importance.

Turnips, too, were confined to gardens until Viscount Towns-hend about 1730 started a campaign to grow turnips as a rotation crop and so provide winter feed for stock. His contemporaries called him 'Turnip' Townshend with the mild disdain that English farmers have always shown for innovators, but 'Turnip' Townshend undoubtedly showed the way to a rural economy capable of sustaining the vastly increased population that followed the industrial revolution. With the help of clovers which had been introduced a little earlier, the four-year rotation of crops became a reality in Norfolk, where Townshend made his experiment. In less than a decade Norfolk became the most prosperous farming county of England; the monotone greys and browns of idle fields almost disappeared from the summer scene. What a contrast this was with the two-field system of the Saxons, when half the ploughland of the country was bare; what a contrast, too, with the mediæval landscape, in which generally one field in three was resting. The brightly-flowering clovers and later the sanfoins and lucernes were as welcome additions to the colour of the English scene as any in the whole history of the countryside.

Another development which had a marked influence on the face of the land in spring was the practice of drilling, first mooted in 1730. Drilling proved to be one of the few innovations that spread across the country with relative speed, though probably half a century elapsed before it was universally adopted. The result, of course, was that the crops came up in neat straight rows from field end to field end instead of in an unevenly distributed carpet as it had when the seed was broadcast. A field of wheat in spring thereafter looked, as it was, a cultivated crop where before it might have been mistaken for a rather ragged grass field.

K

Everything was tending to greater order in the landscape. The English had become a nation of gardeners. Every dwelling place except the smallest cottages had its flower garden as well as its vegetable patch. Right through the seventeenth century the garden accent was on formality. Then gradually the tight rein was released and gardens began to look more like our typical suburban gardens with their bright and glowing colours, their informal arrangement of flowers within the bare formality of lawn and flower bed. New flowers, too, were being introduced and roses, which in their cultivated forms were growing farther and farther away from their natural state, found it more difficult to hold their own as the centre piece of the English garden. There was particular excitement when tulips arrived in large numbers from the Low Countries in Charles I's reign. One writer identified them with the biblical lilies of the field, pointing out that they had more colours than any other of God's creations. And how well adapted they were to the formality of the average Jacobean garden. The laburnum was another flower of unusual distinction which made its appearance in the seventeenth century; but almost every year some new species was brought from the continent. Much later exotic flowers began to arrive from the New World.

Meanwhile park landscapes were developing side by side with the garden landscapes. Nothing, except for a time the civil war, stopped the spate of building which was well under way in Queen Elizabeth's reign. During the Commonwealth, it is true, a few great schemes were postponed or dropped. The utilitarian Puritan doctrines of the Commonwealth leaders made them turn their attention rather to the cottage homes of the labourers than to the further aggrandisement of nobleman and squire. Many groups of rather functional-looking cottages which survive, though often under a suspended order of demolition, in villages of Hertfordshire, Huntingdonshire, and the East Midlands, are testimony to the zeal of the Commonwealth planners. It is unfortunate that the austere lines of these village homes contrast unfavourably with the charming architecture of those built fifty or a hundred years before.

Oliver Cromwell was responsible for one other change in the country landscape, a cutting of the last link with mediaeval life. During the civil war a good deal of opposition had come from Royalist noblemen ensconced in their mediaeval castles, capable even then of withstanding a long siege or of acting as advance bases from which the Commonwealth armies could be harassed and their lines of communication cut. When the war ended in Cromwell's victory the victor not unnaturally decided that never again should English castles stand as obstacles to the will of the people. All were slighted at his command, that is to say their battlements were destroyed, their roofs stripped off, and their fabric left to moulder away as time and circumstances dictated. Their fate was much the same as that of the abbeys and priories. Some were rebuilt as private residences, a few of them as late as Victorian times when most of the fabric had been destroyed. The majority, however, became ready-made quarries from which stone could be taken away by the cartload to repair the roads or build cottages.

Yet in an age which set no store by antiquity as such, the new mansions which were started in 'Good King Charles's golden days' must have seemed a truly generous compensation for the aging profile of the castles. Most were classical in design—in the style we call Palladian after the Italian architect Palladio, whose theories had first been translated into English practice by Inigo Jones and his followers. Aston Hall and Audley End and Hatfield House had been completed before the civil war. So had Inigo Jones's Banqueting Hall, which still stands in Whitehall opposite the Horse Guards' Parade. The tendency after the Commonwealth was admirably illustrated by Greenwich Hospital, completed by Wren and incorporating Inigo Jones's earlier Queen's House in its design. This was a new Thames-side landscape as dramatic in its own way as Wolsey's Hampton Court had been nearly a hundred and fifty years before. It was Wren, too, who was commissioned to transform the Palace of Hampton Court into a residence worthy of the times. He added the Garden Front buildings in the last decades of the seventeenth century and laid out the park with its Long Water and converging avenues.

The pattern of Wren was developed still further by Sir John Vanbrugh, the most grandiose in deed and imagination of all the great architects of the period. Vanbrugh was the architect of Blenheim Palace, presented by a grateful nation to the first Duke of Marlborough. He was given full licence without thought of expense. Not everyone may like the fulfilment of this architect's dream but no one at least can deny that Blenheim Palace today, as two hundred and fifty years ago, is an arresting and ambitious composition.

Vanbrugh did not confine his exuberance to the design of the house. A stream was dammed to form artificial lakes, new avenues were planted pointing to the classical front of the house. The whole of the park land surrounding it, which had once been a 'chase' set aside for the sport of Saxon kings, was reorientated to the new design. Later the gardens were laid out by Capability Brown, who at one time was Controller of the Royal Gardens at Hampton Court and proved in deed if not in title the first of the great English landscape gardeners. No, Blenheim—the palace, the lakes, and the park—may not be the twentieth-century idea of a perfect artificial landscape but it certainly has a breadth and vision greater than any of the man-made additions to the scene that had been achieved before it.

The same in lesser degree was happening all over the country. Vanbrugh himself was the architect of Castle Howard. Moor Park was completed in 1720, Holkham Hall in 1734, and, most remarkable perhaps of all the landscape parks set about eighteenth-century houses, Stowe Park with its monstrous collection of Greek temples and arbours took shape during the century.

The new park landscapes demanded new and more varied trees to set them off; the traditional oak, beech, ash, and elm no longer held absolute sway. These were still planted right down to the end of the era of the parks; so were the birch and willow and the few other native English trees, but now the accent was more and more on trees such as the sweet chestnut and the sycamore, which may have been introduced into Britain in Roman times but probably were unknown, or virtually unknown, in the Middle

Ages, as indeed was the walnut, which formed such a conspicuous feature of many seventeenth- and eighteenth-century parks. The horse chestnut, with its wonderful clusters of flowers and its nuts which have proved useless to man or beast, was the first of the true exotics which arrived in England. It was introduced some time during the sixteenth century, together with the plane tree, from which were developed the species which beautify London and other large towns. A tree which thrives in a minimum of soil and in the bleakest and sootiest of situations has proved a boon to the jaded citizens of the industrial towns.

Towards the end of the seventeenth century the Norway maple made its bow, together with bigger and bigger species of limes to form the sweet-smelling avenues leading to the latest Palladian creation in stone or brick. Different and more exotic species of poplar, too, were arriving—the most striking of them all, the Lombardy poplar, not until about 1750. Once the Lombardy poplar was added to the English landscape it proved a peculiarly dominant feature. It has remained in fashion during the ensuing two hundred years, as witness the Great Cambridge arterial road, rendered by its poplar avenue one of the most attractive of modern roads once it has left the industrial outskirts of London. The cedar of Lebanon, the weeping willow, the Norway spruce; those are just three more of the trees which enlivened the new park landscapes in town and country during the seventeenth and eighteenth centuries. It remained for the nineteenth century to produce the strangest of the exotic trees which found a place more in the public gardens of towns than in country park lands. The arrival of the fascinating monkey puzzle from South America in 1796 showed the shape of things to come. Any and every new tree was welcome in a land in which the devastation of the woodlands had gone on unchecked from the early Middle Ages and which had become the least wooded of all the countries of Europe.

The craze for reshaping landscapes to fit the whim of an architect-designer sometimes reached extraordinary proportions. When the first Earl of Dorchester decided to enlarge the park lands of Milton Abbas in the 1750s he had the whole of the small town which had originated as a market at the gates of the abbey swept away and rebuilt outside the gates of the enlarged park. We should call this an act of vandalism, though age has mellowed the new Milton Abbas, so that visitors today regard it as one of the most attractive of English villages.

If the rural landscape was now increasing its rate of change, the town landscapes of England were beginning to be remoulded with bewildering speed. Strange things were happening with or without the help of nature. The silting up of the Dee estuary was causing the old port of Chester to decline, while a new port called Liverpool was growing apace at the mouth of the Mersey. All the three towns which were the greatest in England in Elizabeth's day—York, London, and Bristol—were holding their own but York was soon to decline into a quiet cathedral city. During the seventeenth and the first half of the eighteenth century, the growth of the navy brought new prosperity and many new homes and public buildings to Southampton and to new townships like Chatham and Woolwich and Deptford. The estuaries of the Thames and Medway were beginning to assume the first signs of their twentieth-century bondage.

The West Riding woollen industry was reshaping the valleys of the Pennine country. Halifax had grown to a town of twelve thousand people, though it was still a scattered community. The concentration of industry was in its infancy and most of the weavers dwelt in semi-rural settlements on the nearby moors. Leeds and Wakefield were beginning to compete with Halifax.

In the reign of Charles II four provincial towns at the most had a population of ten thousand—Bristol, Norwich, Exeter, and perhaps York. Yet by 1700 Birmingham could boast at least fifteen thousand inhabitants, Manchester ten thousand, while there was something more than a shadow of the pall that was soon to fall over the Black Country to the west of Birmingham. The people of London by 1700 numbered about half a million. The old City was now joined to Westminster by an unbroken ribbon development, mostly of large merchants' houses along the Strand, many communicating with the river by a set of steps or a water gate, for the Thames was still London's main artery of private as well as of commercial transport. The Water Gate of York House in the Embankment Gardens, built in 1626, shows vividly how the Thames-side landscape has changed. All that is now the Embankment Gardens and the 'embankment' itself was then included within the river's waterway, a mud flat at low tide but well covered when the stream was running high. The Strand really was the strand, in fact as well as name, a raised riverside boulevard.

Daniel Defoe, when he made his journeys through England, commented that the land was 'daily altering its countenance'. If he had made his travels later in the eighteenth century he would scarcely have recognized his beloved country's face at all. In the towns, the changes might for once have left him speechless. What, one wonders, would he have made of the new Bath which was rising phoenix-like from the dejected remains of the mediaeval city?

In the eighteenth century the horizon of the individual was expanding rapidly. It was a time when one-half the world could at least begin to know how the other half lived. In Defoe's day the roads might still be bad in patches but they had improved tremendously since Samuel Pepys in the course of his duties as 'Clerk of our Ships' must needs hire guides to help his coachman find the way from London to Portsmouth and even with the help of guides lose his way twice on the single journey.

The answer to this seeming paradox in a highly civilized Restoration society was that the roads were a problem which had gone by default. They still consisted for the most part of wide undefined tracks on which following vehicles deliberately took a different course so as to avoid the deep ruts left by those in front. About the same time, in 1669 to be precise, a coach advertised for the first time that it would do the journey to Oxford in a single day during the summer months. Less than a hundred years later the Georgian coach boom was at its height. Travel had become commonplace instead of something only to be attempted of necessity or by the wealthy few. The way was literally being paved to the free communications of the nineteenth century.

CHAPTER IX

Industrial Revolution

1760-1900

◆ ◆

UNTIL THE MIDDLE of the eighteenth century development of the landscape had always been gradual. The process was accelerated from Tudor times onwards, but even then it was a gradual acce-leration, like a train imperceptibly gathering speed on a long level stretch of line.

From the second half of the eighteenth century circumstances lent wings to the evolution of the countryside. In some parts of England the landscape was changed out of recognition in a single generation, as fields gave way to bricks and mortar and valleys were filled with industrial buildings. This was a period not only of industrial revolution; it was equally a period of agrarian revolu-tion the like of which had not been seen before, even in the period following the Black Death.

The two revolutions are linked together. In a sense they were phases of the same movement, to which added impetus was given by the rapidly increasing population. In the last chapter we saw how a rising population necessitated the ploughing of a great deal more land and the partial rationalization of farming in order to keep the people supplied with the necessities of life. The growth of population from the sixteenth to the eighteenth century was nothing compared with that from the end of the eighteenth cen-tury to the twentieth. Between 1800 and 1900 it jumped from about eight and a half millions to over thirty millions (census figure for 1901, 31·4 millions). The reason for the increase, inci-dentally, was not, as so many have said, the industrial revolution itself. All the evidence points to the fact that mortality was at least as high in the towns as in the country, especially in the first half of the nineteenth century, when many of the industrial people were under-nourished, ill-housed, ill-clothed, and obvious victims to every infectious or contagious disease. Rather, the underlying factor was improved knowledge of medicine and surgery, the use of anæsthetics, and all the other miracles of healing which are the most precious legacy of the nineteenth century.

The growth of the population was not, however, the only reason for the revolution in farming which accompanied it. The steady drift from country to town, since it reduced the labour available on the farms at a time of essential farm expansion, also necessitated drastic revisions of the rural economy. Fortunately the same factors which influenced the course of the industrial revolution provided the means of meeting this difficulty. Rural England became increasingly mechanized, so that, although the number employed decreased, production all the time was rising—at least until the critical decade 1860–70.

By the end of the nineteenth century England's rural communities made up no more than ten per cent of the total population. Two hundred years before they had represented between eighty and ninety per cent of it. In a sense that is the whole story of this chapter compressed into two sentences. No wonder that, at the end of the nineteenth century when cheap food was available from abroad and the heyday of English farming was past, the rural people felt that they were survivals of an archaic system, a doomed and diminishing stratum in the population. It is a sardonic fact that but for the crisis of two world wars, the farming community might well have proved to be what strategists call an expendable force.

The first part of the revolution on the land was the spate of enclosure which began about 1760 and was not completed until 1820. Enclosure has figured largely in this chronicle of change since Tudor times. To a limited extent it had been going on all the time, even in the first half of the eighteenth century, which was a period of consolidation and technical advance rather than of obvious innovation. By 1760, however, it was apparent that the

Uffington Castle from the Vale of the White Horse about 1800, with cultivation extending above the line of the Ickleton (Icknield) Way. (Detail from a Vertue print in the British Museum.)

open-field system was a survival that could not be supported on any ground but that of tradition. The open fields, little changed in appearance since mediaeval days, stretched in a broad belt from west Norfolk through midland England to Dorset. Leicester-shire, Northamptonshire, and Rutland were counties in which they were the rule rather than the exception. Most of the enclo-sures made in those districts during the woollen boom were of grazing land outside the common fields and generally outside the common pastures too. Enclosure by mutual agreement between the farmers of the common fields had just about reached its limit. It needed legislation to modernize these strangely out-of-date landscapes of the Midlands.

Hundreds of Acts of Parliament were passed between 1760 and 1815, each dealing with a single enclosure scheme. Commissioners were appointed under the Act to inspect the area designated and to allot it to the various claimants after their titles to a share had been investigated. Many of the commissioners were local men. Others seem to have made a profession of enclosure work rather like modern surveyors. As the task they were called on to perform was at best an uncommonly difficult one, opportunities for bribery and corruption must have been legion. The chief difficulty facing the commissioners was not so much to adjudicate on the claims of those farmers who had been in possession for many generations, as on those of the newcomers to farming in the community who had, as it were, squatted in an outlying part of the parish and had perhaps developed some piece of land which had previously been uncultivated. Many of these squatters had no kind of legal right other than that established by precedent. A number of them were evicted from their holdings.

Others in the average village community were in traditional possession of one or more strips in the common fields which they cultivated as a spare-time occupation, using, as tradition decreed, the common means of sowing and reaping. When their holdings were consolidated into a single field and enclosed, they often found that they lacked the means to work their new land economically. Perhaps the land apportioned to them was not suitable for the kind of tillage which had prevailed in the common fields. In either case, they were only too glad to sell out to one of their more fortunate fellows who had been allotted a larger area of land. The net result was that a great number of smaller farmers were put out of business, while the larger farmers tended to extend their holdings by one means or another.

Some counties were not affected because enclosure was practically complete already. In Kent the landscape had achieved its

Buckinghamshire early in the nineteenth century. Whiteleaf Cross was then, as it is now, the most prominent feature in the landscape. (From a contemporary print by G. Vertue.)

present pattern, or something very close to it, before the end of Queen Elizabeth's reign. Enclosure, too, had been virtually completed in Sussex and Berkshire by the same time. According to Camden it was well advanced in those counties as early as the reign of King Henry VIII.

Many links with the wave of eighteenth-century enclosure remain in the Midlands. First and most conspicuous are the hawthorn hedges which from any high viewpoint in spring look like continuous lines of blazing white stretching as far as eye can reach and picking out the chequerboard pattern of what we have come to regard as the typical English scene, but one which until then was characteristic only of certain parts of the country.

The first boundaries of the new fields were paling fences for which thousands of acres of young woodland were ruthlessly cut down. The first enclosures, too, were effected by a fence round the entire 'estates' of the new farmers. Each farmer sub-divided his holding into smaller fields as time went on. That is why it is so obvious that many of the hedges of adjacent fields were not planted at the same time.

As the prosperity of the midland farming country grew—and

more prosperous it certainly did become in a very short time—the new farmers naturally sought to move their home from the site of the old village community to a farmhouse in their own fields. Hence the great number of compact eighteenth-century four-square farmhouses in the midland counties. Not all, of course, moved at once. Some deferred their removal to the age of greatest rural prosperity in the nineteenth century, when the style of house-building had changed and the far less pleasing Victorian farm-house was replacing older houses all over the country.

In spite of this 'crossing of the trail' by Victorian farmers, the age of the farmhouses is in many districts a clue to the time of enclosure. In Kent, for instance, there are a great many Tudor farmhouses in relation to the area of the county; in the west country farmhouses span the whole range of English building styles; while the vast majority of those in the Midlands are Georgian or Victorian. As a corollary of the general post, consequent on the Georgian enclosure Acts, many of the older houses which the enclosure farmers left for their new homes 'in the fields' were divided into two or otherwise converted into labourers' cottages. That, again, explains an obvious feature of the landscape today— the ancient core of the typical midland village with its Tudor or Jacobean cottages grouped near the church, though the surround-ing country has few, if any, farmhouses of equal age. Almost every traveller on English by-ways will agree that half-timbered or stone-built village homes are aesthetically more attractive than the brick-built farmhouses which replaced them.

One of the duties of the commissioners was to determine the course of the new roads which became practical when large-scale enclosure took place. Here, again, their work is still evident for all to see. The principle adopted was to utilize the mediaeval rights of way dividing one cultivated strip from another whenever it was possible to do so. This was expressed as the road following the furlongs. How often in midland England and in parts of Essex and Suffolk, too, does one come upon a road which goes straight as a die for a quarter of a mile, then turns by a right-angled bend, continuing for perhaps a hundred yards, and then bending sharply again to resume its previous direction. The motorist has reason to treat roads like that with great discretion because the right-angled bends are generally blind corners, and except on roads which are largely used the hedges have not been cut down to give a clear view. Before the motoring era there were many more such roads than there are today. It did not matter very much that a lumbering farm wagon should have to negotiate a blind corner. When motor-cars came into general use the county highway authorities were alarmed at the number of accidents which occurred at these places, even on roads which were very little used, when for instance a delivery van met a farmer's car in a head-on collision, so they 'cut off the corners', that is to say, they built a new length of two or three hundred yards of road which cut into the corners of two fields. Often we can trace these improvements on the commissioners' roads by the sudden disappearance of hedges for a short section while the road changes direction.

In some places it was not possible to use the mediaeval rights of way 'following the furlongs'. When the common pastures were enclosed, generally rather later than the ploughlands, such rights of way were not available. The commissioners, therefore, drew straight lines on the map of the district to represent new roads, and surveyors followed the lines as best they could. The result was straight roads deviating from their set course only to avoid some natural obstacle. In the heavier clay lands the commissioners made an effort to overcome the difficulty of maintaining communications when the ground was waterlogged. Roads in the country were entirely unsurfaced. This meant that when the autumn rains softened the top layer of clay, farm wagons might sink into the mud up to their axles. It was essential that following wagons should be able to avoid these deep ruts. So the commissioners made their roads generally forty feet wide to give traffic, as it were, room to manœuvre. When, a century or more later, the country byways were built up and surfaced, only a fraction of that forty-foot width was needed. Consequently today we have hundreds of miles of attractive byways in which a narrow roadway runs between the wide green fringes, the greens backed by hedges dividing them from the neighbouring fields. A number of these green verges have been enclosed; that is to say, when the roads were surfaced farmers obtained permission to advance the hedges to the new roadside, but it is surprising how often the grassy thoroughfares were left intact.

All who know and love the quiet farming country of central Essex and the Wold of Leicestershire or the tree-fringed byways of Warwickshire, will recognize these obvious links with the last phase of England's enclosure. It was, after all, only a matter of applying to the new roads quite logically the principles which had made limited travel possible on the main roads during the Middle Ages and before the Roman occupation. A road in prehistoric Britain was a track without precise limits, perhaps a quarter of a mile wide where it crossed soft or boggy ground. The mediaeval road in unenclosed country similarly tended to spread abroad. As we have noted before, the Portsmouth road was so vague a thoroughfare in the seventeenth century that Samuel Pepys's coachman could lose the way entirely. The green roads of the enclosure commissioners represented no more than a setting of an arbitrary limit to a road width which, before then, had been undefined.

The landscapes which the Georgian enclosures created were thus something quite new to the English scene, quite different in detail from the earlier enclosure landscapes of Kent or Sussex and still more different from the immemorial fields of the far west. So unobservant are we who live in this twentieth century, which tends to reduce everything to a common level, that the traveller may well fail to distinguish between them because the overall pattern is vaguely alike. Let us take some concrete examples. One might imagine at first glance that the component parts of the view from the high ridge of central Kent by Boughton Malherbe, and of that from the southern edge of Dartmoor looking over the South Hams, were little different from those of the view from the high ground of the Leicestershire Wold near Uppingham. They all reveal a quilted pattern of hedge-girt fields broken up to a

greater or lesser degree by hedgerow timber and scattered coppices, with here and there a farmhouse or village settlement
grouped about a church. In the north country it is the same
except that if one looks over Wensleydale from the summit of the
ridge dividing it from Wharfedale, stone walls take the place of
hedges in the valley scene, as they do in the Cotswold country
and much of the long ridge of oolitic limestone.

It is only when we come to analyse the scene more closely that
the differences are apparent. We then see that the fields of the west
are generally much smaller than those of the Midlands, that the
hedgerow trees of Kent are far older than the hawthorns of the
midland hedges and, above all, that the bank and ditch pattern
essential for draining the fields wherever the soil is heavy, is utterly
different in south Devon from what it is in either the Midlands or
Kent. In the latter areas the banks are low and the ditches, kept
clear by regular excavation, are far more prominent. The legal
boundary of the field in point of fact is more often the ditch than
the hedge bank. South Devon, however, is a country of high
banks often bounding sunken lanes. More often than not the
sunken lane started as a dividing line between two fields and the
banks were built from the earth and stones excavated from what
has become the course of the lane. These Devon hedge banks
have been likened to barricades. For miles on end they effectively
prevent the traveller by road from having a view of the surrounding fields. They may well have been planned originally as barricades, for in mediaeval England most of Devon and Cornwall was
subject to the Norman forest laws. The hardy cultivators of those
times had the problem of preventing the king's beasts from wandering on to their land and devouring their crops, while if they
had the temerity to trap or injure one of the creatures of the forest,
they were liable to the most severe penalties. Tall banks with perpendicular sides and palisades above, later replaced by hedges,
were their only protection.

The completion of the enclosure movement contributed a great
deal to the full use of England's land resources, but it was not
enough to meet the needs of the times. Individual farmers and

he Midland Ouse at Newton Blossomville. *The river here flows through a wide well-
ained valley, very different from the time when the poet Cowper bewailed the permanently
aterlogged fields in the winter. Even now, however, because the river's banks are still largely
natural, the valley is liable to extensive flooding after heavy rain.*

Anemones in partially cleared woodland. *This brilliant carpet of anemones was pho*
graphed in a Kentish wood near Hythe. Already fresh shoots are growing to give the wild flow
the protection from wind and weather which they need.

landowners and a few of the new capitalist class who thought that adventure on the land was as good a means as any of investing the wealth which they had won from urban industries, attacked the marginal lands with admirable vigour. The conquest of Exmoor Forest, though only partially successful, was an example of this tendency in the early part of the nineteenth century. It was one thing to enclose the barren wastes of Exmoor, quite another to turn them into arable fields, which was the initial object of this grandiose scheme. In the event man won a Pyrrhic victory over nature. The poverty of the soil, the ubiquity of the bogs and, above all, the wet, cold, and windy climate proved insuperable obstacles, however much money and labour were lavished on reclamation. Before the full scheme was completed, it became evident that the most that could be hoped for was to turn the forest into grazing land. That is what finally happened. Today the greater part of the original Exmoor Forest is good grazing country where formerly it had only afforded the roughest of pasture.

Although private individuals were responsible for the greater part of the development work of the nineteenth century, changes in the landscape were also achieved through the efforts of public bodies, especially the Commissioners of Crown Lands. The latter authority attacked the mediaeval Forest of Wychwood with the same enthusiasm that Exmoor Forest had provoked. The scrub and undrained land of the old forest disappeared rapidly. When the land was cleared it was enclosed. All that survives of the forest now is the name and the names of surrounding villages such as Shipton-under-Wychwood.

Another kind of reclamation less spectacular but perhaps no less effective was going on in East Anglia, where the Earl of Leicester, more generally known as Coke of Norfolk, showed the way on his Holkham estate to the conversion of sandy warrens into fertile fields. Coke was not really the pioneer of this work, which had been carried on for half a century before his time by small Norfolk farmers, but he attracted the spotlight of publicity by the ambitious nature of his projects and so encouraged many others to follow his example. All in all, it is estimated that two million

L

acres were added to the total of England's agricultural land during the nineteenth century, a fair compensation for the alarmingly rapid loss of land to the growing towns and industrial develop ment.

No one could doubt that the face of England was changing now at an astonishing rate. And now, too, something was happening that had never happened before. The stigma of the industrial areas was no longer confined to their immediate environment. It proli ferated in long straight lines across the countryside, first in the form of canals, then in the guise of railways, until a new criss cross pat tern was superimposed on the traditional pattern of the landscape. How true it is that time heals all wounds, or almost all. It has been pointed out that the new landscapes of the Georgian enclo sure commissioners were once ugly, bare, and featureless, land scapes of tall palings and embryonic hedges, of felled coppices and dull new roads, of decayed old houses and the paraphernalia of new ones under construction. Yet those are wounds which time has healed completely, so that these artificial landscapes have be come as pleasant as any in the whole of cultivated England. So, too, with the canals and the railways. Many of us have an affec tion for the quiet tow paths of the inland waterways. We feel that the channel of water across the landscape is a by no means un worthy addition to it, while the railways we take in our stride as part of the landscape to which we are accustomed, scarcely troubled and sometimes impressed by the skill of those inde fatigable Victorian builders of viaducts and embankments. Cer tainly if we travel by train we welcome with enthusiasm the English spring with its beautiful harvest of primroses and other wild flowers which flourish undisturbed on railway embank ments. But what devastation it must have seemed when these works were in course of construction.

Old prints give some idea of the scene of desolation as a railway embankment was being constructed—a cross between the very worst of the slag heaps in the coal mining areas and the refuse dumps which used to disfigure the outskirts of large towns—naked earth piled high without benefit of grass or other natural covering with all the attendant ugliness of 'major works in progress'. Even the bare ugliness of a slag heap is obscured by time as vegetation takes root surprisingly in that arid environment. Now that any, thing between a hundred and two hundred years separates us from the construction of the canals and railways, little remains to remind us of their initial impact except the Victorian wayside station with its unsightly buildings and the heterogeneous assortment of canal wharves and railway sidings which have become the focal points of the surrounding bricks and mortar.

Let no one imagine, however, because we accept the railways uncomplainingly that that is the end of the matter. It was really only the beginning of a process which dispelled once and for all the unbroken peace and quiet of the English countryside. The railways made one place easily accessible to another. They made it possible for a man to work in London and live in Epsom or Brighton; to work in Manchester and live in the Cheshire Plain; to work in Birmingham and live in Warwick or Leamington. In short, the railways were directly responsible for the rapid and disastrous growth of dormitory towns which encroached as rapidly on the ploughed fields and pastures of rural England as the indus, trial towns themselves.

The chronology of these far-reaching changes is quite unim, portant, but it is worth remembering that, however rapid the change seems in retrospect the time between the building of the first canals and the completion of the railway network was a full century. The canals were, indeed, the consummation of a dream of the seventeenth century, when proposals had been considered to link the Severn with the Thames and also to cut a waterway be, tween the flourishing countryside of East Anglia and the river Trent. Nothing came of these projects, nor is that surprising in view of the time lag between the inception of every progressive idea and its consummation, between, for instance, the first sugges, tion for a Channel tunnel in the last century and its construction, which still seems as far away as ever.

The first of the English canals, if we neglect the Foss Dyke, which Camden says was navigable in the twelfth century, was that linking Manchester with the Earl of Bridgewater's collieries at Worsley. The work was completed between 1759 and 1761. James Brindley, the architect of most of the early canals, was the designer. The aqueducts and tunnels which were built to enable the canals to maintain a reasonably level course won the admiration of eighteenth-century writers. As Thomas Pennant wrote so aptly 'our aqueducts pass over our once-admired rivers, now despised for the purpose of navigation'. Certainly Brindley's aqueduct which carried the Bridgewater Canal over the river Irwell was a very handsome structure, while the work of Telford, who was also the architect of the Holyhead Road and the Menai Bridge, was always arresting, conceived on bold lines and occasionally inspired. Where Telford's Ellesmere Canal crossed the Dee the views for miles around were radically changed.

Nowadays canals have gone out of fashion, and find it difficult to compete in freight-carrying with the railways and the roads. But in their heyday canals and canalized rivers extended to four thousand miles; most of that mileage was completed before the first of the railways was built.

Steam engines had been in use for some time to haul colliery 'trams' and the like but the first actual railway was not completed until 1825, when the Stockton and Darlington line was opened, while the first passenger line was that between Canterbury and Whitstable, opened in 1830 and, ironically, closed owing to competition from the roads in 1952. That bumpy uncomfortable train with its open cattle-truck carriages proved the forerunner of expresses and local trains operating over more than twenty thousand miles of line in Great Britain. Those figures give some slight idea of the immensity of the task which nineteenth-century engineers set themselves and which they achieved in face of all natural difficulties.

The growth of the industrial towns with all the grime which their development brought upon the diminishing countryside is, if looked at from one angle, a human achievement of even greater immensity. In 1800, though the Lancashire and Yorkshire textile industries were well established, they were carried on in the main by the people of still scattered communities. Though the population map shows the shift of the most thickly populated areas from the south to the midlands and the north and there was more than a hint of the blight that became the Black Country, towns like Birmingham and Wolverhampton were only in the first stages of their development. The coalfields, though worked much more vigorously than they had been a century before, were far from being the eyesores that they are today, with their far-seen slag heaps and winding-gear and their innumerable drab villages and small towns. Newcastle was a thriving place but not yet the industrial metropolis that it became during the nineteenth century.

The estimated figures for the production of coal give a clue to the stage of the country's industrial development at any given time. In the reign of Queen Elizabeth production was very small indeed. By 1700 it had reached approximately three million tons annually, by 1800 ten million, a very big increase indeed but a mere baga-telle compared with the two hundred million tons and more which it reached at the end of the century. No more than a twentieth of the full flood of soot and grime was being belched forth from fac-tory and domestic chimneys on to the fair face of the countryside in 1800. The sheep of the Midlands were still middling white, a white-painted cottage retained its colour for a generation in the relatively clear air, the sky was still blue in fine weather, undimmed by the smoke haze which now allows town dwellers only an occa-sional glimpse of the sky as it is seen, for instance, in the pure air of north-west Scotland. Nowadays even the east wind blowing in over the expanse of the North Sea is all too often hazy with the industrial smoke of the German towns along the Rhine.

All the worst phases, then, of our industrial towns were the product of the nineteenth century. They arose from the concen-tration of industry in the vicinity of the new transport. Birming-ham, Manchester and the cotton towns, Leeds and the woollen towns, the Black Country and the pottery towns, all grew up inevitably with their close-packed factories and hopelessly over-crowded residential areas in close proximity to the local means of transport. In most cases the canal terminal or the railway station became the nucleus of malignant growth. The most frightful slums of the nineteenth century are now happily a page torn from the book of the past and thrown away without the slightest regret. Demolition and modernization were well in hand by the turn of the century. Marshal Goering's rather inaccurate bomb-aimers cleared the way for rebuilding in some still backward areas. New blocks of flats are appearing where some of the worst of the earlier tenement homes were situated. Even so, a visitor to any of the big industrial towns of the north can find enough obsolete buildings for him to visualize the squalor and meanness of the 'little streets' that went to make up the working-men's quarter of a typical 'new' town in the nineteenth century. Economic circumstances made it necessary to build the people's homes as near as possible to the factories. As the towns grew the working-class district spread towards the east, because the builders of the time recognized that the prevailing winds in Britain are westerly and that the smoke pall inseparable from industry would most often obliterate the sky to leeward of the factories. The industrialists, the merchants, and later the respectable Victorian middle class had homes in suburbs to the north and west, and as transport improved moved further and further out, most often to a site near the next station down the line.

That is the pattern of development in its simplest terms, a pattern with but few variations. It has been obscured in many places as one suburb has been joined to another until the original reasonably compact townships have become an amorphous ill-defined conglomeration of building, apparently unplanned and still more apparently unbeautiful, their tentacles in the twentieth century spreading out in ever-increasing circles and grasping within their folds fresh country vistas, only to destroy them within an incredibly short space of time.

Even the heritage of the old towns did not escape, for especially in the early part of the nineteenth century people set no store by the precious legacy of mediaeval architecture. In Canterbury, for instance, several of the town gates were torn down for no adequate reason. The castle was adopted by a public utility company and later became the coal dump of the local gas works, while the sacred soil of St Augustine's was occupied by a brewery which used part of the land for a beer garden at which dancing and other entertainments were held. Canterbury may have been an extreme case but up and down the country a similar, if less grievous tale could be told—in Salisbury and Exeter, in Gloucester, and indeed in every town which was maintaining its place in the stern race for expansion and new wealth.

The thoughtless and unrestrained efforts of the speculative builder in the industrial towns is all the more difficult to understand against the background of the truly beautiful towns which had been built during the eighteenth century and the superb architectural styles which persisted throughout the Regency period at the very time that some of the most unsightly slums of north country towns were being erected. The Woods, father and son, had made of Bath an outstanding example of town planning and architectural elegance. Its population had risen to thirty-two thousand by 1800 from a few hundred a century before—and that without any diminution of the standards appropriate to an ancient and famous place. The same tendency was apparent in Cheltenham and Brighton, and indeed in London, where the Regent's Park area was laid out by John Nash, who was also responsible for the building of the attractive façades of the Regent Street which persisted well into the present century. Our own generation has been accused of vandalism in modernizing the frontages and widening the thoroughfare, yet this selfsame 'most beautiful street in England' was being built in the same decades as the slums of Manchester and Glasgow.

During the early part of the nineteenth century, too, industrialists and business men were adding innumerable 'gentlemen's seats' to the environs of the big towns. However unbeautiful one may regard some of the contemporary essays in classical building, however strongly one may feel that elegance was sacrificed to over-elaboration, one is still left with the impression that the ability to create attractive buildings had not died, even though its expression was stifled by other considerations. In the same way though many feel that the parks laid out in the nineteenth century were less successful than those of a century or more before they, too, had their attractions. Many a small stretch of hungry sandstone country was beautified by the planting of hardy trees and shrubs, especially in the range of hills which extend from Oxted to Seven/oaks in Kent. Rhododendron plantations, many of them still a riot of colour in spring, were added to landscapes which before had had only a thin covering of bracken or stunted heather. Still more varieties of foreign trees were introduced, many from the west coast of Canada and the United States, which has a climate approximate to that of the British Isles. The Douglas fir arrived in 1827, the Sitka spruce in 1831. Several kinds of cypress and cedar joined the growing number of trees domesticated in Britain. A number of giant sequoias—the species of which some examples in the United States are said to be four thousand years old—were planted in England from 1853 onwards and now, a little more than a century later, are growing sturdily and promise to become permanent features of our landscape.

The laying out of fresh park lands except for public parks in towns ceased well before the end of the century. Thereafter it was an age of substantial, solidly built, rather featureless houses set in a relatively small garden, to which were added new species of flowers almost every year from every country of the world. The traditional English garden of Tudor and Elizabethan times would not have been recognized as the forerunner of such exotic assemblies.

Not to be outstripped in the race of new building, many farmers of a wonderfully prosperous rural England, especially between 1820 and 1860, elaborated their farmhouses and some of those who had not moved 'into the fields' during the main enclosure period now did so. Farmers who had been living in small Eliza/bethan or Jacobean houses demolished these and built themselves larger and more pretentious homes in the Victorian style. Vicar/ages were remodelled, schools and village halls were built afresh, each larger than its predecessor, though from an aesthetic point of view less satisfying. Village England developed a Victorian look, which it has kept for a hundred years and will probably maintain for the next hundred years, too, however inconvenient, however unsuited to modern conditions its component parts.

In the midst of this exuberant prosperity, with the population growing so rapidly that there was a market for everything that the farmers could produce for sale, a small cloud appeared on the horizon in the form of Free Trade. Its shadow was cast by the Repeal of the Corn Laws, but it was not until about 1870 that the farmers began to feel its effects. Then what was previously a mere trickle of imports turned into a flood of cheap food with which they were unable to compete. The ensuing transformation in the English landscape was amazingly rapid. Within thirty years, from 1870 to 1900, all the gains that the farming community had made in the previous century were lost. England ceased to be a land of smiling cornfields, for the farmers quickly found that at the lower prices prevailing a bad harvest could ruin them financially. Many did indeed fail and sell their holdings to the ever-increasing number of wealthy townsfolk who sought a stake in the land. Hedge and ditch were neglected. Marginal lands were allowed to revert to nature. Grass fields appeared all over the country where for generations the land had been ploughed. It was a change as complete as it was sudden. Every part of the country showed it except the changeless hill pastures of the west and the moorlands of the north. But the areas which showed it most were naturally the heavy clay lands of the southern valleys and the Midlands. There in the valleys of the Ouse, the Trent, and the Thames, in the Weald of Kent and Sussex, in the heavy lands of Essex, and in parts of Northamptonshire and Leicestershire, the story was the same. In the Middle Ages much of this land had been brought under the plough within the sphere of the common fields. Then in the fourteenth century after the Black Death, when sheep became the farmers' most valuable stock-in-trade, fully half of the ploughland was turned over to pasture. By the reign of Queen Elizabeth the mediaeval position had been restored. In the following centuries more and more land was ploughed. Even fields near the river's bank, land liable to be baked hard as earthenware in a dry summer, or to be hopelessly waterlogged in a wet one, had produced their meagre share of corn crops during the Victorian boom. By 1900 all this land had reverted once more to the immemorial green of the pasture fields. And so it remained until the urgent necessity of the twentiethcentury wars spurred farmers once more to drive the plough over the intractable terrain.

CHAPTER X

Our Own Times

◆ ◆

THE PHILOSOPHER of ancient Greece who defined a virtue as the mean between two extremes was certainly wise beyond his time. But the virtue of regarding the present with an unbiased mind is one of the hardest of all to achieve. Every one of us is apt to reflect the optimism or pessimism as the case may be which is dominant in his outlook.

The changes apparent in the face of the landscape over a period of a mere fifty or sixty years do not just happen. They have a meaning. They are the expression of the will of mankind. They are in our own times the reflections of rapid advances in industry and agriculture, of the changing tastes of our fathers and grand/fathers and, indeed, of ourselves. They are, in brief, expressions of the spirit of an age. That is why prejudice creeps into our evaluation of them however much we may try to avoid it.

The pessimists will declare that the changing landscape forms part of a woeful pattern compounded of decadence and misplan/ning. Or it may appear a symbol of the tyranny of capital over labour, of the pleasure of the wealthy few preferred to the good of the many. The development of land usage, the utilization of Britain's natural resources in the twentieth century, can be har/nessed to almost any theme that the chronicler elects to choose. By contrast, the optimists visualize a present that is escaping from the trammels of the past and look forward to a future that is ever brighter, more smiling and more near to perfection. So the chang/ing face of the land becomes the expression of a common will cleansed and purified by the sufferings of the industrial revolution and of two world wars, marching in enlightenment towards still more agreeable vistas. They rejoice, these optimists, at the harvests which are won from land not productive by nature. They point to the work of the National Trust, they acclaim the National Parks. They regard our new forests impartially with pride, whether they are situated on Lakeland fells or on land mutilated only a few years before by open-cast mining. Even when they see the bountiful Essex corn lands and pasture fields swallowed up by the factories and arcades and terrace homes of a new town sprawling over the countryside with all the assurance of a blueprint brought to life, they still contrive a feeling of pride at the achievements of a people so recently racked by the horrors of warfare.

How shall we strike a balance between these two extremes? How shall we look at the bewildering changes that have taken place before our very eyes (some of them forgotten as soon as they were completed) without some strong emotion? It is not humanly possible. Every one of us must for ever be seeking to prove his point in an age in which the very study of history is suspect, for no other reason than because it is apparently impossible to tell the story of the past except in terms of the prejudices of today.

We may have forgotten the world in which it was possible to walk for mile after mile across the springy turf of the Sussex Downs without sight of a ploughed field, or still more remote, the world in which one could walk along the byways of Surrey and Buckinghamshire without imminent peril to limb or life, the world in which the road from London to Maidenhead still had some vestige of beauty, in which Ewell was a quiet country village. It does not necessarily follow, however, that what we have forgotten had no intrinsic value, however well adapted we are to our present environment. The best we can do in a world ruled by economics is to rely on facts and figures and attempt with their help to make a fair selection of good and bad alike.

By 1900 England had ceased to be primarily an agricultural country. Wherever the traveller went in the midlands, in the north-east and in the region of large towns all over the country, there was evidence of that global workshop which Victorian England was proud to style itself. The tentacles of suburbia had grown to hardy maturity as a by-blow of the industrial revolution.

That was a fact beyond dispute. The Victorian outskirts of Leicester, of Sheffield, of London, were downright ugly, an aesthetic offence against the often fertile and always smiling fields that they had displaced. Very few modern critics have a good word to say even for a Sandringham House.

Even worse was to come in the next fifty years—worse, whether judged in terms of aesthetic taste or of rural economics. The increase in unlovely new housing estates was matched by the consequent loss of land to the farming community. Yet, surprisingly, by 1900 a still small voice was being raised against the powerful forces of vandalism. As Dudley Stamp has pointed out, with his usual aptitude for striking the nail on the head, the year 1895 marked the turning point because that was the year in which the National Trust 'for places of historic interest or natural beauty' was founded. That was one of the first steps taken towards acceptance of the thought that something needed to be saved from the landscapes of yesteryear, some hostage given to city dwellers who yearned for the beauties of the countryside from which nine out of ten had sprung a few generations back. For a time, however, the movement for preservation scarcely impinged on the consciousness of the majority, certainly not on the conscience of speculative builders, or local authorities, still less on that of the central government. On the contrary, many who might have known better regarded preservation as a retrograde step, entailing restraint when all must be free to be developed along the sacred lines of private enterprise. It was fully fifty years before the idea of planning on a national scale had genuinely taken root in the stony ground of apathy and commercialism.

Fifty years may be an insignificant time in the history of our landscape, but it was long enough to complete the destruction of many square miles which were once not only beautiful but productive of wealth for the husbandmen and food for the people. How slow public opinion was to join forces with the inspiration of the few who protested against what was happening is illustrated by the fact that the keep of Canterbury's Norman castle was allowed to remain in use as a coal dump well into the present century. With the support of Queen Victoria public conscience had been aroused against the use of the sacred site of St Augustine's Abbey as a brewery storehouse or beer garden. But the public conscience had not yet extended to such profane things as castles, not at least to the extent of overcoming the vested interests of a public utility. It was still an age of industrialism run riot, until in the end travellers by train to the 'city of dreaming spires' were told on an enormous hoarding that 'This is Oxford where Morris cars are made'. That slogan was a true banner of the times. The city of Oxford—the city of Carfax, of the Corn and the High, of Tom Tower and of Magdalen Bridge—was wedged tightly between two excrescences. To the west were the Victorian monstrosities of the station and its environs; to the east the factories and suburbs that made up the industrial complex of Morris-Cowley. They transformed Oxford, if not overnight at least in the space of a couple of decades, from a university city to a midland commercial and industrial town.

Oxford was one of many victims of the motoring age. But what the motoring age did to Oxford was nothing compared with its total effect on the English landscape. The railway engineers of Victorian times had proved competent surgeons. The wounds they had inflicted left only slight scars. The railway viaducts, like the buildings of every age, had been mellowed by time until they seemed somehow to fit into their landscapes, even in some places to give added point to the beauty of nature. The motoring age was a very different thing. It inflicted a grievous wound which has not healed, which cannot ever heal, however hard we try to discount its baleful influence. Where the railways had taken town workers to dormitory suburbs in convenient proximity to the local stations, the motoring age took them to their homes wherever they chose to build them. Where the Victorian dormitories were compact, the twentieth-century ones were diffused; while the former were localized, the latter were disturbingly apparent wherever there was a main road within forty miles of a large town. Mordens and Dagenhams were built between the two world wars but they were unobtrusive compared with the ribbon development that transformed thirty miles of the road to the Lakes from Whaley Bridge to far north of Salford. They were a small change to the face of the land compared with the drastic surgery which first cut the Kingston by-pass road out of the gently rolling fields between Robin Hood Vale and Esher and then lined the road with factories and serried rows of houses so that it was quickly inadequate for the very purpose for which it had been created. They were relatively insignificant compared with the unnecessary ugliness of the Slough Trading Estate, or the interminable ribbon development which has extended along every main road out of London, out of Birmingham, and out of the other industrial towns. One of the worst features of this age of proliferation was that so much of the new building was with alien materials; red brick began to appear in the cobblestone belt of north Norfolk and in the mellow grey stone villages of the Cotswold country. Tiled roofs everywhere replaced the stone roofs and thatch of a bygone age.

Yet all these unpleasing additions to the scene are light shadows compared with the devastating gloom that fell upon Kipling's 'Sussex by the Sea'—the apparently haphazard layout of Peacehaven's bungaloid growth or the strangely pretentious planning of the 'new cities' that line the Sussex sands between Bognor and Littlehampton. Even in the very heart of the country it was the same. In Kent and Sussex and to a lesser extent in Warwickshire the woodlands were faced with a heterogeneous collection of desirable residences each in its own little plot of land.

No district was entirely exempt. The motor-car not only took people to their homes in the country for the night, but took them in increasing numbers to the remote and still undeveloped parts of England for their holidays. Inevitably new hotels, large stuccoed buildings, and innumerable boarding houses, were built to cater for them. Doubtless all this had its economic advantages. When the pilchard shoals, for instance, refused to frequent Cornish coastal waters, holiday-makers proved a satisfactory alternative source of income. Catering for them became a staple industry of south-coast towns and of Lake District villages alike. Speculative builders reaped a rich harvest in such places as Devonshire's Newton Ferrers and Northumberland's Whitley Bay.

Another factor of growing importance in determining the position of land ripe for development (just another way of saying suitable for erasure) was the ubiquitous motor-bus which gave the town worker who could not afford a motor-car rapid access from the nearest railway station to his chosen lodgement in the country. Though rich agricultural land was the chief sufferer, the beautiful sandstone country of the south was equally mutilated. Hindhead sprang up mushroom-like on the Portsmouth road in the midst of Surrey's loveliest commons and heather-clad heaths. Haslemere pointed a long finger towards the heights of Blackdown. High Wycombe spread in every direction up the Chiltern valleys which converge on the Wye, and villas began to line the little roads in many counties. To be fair, a number of the new settlements were not ugly in themselves as their Victorian counterparts crammed into the narrow valleys of Yorkshire and Lancashire had been. Certainly many bastard styles of architecture emerged, especially the unfortunate 'by-pass Tudor', and the baronial hall homes which misguided builders made to their own designs on the outskirts of many a town. But in general the style of building was negative enough except in a slough of despond such as Peacehaven or Pitsea or Canvey Island.

No, it was not the buildings themselves so much as their relation to the environment that offended—the replacement of pleasant countryside by an endless suburbia. Some of the new townships were in advance of their times, pleasing in appearance and suitable for their purpose, the very antithesis of the building estates of the Victorian north country which all too soon became slums. Frinton was a good example of careful design, so was the enlarged Broadstairs. More self-conscious efforts were made just after the turn of the century at Letchworth and between the wars at Welwyn Garden City. These two towns differed from Frinton and others like it in that they were designed as self-contained communities with their own industries, shopping centres, and entertainments, while Frinton was designed solely and simply as a

The changing mountain scene. *Extensive plantations of coniferous trees near the Whinlatter Pass in Lakeland.*

ntrusive pylons. *Here on the Shap Fells the pylon merges remarkably well with the un-yielding contours of nature's pattern.*

An old town lives on. *Rye, with its many half-timbered houses, its steep cobbled street, above which hangs the sign of the Mermaid famous smugglers' haunt, retains to a remarkable degree the appearance and atmosphere of at least a century ago.*

dormitory town. Neither Letchworth nor Welwyn were particularly successful, yet they showed the way. They proved to be the models on which the new towns of the present decade were fashioned.

So there were good features as well as bad in this extraordinarily rapid change in the face of England, a more rapid one and more widely spread than even that of the industrial revolution. Throughout the last fifty years there has been a shift of industry from the coalfields southward, or rather a shift of accent. The Lancashire and Yorkshire, Northumberland and Durham industries based on the coalfields have continued to expand but only very slowly, while the expansion of the Birmingham and London areas has been much more rapid. Here again the internal combustion engine is the primary cause of the change. Transport by road proved so reliable that it became a matter of course to establish factories far away from the coal measures and even at considerable distances from main railway stations, which would have been quite impossible before the advent of motor lorries. The significance of this change of accent was shown by the discrepancy in figures for unemployment between the old-established industrial areas and the new during the years of depression. Several of the traditional centres of industry after a long period of neglect were christened 'special areas' but continued in a state of depression until a world-wide conflict of metal and explosive brought employment once more to everyone fit to work.

It follows that in these last fifty years the greatest change has been in south-east England. The pessimist might say that the nineteenth century destroyed one-half of the country, the twentieth century the other half. 'What nonsense', replies the optimist, 'all we need is more numerous and broader highways to take us out of the towns into the unspoilt country.' It does not matter, one supposes, that the new roads will be cut straight across country—surveyors' lines drawn from point to point and taking away a few thousand more acres from the slender resources of Britain's wealth, like strips of adhesive tape stuck down on the face of the land. Must new landscapes be built from those novel ingredients des-

M

cribed in the American language as flyover crossings and clover-
leaf junctions, not to mention a few thousand concrete bridges and
viaducts? And, of course, a few more score of petrol storage
dumps like that which disfigures the port of Colchester, where the
old sailing barges still ply up and down the tideway?

These I gather are the scenic penalties of progress. It is sheer
sentimentalism to have vain regrets. I am just an old fossil seeking consolation in the past, like a certain *laudator temporis acti* who
provoked the shafts of Roman satire two thousand years ago.
Old fossil or not, I do claim to be a factual recorder of the changing scene. What has been written in these pages is fact and not
fancy, sober truth and not a Wellsian glance into the crystal ball
of the future.

So far our sad tale has been chiefly that of the obliteration of
well-loved scenery by man-made homes and factories. What,
then, of the country itself, or what is left of it? There, too, the
changes in the last fifty years have been startling, determined for
the first thirty-nine years of the century by a progressive decline in
farming, followed by a remarkably swift recovery.

Few will accept without question the fact that between 1919
and 1939 more than a million acres of farming land were lost to
urban development, about one and a half times the acreage of an
average-sized English county—a million acres out of a total of
thirty-two millions, including the mountains and moorlands and
commons. The loss of land was matched by a still more rapid
loss of labour. The farmers of England therefore had little choice
but drastically to revise their method of working the land. They
achieved equilibrium by two methods. Large-scale farmers, especially those of the traditional grain-bearing counties of East
Anglia, turned over more and more to mechanization, on the
principle that one machine can do the work of several men. The
others met the changing circumstances by converting still more of
their ploughland to grass, thus continuing the process begun in
the last three decades of the previous century.

There was another way in which the farmers reacted to changing conditions and that, too, made for variations in the landscape.

In the heyday of nineteenth-century farming a great deal of land had been recovered from the fringes of the moorlands and commons, especially in the west country and the northern counties. As more and more of the ploughland reverted to grass, so more of the marginal lands reverted to moorland or rough grazing land. Bracken and heather are indomitable enemies. However thoroughly they are extirpated they will creep back once the defences against them are lowered. Many of the rich hill pastures of the west were made good farming land by efficient drainage. Once the ditches began to fill in through neglect, the land quickly reverted to swamp or bog (and, incidentally, some of the wild birds previously driven out by reclamation returned to their old nesting-places).

Thus all through the first thirty-nine years of the present century the frontiers of cultivation were being gradually but perceptibly thrown back. Nature in the wild was reasserting herself, as she is ever ready to do. To the million acres lost through urban development were added an unknown but probably no smaller number of acres lost through neglect. In the valleys grass carpeted fields which were still ridged with the furrows made fifty years before. Even today hundreds of fields in the immemorial grazing grounds of Creslow, in the country beneath the hill of Brill and around Bicester, show these telltale marks of a changing landscape, furrows which nearly a century of grazing has not erased. Probably time will never erase them any more than it has the furrows made by mediaeval ploughshares in Leicestershire and Northamptonshire.

The many competent observers of the English scene who painted such gloomy pictures of its once prosperous farming country were thus recording sober fact. They can be forgiven for despairing of its future. The food shortage of the first world war had produced a short-lived spurt in production, especially of cereals; but profound apathy had quickly redressed the balance. The great contribution which another revolution on the land made to victory in the second world war was carefully planned, but none the less unexpected even by most of the farmers themselves. Of the resultant transformation of the landscape in many parts of the country we shall have more to say later.

A characteristic phase of the twentieth century is the dis-afforestation of the two world wars and the compensating new forestry undertaken chiefly under the auspices of the Forestry Com-mission, which came into existence under the Forestry Act of 1919. The Forestry Commission has already acquired a great deal of land, so that the words 'national forest' are commonplace in many parts of England.

The indiscriminate felling of trees, mature and immature, during the first world war brought home to the government of the time the need to replace the haphazard economy of the trees with a definite plan. In five years under the insistent demand for timber the remaining plantations of England had been decimated. Timber had been a wasting asset ever since the trees of the Weald began to be felled to supply fuel for the furnaces of the Sussex iron-working industry, but far-reaching as had been the changes to the mediaeval forest scene, the effect of the first world war was no less spectacular. Even scattered coppices and the trees which graced the remnants of the English park lands were not exempt. An eco-nomic factor contributed to the change. The price of timber was high. With all the nation's timber resources (except for the Crown woods) privately owned, it was a case of cashing in on a valuable asset when the price was grotesquely inflated, as well as of responding to the patriotic duty to supply timber for the national welfare. How great was the change in some districts is shown by the now bare hillsides of Gloucestershire amid the surviving frag-ments of the Forest of Dean. In parts of Kent and more widely in the west country, especially under the bulwark of the Malvern Hills, the only reminders of woodland which formerly covered the hillsides are carpets of anemones and wild violets and prim-roses which produce a spring-time colour scheme of incredible brightness. Alas, without their natural protection of trees the delicate petals of the anemone soon shrivel under the direct rays of the sun, or are twisted and turned by wind. They are essen-tially woodland flowers; the beauty that was the pride of the woodlands does not survive for many years such drastic change of habitat. Either the land is turned over to some other purpose and the wild flowers prove inevitable casualties, or if the ground is neglected coarse undergrowth creeps over it ruthlessly, covering and ultimately killing the plants that flourish in the relatively open ground beneath the trees.

By every standard the indiscriminate felling of England's timber was a tragedy—a loss to the beauty of the countryside as surely as it was a wastage of its potential wealth. When we turn to the work of the Forestry Commission and the great new forests that are growing so rapidly, we can only join forces with the optimist and rejoice that so much has been done in so little a time. But a small voice asks 'Is everything as it should be, even here?' Are these national forests really replacing the woodlands of fifty years ago or of five hundred years ago?

Economically the answer is probably 'yes'. Forestry today is a science with its own curriculum of research. Science has proved conclusively that this or that tree grows best in this or that soil, that this tree will give a bigger return of timber in a shorter time than any other. The national forests reflect the development of scientific research. But if anyone tells me that the Forest of Breck-land which lies between Brandon and Thetford is ever likely to have the beauty of a New Forest or a Sherwood Forest, I shall call him a liar, and a conscious and deliberate one at that.

The scenic loss is the change-over from deciduous trees to coni-fers, from the varied colouring through the seasons of the oak and the elm and the ash and the beech to the comparative monotony of the conifers which bulk so large in recent forests. The Breck-land forests are an extreme example. One knows full well that the traditional forest trees of England would not grow in that thin sandy soil. One does not need the eye of an expert to see how well the conifers are doing. They are growing so thick and tall that their lower boughs are withering away, while as they shoot up-wards their interlacing foliage is so thick that not a glimmer of sunlight penetrates to the ground beneath them. So nothing, posi-tively nothing, grows on that ground, thickly carpeted with the fallen fruits of the conifers and with their dead spiny leaves. From the air the forest looks like a green carpet spread over the land; from road level it seems as though one is looking down infinite shadowy avenues into an even darker and less hospitable distance. Yet here is wealth in the making. How can one deny its virtue even though one regrets the sandy warrens of yesteryear and the breezy commons with their thin covering of bracken and heather?

In my own lifetime I have seen the 'forest' that lies between the main Guildford-Leatherhead road near Clandon Church and the summit of the Surrey downs at Newlands Corner planted and grow to the promise of maturity. I remember my regret at the passing of yet a few more acres of unspoilt downland. I remember thinking how out of place the carefully aligned saplings looked. Yet now, that little forest has become part and parcel of my picture of the North Downs country as surely as the ancient oaks and beeches that lie on either side of the old Drove Road a few miles to the east. One would, I think, be sorry to see that new piece of woodland stripped, as sorry as one was to see it planted twenty-five years ago. After all, the South Downs in West Sussex, especially round Goodwood, are singularly well wooded, many of the plantations of comparatively recent origin; though their beauty is quite different from that of Kipling's 'blunt bow-headed whale-backed downs' the fact that they have a real beauty of their own is undeniable.

Many people think of the conifers as somehow foreign to the English landscape. Of course, they are nothing of the sort. In prehistoric times they played an important part in the building of our landscapes long before the oak and the ash and the elm made their appearance. When the last of the glaciers retreated and new life was burgeoning in the lowlands of the south, hundreds of thousands of acres of the Weald and of the Downs must have been covered in dark forests of spruce and pine. It is not very helpful, therefore, to regard conifers as foreigners, even though the actual species of today may be recent additions to the scene. In the last few years national forests of deciduous trees have been planted side

by side with the conifers; England is not destined to be entirely
bare of its 'native' trees.

The proposed afforestation of the Lake District is a problem
radically different from most that have arisen out of the national
policy of renewing Britain's vanished woodlands. Lovers of the
bare fells, visitors as well as residents, rightly realize that afforestation on a big scale would change entirely the very spirit of the
landscapes they love. Just how great a change can be effected is
something that can be judged by any motorist who drives over
the Whinlatter Pass and a few miles before approaching Keswick
is confronted by the State Forest. There on the left of the road
the essence of the mountain scene has been lost. Densely wooded
slopes appear to lose height just as they lose grandeur. The once
majestic moors and fells become parts of a very ordinary landscape
which might just as well be in the heart of the Surrey hills as in
the incomparable Cumbrians. Here it is not so much the choice
of tree as the very fact of afforestation which effects the dramatic
change. And, in these surroundings, there can be few who do
not regret the change.

The years between the two wars produced some other local
changes in the landscape which by now we tend to overlook.
Those years were the era of the new-style smallholding derived in
spirit, if not always in actual planning, from Mr Lloyd George's
policy of a return to the land. The Fylde of Lancashire—that level
green expanse which lies between the industrial towns of Lancashire and the urban complex of Blackpool and its satellites—became the most important poultry-producing area in Britain. Hundreds of new homes were built—half-villa, half-farmhouse.
Optimistic ex-servicemen invested in them and the plot of land
attached and set to work rearing chickens on a scale never previously attempted. The majority of them were no more fortunate
than those who invested in wayside garages in the early days of
the motoring era. Demand did not keep pace with the increased
supply. There were deficiencies in marketing arrangements and
in the end a large proportion of those who had settled in the green
land of the Fylde—many of them, it must be said, with no expe-

rience whatever of the country or its ways—gave up their holdings minus their capital to seek again a living in the towns. They
left behind them, however, a tradition which has persisted. The
Lancashire poultry industry today is still an important one; the
landscapes of the Fylde modified and by no means improved by it.

The smallholdings of Suffolk, each with its greenhouse intended to produce tomatoes and provide a living for the returning
heroes and their families, have suffered similar vicissitudes of fortune. They remain, like the wayside garages, like the hen coops of
the Fylde, a permanent addition to the rural landscape.

As one writes, one feels more and more like an historian recording one blow after another inflicted on the fair face of a long-
suffering land. Nor is this an entirely fanciful interpretation of the
development of the English scene, for which the pattern was set
by the industrial revolution. The appearance of wire fences (in
place of the now obsolete hedge) surrounding newly cultivated
land, and the indiscriminate lopping of trees which, one would
say, are a danger to no one, are part and parcel of the same cycle of
change.

The diminishing number of hedgerow trees and the growing
threat to the existence of the hedges themselves are all the more de-
pressing because of their value as shelter for wild animals (already
nearing extinction in many parts of Britain) and as nesting places
for birds whose activities are beneficial rather than otherwise to
the farmer. Hedges, too, have proved their worth in preventing
the erosion of light or sandy soils, while trees, even singly or in small
groups, have helped to bind together with their roots and decaying
foliage much fertile but unstable land. The story of the 'Dust
Bowl of the Fens' might never have had to be recorded if the fenland fields had been marked out by continuous hawthorn hedges
like the fields created from the arbitrary boundaries of the Georgian
enclosure commissioners.

Perhaps the farming community and local authorities are not
likely to attend overmuch to the plea of nature lovers that the felling of trees, the substitution of wire fences for hedges, may also
change at least locally the character of the flora, when the birds

responsible for carrying the seeds of many wild plants are driven from their nesting places. But at least when farmers fell hedge-row trees in order to take the plough right up to the edge of a field (especially in these days of tractor-drawn ploughs) they might think seriously whether they are gaining or losing by thus expelling birds that may be helpful to them and destroying for ever a wind-break that may protect their crops to a far greater extent than they imagine.

The grid must be accounted another threat to the beauty of the landscape. When first the grid lines climbed over the Chiltern Hills behind Amersham, when a grid sub-station made its ap-pearance on the Hindhead Hills, many felt that this was a fatal thrust to the heart of the country. Once again compromise has won the day. There are no pylons or grid lines in some districts that were threatened because public opinion was determined; the authority responsible found alternative sitings and in some few cases carried the lines underground. Elsewhere we have become accustomed to the grid as we have to the railway lines. In the moorland country of the north one might even make a case for their gaunt lattice work adding to the austere beauty of the scene. As one climbs the long hill from Kendal towards Shap Fell, one of the wildest and grandest of English main roads, one takes the pylons in one's stride. One feels they contribute a not unpleasing feature to the landscape. More remarkably, the feature they add is strangely in conformity with the spirit of the landscape itself. That is something more noticeable perhaps in Scotland, for in-stance in the unrelieved moorlands that hem in the Pass of Killie-crankie.

One cannot accept the pylon in the same spirit as part of the rural scene in the southern lowlands—straight lines cut across the black earth of the Fens, or piercing the wooded beauty of the Vale of Blackmore. The next generation will never have seen these landscapes without their superimposed tracery of power line and pylon, any more than we have seen the crossing of the Esk above Whitby without its complex of viaducts and railway lines. To them that will be the Vale of Blackmore as it is, the fen landscape without qualification. To us they still seem in some way strange, not quite as we remember them when we were young.

The countryside, of course, retains many actual battle scars, the legacy of the two world wars and of the defence preparations which assured Britain's victory. Anyone who has walked over the cliffs from Folkestone to Dover must have noticed the concrete bases of the gun platforms which did service in both world wars. Even though the shelters and the pillboxes have been dismantled, the disfigurement of the turf remains. It is the same on the farther side of Dover towards St Margaret's Bay, where the Dover Patrol Memorial, unhappily placed but curiously impressive, looks down on the greensward of the cliffs.

The bombardment of Dover by long-range guns from the French coast has changed beyond all possible recognition the façade that the town once presented to the sea between the two white cliffs that shelter its harbour. That is scarcely a loss. What-ever the nature of the new façade that takes shape in the years to come, it is not likely to be less beautiful than the heterodox assort-ment of eighteenth-, nineteenth-, and twentieth-century houses which formerly stood along the front. A world of reconstruction is inevitably a changing world. It would be no more appropriate to rebuild Dover's jumble of front-line houses as they were than it would be to try to replace Coventry's cathedral stone for stone.

No part of the cliffs of the south-east coast has escaped the marks of war. The radar station on Beachy Head, the gun em-placements on Seaford Head—these are all part of the price which Britain had to pay for victory. Nor, looking back, can one see how it could have been otherwise.

It is perhaps significant that we have developed a sentimental affection for the symbols of another victorious war—the struggle against Napoleon and the French armies. The Martello towers which a panic-stricken government had built as part of the master plan of coastal defence are decaying fast. But these, people say, with utter lack of logic, are scars of war which ought to be retained, though why on any ground but sentiment it is impos-sible to say. A hundred and fifty years have hallowed these useless towers which must have shocked the country-lovers of the time as profoundly as the pylons of Beachy Head disturb our own generation. The Royal Military Canal, constructed during the same invasion scare, to facilitate the transport of materials along the coast, has become in our eyes an integral and attractive feature of the Kentish scene.

The changed and mutilated character of the Salisbury Plain area seems far less inevitable than the battle scars of Kent and Sussex. It is not so much that the building of permanent military camps in quiet hollows of the plain has destroyed the character of limited areas beyond repair. Presumably the military machine must have training grounds. The relatively unfertile country of Salisbury Plain seems as good a choice as any. No, it is not the camps, nor the comparatively small area from which the public is excluded that are a matter for profound regret. It is the wider field in which the training exercises are held, the thousands of acres in which every grassy track is ploughed deep by the furrows of tracked vehicles. Because sheep no longer pasture there, the green close-cropped springy turf of the chalk has been transformed into rank, soggy and almost colourless grass. So it always is in the downland country whenever sheep cease to graze over it. Hundreds of generations of Southdown sheep have given us the smooth turf-covered slopes of east Sussex and Hampshire. Without them the grassy covering would be no different from that of the sadly neglected areas of Salisbury Plain, some of which chameleon-like has assumed yet another character in the guise of ploughed fields and growing crops.

Wiltshire is not the only county concerned. A vast gunnery range stretches across the Northumbrian Moors from Otterburn to the headwaters of the Coquet. There in the midst of the grey fells of Northumberland few regret or even notice the loss of open countryside. The dull reverberations when the firing range is in use, echoing and re-echoing as they roll down the valley which carries the main road from Carter Bar to Otterburn, evoke thoughts of warfare through the ages. Nor could one imagine a more appropriate place than this, where for hundreds of years the

Percys were leading armies to avert the threat of Scottish invasion and the Battle of Chevy Chase was fought.

The valley of the Rede in which Otterburn is situated has other signs of the changing times. The Forestry Commission village of Byrness on one side of the valley matches the military camp on the other, while the conifer forests towards Catcleugh, itself a man-made reservoir, are intrusions in a landscape which is characteristically bare of trees. But the distances involved are so great, the landscape otherwise so featureless, that these few signs of man's handiwork serve only to accentuate the loneliness of the rest. No traveller along the finest of all roads into Scotland will ever feel, when he comes to the summit of Carter Bar and looks down on the rolling green hills of the southern uplands, that his journey over the moors has been marred by human intervention. The overall impression is still one of nature triumphant—of barren hills and wild beautiful landscapes.

Unfortunately warlike preparations go on with equal vigour in far less suitable places. The abandoned airfields of East Anglia and Lincolnshire are once more manned by the American Air Force. Many of the airfields of the south, although deserted and derelict, remain only too obvious scars on the landscape. One example will serve to typify them all—that of the extensive runways and unsightly hangar on the Stoney Cross plateau in the midst of the New Forest. Though nearly a decade has passed since this airfield was busy with the comings and goings of military machines, neither time nor the authorities show any sign of erasing the concrete or macadam runways. Here and there the surface is cracking and a little grass is taking tentative root. But can nature, at least in our lifetime, absorb completely such monstrous wounds?

It is a real pleasure to turn from the ugliness that war has produced to its only legacy of uncomplicated beauty. To William Cobbett the loveliest thing in the world was a well-tilled landscape filled with growing things: the white splash of a potato field in blossom, the waving fields of corn turning from green to gold in the late summer sunshine. There are many William Cobbetts still among us. Everyone who has the slightest sympathy with that great observer of fertile nature will rejoice at the change, the most striking change which the nation's need for increased cereal production during the second world war has brought to many well-known landscapes of the south and midlands. Thousands of acres of the Sussex downs have been ploughed where the plough has never been before, at least since the heyday of Roman Britain. Hundreds of thousands of acres of the heavy clay lands of the central lowlands which bore crops in the golden years of the middle nineteenth century and then were put down to permanent grass once more yielded their quota of wheat and oats and root crops. The transition of the fenlands from the finest area of pasture land in Britain to its richest area of arable farming is complete.

The limit of cultivation advanced a few hundred feet towards the plateau of Dartmoor, where crops of rye added their quota to the national loaf in the latter years of the war. Thousands of prisoners of war drained clogged ditches and trimmed hedges so that waste land became fertile again. By 1947 the pattern of farming had reverted to the model of 1870, with many additional improvements in detail.

Although the next ten years saw some regression, the pattern in general remains. Moreover, the soil has been enriched by modern methods of cultivation and manuring, and especially by the addition of lime. Cobbett just over a hundred years ago deplored the starveling oats of Northumberland and complained bitterly that man was trying in vain to reverse the law of nature, growing crops that never matured in soil intended by providence for grass. These selfsame fields today are sown with early maturing crops which though they may be harvested late nevertheless yield an adequate return for the farmer's labour. On the high ground of the north country a good harvest is as often gathered in at the end of September as a month earlier. The smiling fields of Coquetdale under the rocky outcrops of Rothbury Forest are the complete answer to those pessimists who forecast in 1940 that the wealth of England would be halved by the misplaced zeal of government planning for better use of the land.

Ten years after the end of the war if one climbed the Downs behind Kingston by Lewes to the broad green track that follows closely the edge of the escarpment then looked southward to the sea the results of wartime planning were as evident as ever. In place of the unbroken expanse of grassy downland that once sloped towards the distant Telscombe hollow, there was a seemingly limitless field of wheat, unenclosed and undivided, carpeting the folds of the downs in a mantle that changes colour with almost every week of the spring and summer. It seems as though such 'new' landscapes are to be a permanent feature of the countryside.

Though the damage done to growing crops by rabbits in England, at least, is often exaggerated, it is certainly true that corn crops have grown much nearer to the edges of the fields since myxamotosis virtually wiped out the rabbit population in the south country. Nowhere is the change more evident than in the downland 'prairies' where rabbits were most numerous. The difference may be just enough to swing the balance to economic working of the land even in a succession of lean years.

When the chalk country is newly ploughed the poppy is always the first tilth of the freshly ploughed land, try how the farmer will to eradicate it. I remember standing on the ridge south of West Dean in the July of 1943, before the crops had started to ripen, and marvelling at the apparently solid mass of bright red poppies whose tall heads reared above the corn on the opposite slopes like a closely-fitted carpet overlaid on the green floor of the cornfield. As the years have passed the number of poppies has diminished, the carpet has grown worn with many holes, but they still make a bright splash here and there in the southern downlands—a very cheerful if uneconomic addition to the colours of the downland vistas.

Figures often make dull reading but in this case they speak for themselves. Between 1870, the peak of Victorian prosperity, and 1906, the trough of the pre-war depression in the land, the acreage under the plough had fallen by fully three million acres, the equivalent of one-fifth of the whole arable countryside in 1870, while wheat, most characteristic of all the English crops, had fallen by almost half—from just over three million acres to less than a million and three-quarters. The 1914–18 war just about reversed this trend. Something like three million acres of grass-land was turned over to the plough, while the production of wheat was increased by fifty per cent, an aim achieved with the help of legislation to ensure that farmers reaped a fair return in cash as well as in crops and with the assistance of a Women's Land Army, prisoners of war, and volunteer workers on the land from the towns at harvest time.

Between the wars the pendulum swung backwards again, though two factors combined to retard its movement. One was the guaranteed price of wheat in the 1930s, which resulted in a big increase in the production of wheat during the six years 1932–8. The other was the introduction on a large scale to the British countryside of an almost new crop, sugar beet. Sugar beet is not by any manner of means a beautiful crop. It has none of the charm of the cereals nor the spectacular seasonal beauty of potatoes in flower. But it certainly acted as a buffer to protect the midland and eastern counties from submersion in the economic depression that followed the first world war. The sugar extraction factories were a new rural eyesore in eastern England, though their number was limited and the inevitable mellowing of their buildings has left them no more conspicuous than the average large Victorian farmhouse. It seems amazing now that we are accustomed to the green drooping leaves of the sugar beet and the mountains of roots by Essex and Cambridgeshire and Lincolnshire waysides await-ing collection in the autumn that in 1925 sugar beet was an experi-mental crop, its acreage in Britain numbered in hundreds. Its now assured place in the rotation of the eastern counties made a change in the landscape comparable with that of the large-scale introduction of field potatoes a century before.

Other strange crops made their appearance, or rather their re-appearance, between the two wars, including the ever-welcome flax with its bright blue flowers, its attractive foliage, and its en-gaging ability to transform a whole landscape with a single small field. Flax, of course, has been cultivated for many hundreds of years but it needed a government subsidy for it to be reintroduced on an appreciable scale. The latest news is that the government scheme is coming to an end and the bright blue flowers may soon disappear from the East Anglian scene.

All these changes, all these welcome signs of the rebirth of English farming, were as nothing compared with the gigantic efforts of farmers during the second world war. Some treasured landscapes, of course, have fallen by the wayside, especially those of the typical English park lands, many of them young in years and dating only from the beginning of the nineteenth century, others going back to the heyday of park building in Elizabethan and Jacobean times. Most of the parks were originally wooded; then the woods were cut down but single trees left standing to give the characteristic tree-studded appearance that represents our ideal of an English park—apart, of course, from the self-conscious land-scape-gardening schemes of men like 'Capability' Brown. In the crisis of the second world war these parks had to bear their share of the national effort to grow more food. Where the soil was suit-able they were ploughed up, as surely as the immemorial grass-lands of the downs. Whittlewood Park, on the way to Towcester, was transformed in a single season and produced some of the finest corn crops of the midland counties. The king set the example on the Sandringham estate and in Windsor Park. The example was followed in most of the parks of the few remaining great land-owners. But it must be remembered that this was only a speeding up of a process that was already well started through the incidence of taxation and the changing structure of society. Many great estates with their parks had already been broken up. Only a few like Woburn Park remained well kept, well stocked with orna-mental trees, and maintained in the tradition of the previous century.

That, then, is the twentieth-century scene, a scene which reflects as vividly and violently the changing pattern of social life as any other facet of the world today. The pendulum has swung first to left then to right but the net result is something tangible and in

The vanishing Broads. *If nature is unchecked lakes and rivers tend to fill in. This view is of Filby Broad, near Yarmouth.*

Under Northumberland Fells. *The valley of the river Coquet shows the abundant crops which can be produced by modern methods, in contrast with the 'starveling oats' which William Cobbett noted on his journey through Northumberland.*

New man-made landscapes. *The builders and road engineers of the twentieth century a[...]
producing new landscapes as functional, if not as dramatically ugly, as those of the nineteen[...]
century. Above, a suburb of the historic and beautiful city of Bath sprawls disturbingly up t[...]
hillside; below, the broad ribbon of the new road between Leatherhead and Dorking chang[...]
utterly the natural scene between the slopes of Boxhill (in the foreground) and Ranmore Common.*

some ways admirable. It cannot blind us, however, to the horrors of ribbon development and wayside hoardings, or make us insensitive to the throbbing roar of internal combustion engines that has destroyed for ever the quiet of English country roads. Only the moorlands and mountains of the north and west stand out as they have done from the beginning of time, bulwarks against change, impervious to the pattern which man has superimposed on nature. Broad ribbons of main roads cross Rothbury Forest and Dartmoor and Bodmin Moor and the Pennines but they have wrought no havoc; out of earshot of the roads it is as if they did not exist. Time stands still on the heather moors and the rock-strewn bracken-covered hillsides. But in the midlands and the south-east, wherever in fact there is easy transport and a suitable terrain for building, the changes that began two hundred years ago have been speeded up in front of our very eyes until it is almost impossible to imagine the peaceful scenes of yesteryear. We have no option but to be thankful that it is still possible to escape, in the errant schoolboy's immortal words, from the 'maddening crowd'—that even in the lowlands there are still hundreds of square miles as beautiful as ever—that one can walk for many miles through Essex cornfields, or over the Leicestershire Wold or along the Icknield Way without meeting another wayfarer, still less seeing any imminent or drastic sign of our developing economy.

We have shown in this chapter that the last half-century of change has a bright as well as a gloomy side—the brightness of a more intelligent use of the land for farming as well as the gloom of unregulated building to house the population of towns which no longer have natural limits. We cannot leave the scene of today without referring briefly to one more insidious change—the development of quarrying and mining. From every point of view except the aesthetic these modern rural industries have value. The materials which are won from the land are essential to the life of the nation, the building stone, the lime, the cement, the open-cast coal, the bricks. Yet all these inflict new wounds on the face of the land, wounds that in many cases can never heal. The brick-

N

fields of Bedfordshire have devastated a tenth of the county. Everywhere there are quarries, some inconspicuous but others like the great quarry on the southern side of Shap Fell which is carved out of the beetling cliff where once there were grass-covered fells. The valley of the Thames between Gravesend and Strood, the valley of the Medway where it cuts through the Downs under Bluebell Hill, the valley of the Ouse between Lewes and Seaford, all these have been changed within living memory by the tall stacks, the functional buildings, and the belching smoke of cement works which lay down a thin covering of white dust over the countryside around.

The new National Parks are protected to some extent from indiscriminate new quarrying, but even in National Parks an industrial world must be served and the necessary licence will undoubtedly be given for some fresh quarries to be made. As for the open-cast coal sites, perhaps the least said, the soonest mended. It is always an unhappy experience to see the mechanical grabs scooping out great slabs of fertile soil and turning, for instance, the park lands of Wentworth Woodhouse within a year into something worse than the devastation of the Somme battlefield. The National Coal Board makes valiant efforts to restore the land but let no one suppose that an open-cast site can ever return to its former beauty. The best way perhaps to treat it when it is levelled is to plant it with a negative covering of conifer so that in a hundred years' time there will be at least a useful forest.

But what can one do? For better or worse ours is an industrial country whose continued existence depends on subordinating every other consideration to the needs of industry and commerce. If we look at the problem in those terms we must accept the changes we see, however much we dislike them, as an inevitable part of the birthright we have inherited. There is no turning back, indeed no possibility of it. Even our wayside wild flowers must perish. Many of our wild flowers are weeds which the efficient farmer must exterminate. What if our hedgerow beauty suffers from the weed-killing sprays that are scattered over the fields from the air? What if a typical facet of English beauty is destroyed by the deliberate burning of wayside vegetation (and some types of wild birds are deprived thereby of their natural food supply)? All we can do is to voice the thought that the country lover has a place even in an urban society, that beauty has a value of its own, that much of the spoliation of natural beauty in the last century and a half has been unnecessary and insensate. Even so, the interests of preservation will always be at war with the interests of national development. Though the rate of change has slowed down in the last ten years the scenic pattern is still changing, the strongholds of nature are being gradually overwhelmed—a new reservoir here, a new town there, a housing estate over the hill, and most of them in that part of England which has least room to absorb them, the fertile wealthy landscapes of the midlands and the south-east. The outline pattern is drawn all too conclusively, only the detail remains to be filled in by a process as remorseless as the advance of the incoming tide.

CHAPTER XI

A Glimpse of the Future

* *

THIS IS AN AGE of planning. Once the population had grown greater than home-grown food could sustain, planning the use of the land on a national scale became essential. The wonder is that its consummation was deferred for nearly a century. Now town and country planning is a new branch of science. But it is one thing to know how to plan, quite another to make a plan and carry it out so as to satisfy even a fraction of the people. All the planning in the world will not allow a quart to be put in a pint pot. Indiscriminate private speculation has been exchanged for bureaucratic control. It depends perhaps on the measure of one's faith in bureaucracy whether one really believes that the future planned landscapes of Britain will be as bright and beautiful as they sound when a highly-salaried official is expounding plans for the next fifty years.

Some things are behind us for ever. There will be no more wayside hoardings, no more pitched fights on Kinderscout between ramblers and gamekeepers, no more ribbon development (we hope), no more obvious offences against good taste—at least without a lot of people having said a great deal about them in advance. Yet no ministry can wave a magic wand, still less a local authority, in which vested interests of one kind or another bulk so largely.

Let us try to face the facts, which spring quite inevitably from the account of the landscape given in the previous chapter. England has an area of about thirty-two million acres, including the mountains and moorlands. Its population exceeds forty-one millions and is still rising slightly, though at nothing like the rate that it has risen in the last hundred years. Barring mass migration or atomic warfare it will be about the same in fifty years' time. In the words of the arithmetical catch-phrase of childhood 'forty-one millions into thirty-two millions won't go'. It works out at about three-quarters of an acre per head of the population and not much more than half an acre if one is speaking of the really fertile parts of the country. The minimum 'living space' required for national self-sufficiency with all modern aids to intensive agriculture is at least one acre per head. It follows that England is a grossly overcrowded country which must literally export or die.

A fact which aggravates the position is that the bulk of England's forty-one million people are enjoying an improving standard of living, of which the most salient characteristic is more spacious living accommodation. They demand semi-detached houses with gardens, and playgrounds or parks in the midst of urban development. One will not hear a single voice raised against such a modest ideal. But what does it mean in terms of the country? It means that the town and country planning authorities looking forward twenty years are calculating that in each of those twenty years an average of thirty to thirty-five thousand acres will be lost to agriculture through the re-housing programme, and the building of new towns. The official encouragement of this movement stems, of course, partly from the strategic policy of dispersal to minimize the effect of aerial bombardment. But the cause is less important than the fact, and the fact is that during the next twenty years approximately 700,000 acres of the English lowland landscape will disappear. That is the equivalent of an average-sized English county and the figure quoted is not much more than half the loss during the twenty years between the wars. We are firmly committed, therefore, to a change from rural to urban landscapes about half as great as that which took place during the years 1919-39.

What a gloomy prospect! But there is nothing, positively nothing, that can be done about it. Even the most extreme among those who work for countryside preservation would not wish for another Black Death to cut the population by half, or an atomic war which might sweep away the whole of civilization as we know it. The latter, of course, is a possibility which no one discounts. It is just one of the factors which makes forecasting the world of the future uncommonly difficult.

At least, one hears it said, there will be the National Parks. There will be, of course, and there is no doubt that these limited areas—Dartmoor, Exmoor, the Peak District, the North York Moors, the Yorkshire Dales, and the Lake District and the others—will have rather specialized development plans. Yet it is significant that most of the National Park areas are highland areas and quite unsuitable for the kind of development which has revolutionized the lowland landscapes during the last century and a half. Yet even National Parks are not sacrosanct. Almost before they had been designated at least one member of the National Parks Commission was complaining bitterly in public that the National Parks Act was not being carried out in the spirit of those who drafted it. There were public protests at the proposal to make new quarries in the Peak District Park, and at the proposal to inaugurate fresh hydro-electric schemes in Snowdonia. The latter turned out to be a triumph for the ramblers' and other organizations which intervened, for the scheme was shelved—but only for the time being. It is surely not unduly cynical to forecast that the face of the land in the National Parks will change during the next twenty years, though only slowly and after much talk.

For the rest, quite apart from the many square miles fated to disappear for ever under bricks and mortar, everyone who has walked or cycled or motored through the byways of southern England will have realized that already since the end of the second world war there is scarcely a village whose profile has not changed. The new row of trim labourers' cottages may be a great amenity; their new homes may or may not be appreciated by the countrymen according to the extra rental which they are required to pay, but they do represent the pattern of living in the country today. The old village is doomed. Many of its old cottages though still inhabited are condemned, were indeed condemned in the period between the two wars and then given a new lease of life because of the great shortage of rural housing.

Understandably the rural housing authorities seek good and healthy sites for their new homes. All too often this means that they are built on the brow of a hill, whereas the old village is on lower ground. So the charm of the old village is swamped in the spate of new building which dominates the whole landscape. The fate that overtook the village of Great Munden in Hertfordshire, to name one example out of hundreds, between 1919 and 1939 is a fate that awaits almost every village in the fertile lowlands during the next twenty years, except those like Chiddingstone and Lacock and Castle Cary, or like West Wycombe and High Roding, which are preserved more or less as museum pieces, with or without the help of the National Trust.

No one regrets that electricity is being made available to every villager in England who can afford it. Yet every amateur photographer knows how difficult it is becoming to take a photograph of a village without the ubiquitous power lines being the most obvious feature of the finished print, a complex pattern which cuts across the natural composition of the village and effectively destroys its photogenic quality. Too much depends on the varied enthusiasm of local authorities. One may refuse to allow a discreet new sign announcing 'Teas' to be set beside the already resplendent signs of a garage, while another will approve the building of four new cottages in a position where they become the dominant feature not only of their own hamlet but of every view for miles around. It is a brave new world but sometimes a very strange one.

Nothing illustrates this more clearly than the postwar rebuilding of Canterbury, always the touchstone of public opinion. A local election after the war was fought virtually on the platform of town planning. Debate after debate in the City Chamber has been on the conflict between those who desire to preserve the oldworld atmosphere of Canterbury (which their opponents describe as reducing it to a living museum) and those who desire it to develop on modern lines (which the others describe as desecrating the holiest shrine of Christendom). The upshot strangely is that the tower of the destroyed St George's Church is solemnly dedicated as a permanent feature of the new urban landscape, while as heterogeneous an assortment of new shops, offices, dwelling‑ places, cinemas, and the like are built within a stone's throw of it as one could possibly imagine. Presumably as long as the tower of St George's remains, honour is satisfied.

Road building provokes the same kind of conflict between those who declare that new roads destroy the peace of the country and those who say that the old roads are throttling commercial development and causing a sort of thrombosis in the circulation of the country's industry. How this conflict will be resolved is already becoming obvious. In a recent issue of a London evening newspaper under the banner headline 'Surrey hurries new roads', one reads 'Surrey aims to put itself in the front ranks of the Home Counties with nearly a hundred miles of fast new motoring roads. A hurry signal is already being flown by Surrey's road builders because of the rapid building development going on all over the county. They fear that new homes will be built astride the new motoring roads.' There is the whole story in a nutshell.

Once again we turn to the brighter side of the account, to the rich promise of agricultural development which complete mechanization of the farm and modern methods of soil improve‑ ment have brought near to fulfilment in the lowlands. Farming is admittedly a noisy business compared with a hundred years ago. The whirr of tractor‑drawn ploughs can be heard in the arable country of the east at any time between September and April when the weather is suitable. The drone of the combine harvester carries for miles through the clear atmosphere of a fine August day. So ubiquitous is the internal combustion engine that the traditional horse‑plough matches that used to be held all over the country are falling into abeyance for no other reason than lack of local com‑ petitors. But we grow accustomed to noise and there is every reason to rejoice that the tractor has ousted the horse and that lowland Britain is one of the most highly mechanized farming districts in the world. How else would farming on its modern scale have been possible?

Thinking once again in terms of the twenty years ahead—the most that can be comprehended with any degree of certainty—one can say with some assurance that the pattern of agriculture will change only in detail. It is unlikely that the new ploughed land will be allowed to revert to pasture on a large scale. It is equally unlikely that the marginal country which has been hedged and ditched for the first time in generations will be permitted to decay once again through neglect. Rather under the aegis of the county agricultural committees it is likely that some further marginal lands will be reclaimed and that cultivation will climb a little higher up the hillsides of the west and north.

It is possible, though scarcely likely, that some great experiment will be initiated to reclaim the uplands of a Dartmoor or a Bodmin Moor. What has been achieved in the case of Exmoor presumably could be achieved in these other districts, and perhaps also in the North York Moors. What is now heather-covered moor or bracken-covered common could be converted into fair pasture. The obstacle is the cost. The capital investment needed to reclaim the Forest of Exmoor, though it brought into existence a completely new parish and added appreciably to the food production of the south-west, could never be considered an economic one. It was a rich man's dream, like the draining of the strath floor under the slopes of the Reay Deer Forest on the Duke of Westminster's Scottish estate.

It is much more probable that the area available for cultivation will be increased, however slightly, by the reclamation of new land now being built up by the tides and the silty outflow of rivers at several points round the coast. A few thousand acres round the Wash will be added to the ploughlands of Lincolnshire by the building of fresh sea walls. The salt marshes of the North Norfolk coast will ultimately become permanently dry land—a new Romney Marsh or Fylde. But that may be many years ahead, especially as the area is of special interest to ornithologists and part of it has already been converted into a bird sanctuary.

There will, however, be one big difference clearly visible within the next twenty years—the cumulative impression of the new forestry. Here facts and figures once more come to our assistance. The national plan for forestry published shortly before the end of the second world war set a target of five million acres of new forestry and re-afforestation in Great Britain. That is a terrific acreage, even allowing for the fact that some of the new forests are planned for Scotland and Wales. It can be judged in its proper perspective by comparison with the total acreage under woodland, which was less than three and a half million acres in 1947 (less than two million acres in England). These latter figures include not only true woodland but coppices and woodlands in which the bulk of the trees have already been felled. The programme means, then, that by the time the target is achieved the area of woodland will have been nearly trebled. In its latest published plan (1956) the Forestry Commission envisages the planting of five million acres in the next fifty years.

That, indeed, is a radical change in the face of the land. Within our twenty years not only will the forests be far more numerous but their character will have been changed. In 1947 only about a third of a million acres in England were planted with conifers, but on the present basis of planting not less than ninety per cent of the new trees will be conifers, the bulk of them Sitka or Norway spruce and Scots pine. A large proportion of the new forests are being planted on marginal lands, or in areas where there is no possibility of cultivating the soil in any other way. So forestry is a symbol of the gradual ascent of cultivation and the recession of heaths and common lands—yet one more stage in the battle that man has waged since prehistoric times against the intractable strongholds of nature.

We have traced the shape of things to come in the next generation. The outline may well persist for generations beyond that. Is it possible to look into the more distant future? The common-sense answer is that a forecast is possible, but not a detailed one in a world of so many imponderables. Just as when we look back through the past the picture of our country grows less clearly defined, so the further we look into the future the more blurred our vision becomes.

We can say, however, without fear of contradiction that coastal erosion will continue and in the course of a few hundred years will have changed much of our coastline beyond the recognition of people living today. This is an age of magnificent coastal defence works, but again and again the strongest works prove unequal to their task. So many changes have happened in living memory, the great landslide by Lyme Regis, the crumbling of the Suffolk cliffs, the gradual eating away of the chalk headlands of the south, that it seems as certain as anything can be that much greater changes will take place within a century or so. The sea more than any other natural force makes mockery of man's handiwork. Travellers through the fenlands will have noticed how far below the surface of the artificial rivers is the black earth of the rich fields. A high tide in 1954 gave grim warning of the inundation possible in a single night, not only in eastern England but in the corresponding level lands of Holland. Can the whole of Britain be made into an embattled fortress to resist the implacable battering of tide and storm? It seems an improbable conception.

Other factors are likely to influence the outcome of this struggle, the most important of them possible changes in climate. Many believe that northern Europe is enjoying the comparative warmth of a period between two ice ages. Certainly there is some evidence that the English summer and autumn are gradually becoming warmer and the English winter no colder. If the tendency continues and the southern limit of the Arctic ice recedes; if, above all, the Greenland ice cap melts away, the time will come when the southern counties will bear a sub-tropical vegetation, when palms and fuchsias will be as common a sight as they are today in the South of France. Perhaps maize and cotton will be added to the rota of English crops. If, as some believe, the amount of polar ice is diminishing over all, then the level of the sea must rise and bring new pressure to bear on the country's coastal defences. Ultimately the coastal plains which have been reclaimed at such cost and labour might be submerged and with them the sites of many of our largest towns.

On the longest-term view one thing stands out as certain. The forces of nature are still at work with undiminished activity. So long as there is rain and frost—so long, that is, as the circulation of the atmosphere continues—erosion will go on in the hills and valleys of England as well as around the coast. Gradually the highest hills will be worn down. Gradually the river valleys will widen, the flow of the streams grow more sluggish, while new land is built up in the river estuaries. If the process were to continue indefinitely, the time would come when the whole of England was a level plain, or at least as level as the plain of East Anglia today.

That, of course, is looking millions of years into the future to a time when the human race may itself have changed its nature by continuing evolution. Yet it is no mere idle speculation but a forecast which will certainly come true unless before then fresh spasms of the earth's crust, still imperfectly understood, produce new mountains, new continents, as they have done so often in the past.

CHAPTER XII

Exploring Your Own District

• •

IT MAY BE slightly misleading to say that wherever you live you can find links with the story of England's changing face within a mile or two of your home. It is, of course, literally true, but the links may be few and rather uninteresting. If the statement is amended to read 'within an hour's journey of your home', no one will be disposed to question it.

Most of us, as statistics show, are town dwellers surrounded by all too generous an exhibition of the handiwork of man the builder. Most of us, however, have our favourite excursions into the country. The pleasure of such excursions will be doubled if we re-explore the countryside with an eye to the many significant features discussed in this book. Even if circumstances prevent our going often into the country we may still be fortunate enough to find within easy walking distance of our home many of the tell-tale signs which illustrate how the appearance of our homeland has altered in the course of the last thousand years.

Here is a concrete example. Before the last war I lived for a time in one of the many little streets on the north of London's Theobalds Road, a bare mile away from Charing Cross and Piccadilly Circus—and little more from the City. A less promising position for observing the changing face of England it would be hard to imagine.

For anyone specially interested in architecture and town planning through the ages it was, of course, a paradise. It offered an amazing contrast between the row of Queen Anne houses in which I lived, then far degenerated from their former elegance and now completely wiped out by enemy bombardment, and the new blocks of flats and offices which were being built in the next parallel street. There was, too, the contrast between the narrow Georgian roads which radiate from Queen's Square and Meck-lenburgh Square and the broad, straight, twentieth-century high-way which is called Kingsway and which was cut straight through the slums into which the area eastwards of Drury Lane had degenerated. One could trace the outward spread of London in the critical seventeenth and eighteenth centuries by the age of the new parish churches that were built to serve the growing suburbs.

When in later years I have returned to this corner of London to see what has happened to the site of the sadly dilapidated old house in which I lived, I have had the rather sardonic pleasure of seeing one of the most modern essays in urban re-housing taking shape. The block of flats that has been built is vastly more pretentious than any that were there before the war, while around it many a bomb-site has developed spontaneously into a garden of nature in its own right without the slightest intervention by man—a bright blaze of pink when the rosebay willow-herb is flowering, as surely the first flower of the bombed sites as the poppy is the first flower of the newly ploughed chalk lands. I can even see with my own eyes the brick and stone of the rubble being turned into an amor-phous mass as the rain and the frost and, above all, the windborne vegetation, gradually break it up. In such inauspicious surround-ings it is quite a shock to see a few young saplings strong and vigorous in growth, as tall after their ten years' life as they would be if they had been planted in a specially selected site.

So I feel that I am seeing a practical illustration of two major themes of this book—the tangible evidence of man's work in moulding and remoulding the urban landscape, and side by side with this the tendency of nature to re-assert herself wherever she has the opportunity, however unfavourable the terrain, however improbable the result. And what a strange contrast there is be-tween these tiny gardens amid the foundations of bombed build-ings and the planned garden landscapes of the squares nearby—of Red Lion Square, for instance, just across the Theobalds Road, or of Lincoln's Inn Fields a quarter of a mile away where the crocuses by the tennis courts are ever-welcome harbingers of spring and the plane trees minus almost all their bark keep their clusters of fruit into the dullest and greyest of the winter months. One knows that every tree and every shrub has been planted and tended by man. The whole thing is an artificial landscape, carved out of the open fields which until the end of the sixteenth century reached almost to the mediaeval walls of London.

And so one can go on indefinitely reconstructing the history of many ages in this small corner of one big city. In an hour's walk I could see a great deal more that was linked still more clearly with the changing face of the country through the ages. I could walk down Kingsway and cross the Strand, reflecting as I did so how strangely time has used a thoroughfare which started as a track between the gates of the mediaeval city and the Palace of Westminster. Its course was determined by the fact that it was the nearest point to the river which could reasonably be called dry land. It was, literally, the 'strand', a riverside thoroughfare. In my mind's eye, I could visualize its development in the sixteenth and seventeenth centuries until it was lined on one side by fine merchants' houses and on the other by the town estates of the nobility, whose gardens reached down to the brink of the river and to the inevitable water gate where they stepped into their private boats, still in Pepys's time the most usual means of travel- ling from one part of London to another.

Then wandering down some of the side-streets, most of them bear- ing names of people famous in history who had their homes there, I could see the few mutilated Georgian houses which are all that remain of the reconstruction carried out by the Adam brothers, which gave the name Adelphi to an area between the Strand and the river. One might recall the words of John Evelyn, the diarist, describing the entry of the new king, Charles II, into London, when in the Strand 'the windows and balconies were well set with ladies, the streets hung with tapestry, the bells ringing'. That was just ten years before the new Temple Bar was built to the design of Sir Christopher Wren at the point where the end of the Strand marks the beginning of the City, and where it remained until 1878.

Against the background of such memories of long ago the very new stands out with a startling clarity, for the Strand of Queen Victoria's day has suffered much the same fate as the older more historic Strand. The demolition of the Hotel Cecil is within the memory of many Londoners. That great hotel, which claimed to be the finest in Europe, was only built in the last decade of the nineteenth century. After less than forty years it was demolished to make way for the ten-storey building in steel and concrete which is the London headquarters of an oil company as dominant in its own sphere as the building which houses its headquarters staff.

Leaving the Strand, I walk down Savoy Hill to the Embankment looking across the river to the Royal Festival Hall and the utterly new skyline which has appeared between Waterloo and Westminster Bridge since the turn of the century. Then I walk through the Embankment Gardens towards Charing Cross and St James's Park. By that route I pass one of the surviving water gates, that of York House, inscribed with the date 1626, one of the many additions which Inigo Jones, the Renaissance architect of inspiration, made to the London scene. That gate, well below the level of the Embankment Gardens, gives me my bearings, for it marks the point with absolute certainty to which the waterway of the Thames reached at high tide only three hundred years ago. All that I see around me, the pleasant gardens with their lawns and flower beds and statues and, latest addition of all, the bandstand in the modernistic style—all that, and the broad embankment beyond it, stand for the chief theme which runs through the whole of this book, the reclamation of fresh land in spite of nature's will, the remoulding and remodelling of the natural scene by man's work and determination.

Still more of the river's course has been reclaimed on the other bank within the present generation; still more is due to be reclaimed, for instance, in the stretch above Chelsea Bridge, where a wide expanse of mud is exposed at low tide and a strange assembly of boats and junks are moored beside one of the few corners of London which has not yet assumed the new look of the twentieth century.

Continuing my walk past Whitehall Court and Inigo Jones's Banqueting Hall of the Palace of Whitehall, with its window from which Charles I is said to have stepped on to the scaffold erected in Whitehall, I cross the roadway to the Horse Guards Parade and so enter St James's Park. There I am looking at another entirely man-made landscape, in which every single feature is artificial, or rather in which every natural feature is artificially contrived—the arrangement of the trees, the flower beds, the shrubs by the lake and, above all, the lake itself, which was formed by damming up the river Cranbourne, a branch of the Westbourne, which was itself dammed to create the Serpentine in Hyde Park on the order of Queen Caroline, wife of George II.

St James's Park was a swamp which only dried out for a few months in the year until the fifteenth century. Henry VIII had it drained, when he built St James's Palace, and turned the new green meadow into a deer park. More than a century passed before Charles II transformed it into a landscape of flower beds and shady walks, with the help of a famous landscape gardener, Le Nôtre, who had laid out the gardens of Versailles.

So far as the last few centuries are concerned, old prints which can be bought in many of the little shops in the byways of the West End give added point to one's own reconstruction. They often bring to vivid life a picture of which one has oneself only been able to reconstruct the bare outline.

It may be said quite reasonably that the foregoing is an historic tour which could only be undertaken in the centre of Britain's capital city. It is true, of course, that there can be few areas of equal size in the world, let alone in England, which have quite so many historic memories, or show quite so clearly how the landscape has been changing through the centuries. Certainly if one lives in the rather characterless suburbs of the late nineteenth or twentieth centuries, in the distant outskirts of Manchester or Birmingham, or in a Dagenham or a Morden, one will find far less of interest. But there the compensation is that the countryside is much nearer to hand and the open country, as we have seen,

O

wherever it is, however unexciting it may seem, has in it for the imaginative observer all the elements of a drama.

Yet if one lives in a country town, the signs of the times may not be so clearly marked as in London, but they are probably there none the less. Almost all England's country towns are ancient ones which had their origin before the Norman conquest. Starting from the old market centre by the mediaeval church, or, if one is fortunate, by the cathedral, one can mark the outward spread of the town from the time when the church was built to the present day. The different periods of architecture represented in the church itself may give a clue to successive enlargements corresponding with the growth of the town. There will probably be a few old buildings in close proximity to it, with some Georgian houses a little way away, and then farther from the centre the Victorian and later suburbs. There is almost certainly a river nearby, which may have been canalized two hundred years ago, and which, if that is so, has artificially raised banks and flat meadows just outside the town where centuries ago there was only impenetrable swamp. Probably, as in the case of London, old prints are available to show how the place has developed, or perhaps a museum like that of Canterbury, in which successive 'panoramas' of the city provide a speaking commentary on the work of man through many centuries.

When it comes to exploring one's own locality in terms of the open countryside, there is literally no limit to what we shall find, much of it illustrating the various chapters in this book but much, too, that throws other light on the story of the countryside, too local in its import to be described at length in the foregoing chapters. The right attitude is to start out with the eye of a detective, trying to interpret everything that is seen—the woods, coppices, and single standing trees; the wild flowers; the hedges and banks and ditches; the layout of the roads and lanes and footpaths; the banks of the rivers; the nature of the soil and its origin; the farms and farmhouses; the village buildings; and, indeed, every man-made object in the landscape.

Occasionally one will be rewarded with something quite out of the ordinary. I still remember the thrill I felt years ago when, walking over the boggy tableland of the Tweedsmuir Hills, I came upon a little depression, shallow but steep-sided, and there separated by only a few yards I saw one slight but perceptible stream flowing westward from a hidden spring, another, on the other side of the hump, flowing eastward. Each was biting deeper and deeper into the hillside, each making its own channel—one to right, the other to left. In a few years I could see the sources of the two streams would be clearly one, and in a few thousand years there would be a deep valley through which flowed a single river, draining the higher ground to the east and absorbing the spring which at that moment was giving birth to two separate streams. There, I felt, was the most perfect of all examples of nature building the landscape.

The interest of the lowlands is very frequently more sustained even if it cannot from its nature show such highlights as this. Once more, a concrete example will help to show what can be found if one is prepared to search. I lived for a time near Tunbridge Wells on the borders of Kent and Sussex, almost half-way between the rim of the North Downs and the corresponding escarpment of the South Downs. Within easy walking distance (or, for that matter, though for me with less enjoyment, in a single afternoon's car ride), I could find illustrations of almost every phase in the changing landscape, from prehistoric times down to the present day.

First of all, I could see the terrific contrast between the soils that were mainly of sandstone and those of the valleys, which were mainly clay. I could see the sandstone rocks exposed at one point near the Wells and cut through by modern roads and mediaeval sunken lanes in several other phases. I could compare the typical vegetation of the sandy commons and pinewoods of the Royal Broadwater Forest with the lush meadows and deciduous trees of the valleys to the north of the Eden and the Medway, which have been cultivated since Saxon days and show clear evidence of their rapid development in the sixteenth century. On the heights of Ashdown Forest I could find the faint marks of prehistoric entrenchments, one at least pin-pointed by a circle of pine trees planted by romantic antiquaries of the last century. Nearby the skyline has been transformed by the tall masts of a wartime radar station.

The very existence of the prehistoric entrenchments proved to me that what we call Ashdown Forest stood clear of the wealden forest of oak four thousand years ago. That, of course, is what I would have expected, because sandy country is no sort of environment for oak trees, whereas the clay soil of the valleys on either side is ideal.

Wherever I went in those clay valleys I could find no sign of prehistoric man. Even now the valleys look densely wooded from a distance. In fact they still are relatively well afforested, even though no trace of the primeval forest remains. That is a continuing feature of the landscape specially well seen from viewpoints like Camp Hill on Ashdown Forest.

Standing on that high point, I could reconstruct the process by which the chalk dome (which was once overlaid on the whole Weald and linked the scarp of the South Downs with that of the North) was worn away by erosion. As shown in Chapter I, the roads and paths which traverse the Weald from north to south reveal a wonderfully complete cross-section of the various layers of sedimentary rock which were raised up at the same time as the chalk. They show, too, the modifications which the many rivers and streams of the Weald continue to effect by carving out ever deeper valleys for themselves and by carrying rock fragments in suspension from the higher ground to the lower.

The place names of villages and small towns within a few miles of the Wells are clues to the various stages of clearing the forest land in Saxon times and later. Places like Lamberhurst and Ticehurst and Hawkhurst I knew represented early clearings in the forest. I went to visit them and noted their position; I could see just why their sites had been selected by those distant ancestors of ours for special treatment, for they are situated on relatively high ground where the soil is light by comparison with the heavy clays in the troughs of the wider and deeper valleys. Most of the place names in the heavy land, I found, represent later clearings, though considering that the Saxons founded so many villages near the courses of rivers, I could find surprisingly few settlements with Saxon names in the troughs of the deeper valleys such as that of the Rother. Clearly, therefore, that part of the Weald proved especially intractable by comparison, for instance, with the well-settled Eden valley on the other side of the Tunbridge Wells ridge.

It requires no particularly vivid imagination to see in the present appearance of the landscape some carry-over from the distant past —to observe that the valley landscapes of the Weald by Penshurst and Hever are comparatively open, that most of the prosperous farmhouses stand clear among the fields. In the other direction towards the South Downs, by contrast, the ploughland is still in the form of islands in a sea of wooded country, while the many half-timbered or stone-built farms have something of the character of farming outposts in a relatively thinly-peopled country.

A short and exceedingly pleasant footpath walk from Tunbridge Wells would bring me to Tonbridge and one of the most historic fords over the Medway guarded by its Norman castle, which may well have been a castle for a generation or two before the Norman occupation. I could see why this place was a traditional ford in that the valley narrows here, and relatively dry ground is near the river on either side, whereas a few miles farther up and down stream the flat fields bordering the river extend for many hundreds of yards from either bank. Before the river was taught to flow in the channel determined for it by man those fields must have represented impenetrable marshland. I recalled in this connection how difficult the country hereabouts was for the traveller even as late as Tudor times, when Henry VIII found such difficulty in reaching the home of Anne Boleyn at Hever over the waterlogged tracks—and that although Henry was riding on horseback, which was, in fact, the only practical way of negotiating such waterlogged country in the winter months. To revert to a suggestion made earlier, I found some early eighteenth-century prints hung in the public lounge of a Tonbridge hotel which showed conclusively that the castle was the dominant building and that the town grew up literally in its shadow.

Within equally easy distance I could find a typical monastic ruin in Bayham Abbey; a typical manor house in Penshurst Place. I could see the effect of Tudor enclosure in the building of a complete new village at Chiddingstone. I could even on my own doorstep see how Tunbridge Wells, founded almost accidentally as a spa, spread outwards from its centre at the Pantiles and the Pump Room into the ever-growing market centre and dormitory town that it has become. In fact I could find within the limit of a day's walking illustrations of almost every facet of change through the centuries except perhaps of the agrarian revolution carried out by the Georgian enclosure commissioners. The reason why that evidence is not so plain to see as in many other parts of the country is that by the seventeenth century the greater part of Kent and Sussex was already enclosed and there was no room for the complete remoulding of the landscape carried out, for instance, in Bedfordshire or Northamptonshire.

I do not mean to suggest that this fascinating corner of England on the borders of Kent and Sussex is typical of the country as a whole. I do suggest, however, that any other corner of rural England will reveal almost as many interesting associations with the past, though they may be quite different in kind.

Finally, here are a few pointers, a few questions which one may ask oneself when setting out to rediscover one's own neighbourhood:

What is the composition of the soil and the underlying rocks? What signs, if any, are there of the ice age? What developments in nature's moulding of the landscape are still evidently going on? What is the history of the nearest river? Has it ever been canalized? Are its banks clearly artificial? If so, when was it brought under control? Where are the nearest prehistoric monuments? The nearest Iron Age fortified village? What was the country like when those defences were built? Where was the nearest Roman road, town, or villa? What part, if any, did this district play in the organization of Roman Britain? Are the Saxon village names early or late? What reasons led the Saxons to found villages where they did and at the time at which they founded them? Are there any signs of the Norman occupation? What is the history of the nearest castle and abbey? What story can be inferred from the mediaeval churches and their periodic enlarge, ment? Is there any marked local style of church building? If so, does it have a special significance? Is there a nearby mediaeval manor house or farmhouse earlier than the seventeenth century? If so, why were these built and what is their history? What still, present links are there with the various periods of enclosure? What is the origin of the present roads? What signs are there of past differences in the relative proportion of ploughed fields and pasture land? Are there any fields which show the characteristic ridges of early ploughing? If so, in what period was this plough, ing carried out? What signs are there of mediaeval forests? What is the date of the more modern plantations? How far has the in, dustrial development of the last century changed the face of the land? What plans are on foot for the future 'development' of the district? How will it look in twenty years' time?

There is really no end to the number of questions one can ask oneself and certainly no end to the variety of answers possible to these questions. All that is needed is an inquiring mind and real enthusiasm for understanding the country. Therein and in the will to explore on foot lies one of the secrets of perpetual youth.

BIBLIOGRAPHY

For the preceding chapters the principal source books (each of which needs a good deal of interpretation to be intelligible to the present-day reader) are the "Domesday Book", John Leland's *Description of the Realm of England*, William Camden's *Britannia,* Daniel Defoe's *Tour through the Whole Island of Great Britain 1724-7*, and William Cobbett's *Rural Rides,* supplemented by old prints, a few of which are reproduced here, though the vast collection of eighteenth- and nineteenth-century prints in the British Museum furnish a speaking commentary on the changes which have overtaken the landscape during the last 250 years.

Cobbett's *Rural Rides* has been published in full in the Everyman's Library (2 vols., 1912) which also includes Defoe's *Tours Through England and Wales*, with a most helpful introduction by G. D. H. Cole (2 vols., 1928). No such convenient editions exist of Camden or Leland, still less of the "Domesday Book". Camden's *Britannia* was published in Latin in 1586; the standard translation is that of Bishop Gibson, first published in 1695 and reprinted in 1722. The definitive edition of Leland is that by L. T. Smith published in 5 volumes between 1908 and 1910 under the title *The Itinerary of John Leland in or about the years 1535-1543*. As for the "Domesday Book", it is quite useless for anyone but a specialist to attempt to read a detailed transcription of the original. The edition usually quoted is that in 4 volumes by Abraham Farley and Henry Ellis (1783-1816). Of these volumes the first two contain almost all that is relevant to our theme. F.W. Maitland's *Domesday Book* (Cambridge University Press, 1897) is a valuable interpretation of the story that Domesday reveals for the serious student.

E. F. Lincoln's recently published *Story of Canterbury* (Staples Press, 1955) is an admirable commentary on the development through the ages of a typical English town, an inexpensive little book which is clearly and simply written as well as scholarly and authentic in approach. In the same category Brian Vesey-FitzGerald's *Winchester* (Phoenix House, 1953) is strongly recommended. A. Harvey's *Castles and Walled Towns of England* (Methuen, 1911) paints a larger canvas in much less convincing detail. Clive Rouse's *Old Towns of England* (Batsford, revised edition, 1950) is interesting, chiefly on account of its outstanding collection of photographs showing still existing mediaeval features of towns in all parts of the country. The same is true of *The English Abbey* by F. H. Crossley (Batsford, 3rd edition, 1949). Edith Bradley's *Story of the English Abbeys* (Vol. 1, "The

Northern Counties", 1938; Vol. II, "The Eastern Counties", 1939; Robert Hale) is a far more ambitious work which recreates with some success the landscapes and people of pre-Reformation England. *The English Mediaeval Parish Church* by G. H. Cook (Phoenix House, 1954) deals in great detail with the origin and development, both architecturally and socially, of the parish church throughout five centuries. Sidney Toy in his *Castles of Great Britain* (Heinemann, 2nd edition, 1954), though he only sets himself the task of describing the developments in the art of fortification, tells his story effectively against the background of the times.

I have found a great deal relevant to the theme of England's Changing Face in G. M. Trevelyan's *English Social History* (Longmans, 1944), and in Arthur Bryant's *Story of England* (Vol. I, *The Makers of the Realm*, Collins, 1953). L. Dudley Stamp's *Man and the Land* (Collins, 1955) is one of the finest books which this brilliant scholar has written and is particularly valuable in its review of the present and the immediate past. C. S. Orwin's *History of English Farming* (Nelson, 1949) is a small and cheap book, but the best on the subject that I have found. At the other end of the scale is the *Historical Geography of England before A.D. 1800*, a collection of studies edited by H. C. Darby (Cambridge University Press, 1936)—nearly 600 large pages of closely packed, fully documented facts and figures. *The Oxford Dictionary of English Place Names* (3rd edition, 1947) is my constant companion in recreating the early history of English villages and hamlets and of the countryside in which they are set; Sir Banister Fletcher's *History of Architecture on the Comparative Method* (Batsford, 16th edition, 1954) has been equally indispensable in its own sphere.

When we come to books dealing only with limited periods in the story of the countryside, their number is legion. The following are a few (and only a very few) which stand out by contrast with the majority.

For the subject of Chapters I and II, geological time, Walter Shepherd's *Living Landscape of Britain* (Faber, 1952), written primarily for week-end ramblers, though rather expensive, is certainly one of the best. Others strongly recommended are L. Dudley Stamp's *Britain's Structure and Scenery* (Collins, 1946) and A. E. Trueman's *The Scenery of England and Wales* (Gollancz, 1938).

An indispensable book to take further the story of Chapter III—Britain in Prehistoric Times—is *Archaeology in England and Wales 1919-1931*, by T. D. Kendrick and C. F. C. Hawkes (Methuen, 1932). Do not be misled by the dates in the title of this book, for though later research has thrown additional light on some of the topics discussed, very little has been falsified. Another book by C. F. C. Hawkes in association with Jacquetta Hawkes, *Prehistoric Britain* (Chatto and Windus, 1947), is a good popular but less informative account of the subject. The other indispensable book to help the reader bring Prehistoric Britain to life is O. G. S. Crawford's *Archaeology in the Field* (Phoenix House, 1953).

For a reconstruction of Roman Britain I regard *Roman Britain and the English Settlement*, by R. G. Collingwood and J. N. L. Myres (Oxford University Press, 2nd edition, 1937) as by far the best general study available. Ivan Margary's *Roman Roads in Britain* (Phoenix House, 1955), of which I have only seen the first volume, is equally outstanding in its own sphere and also, of course, completely up to date. Among the volumes of the valuable pre-war series of *County Archaeologies* (Methuen) I have found Cecil Curwen's *Sussex* (1937) the most stimulating and constructive.

The mediaeval period is well covered by Marjorie and C. H. B. Quennell's *History of Everyday Things in England*, Vol. I (10th edition, 1941), and *Everyday Life in Anglo-Saxon, Viking, and Norman Times* (Batsford, 3rd edition, 1952). F. M. Stenton's *Anglo-Saxon England* (Oxford) is precise and scholarly, while Arthur Levett's *Studies in Manorial History* (Oxford University Press, 1928) is admirably written and far less forbidding that its title suggests. Thomas Stapleton's translation of *The Ecclesiastical History of the English People* by Saint Bede the Venerable (Burns Oates, 1935) gives many interesting sidelights on the state of the English countryside before the Norman conquest; so to a lesser extent does D. P. Capper's *Vikings of Britain* (Allen and Unwin, 1937). Vol. VII of the Cambridge Medieval History gives a fine picture of pastoral England in the thirteenth century. L. F. Salzman's *English Industries of the Middle Ages* (Oxford University Press, 1923) fills in another corner of the outline.

So far as the early Tudor period is concerned, L. F. Salzman's *England in Tudor Times* (Batsford, 1926) has not yet been superseded. For the later Tudor period A. L. Rowse's *The England of Elizabeth* (Macmillan, 1950) is the most brilliant and the most relevant to our theme of all the books mentioned here. I feel particularly fortunate in having read the first volume (*The Structure of Society*) before writing this book, for it gave me a new perspective on a scene long studied but still in part obscure. Based on the finest traditions of scholarship and compiled from the results of original research in many districts of England, it paints an incomparable portrait of the age in country and town with an insight and interpretative genius matched by no other author.

The literature of the last three centuries in relation to the countryside is unrewarding by comparison. Jack Simmons's Anthology *Journeys in England* (Odhams, 1953) is helpful. Godfrey Davies's study of *The Early Stuarts* (1937) and G. N. Clark's companion work on *The Later Stuarts* (Oxford University Press, 1934) are standard works but not specially illustrative of the Changing Face. For the general reader the Quennell's *History of Everyday Things in England*, Vols. II (10th edition, 1954) and III

(6th edition, 1954) (Batsford) is more illuminating. A vast number of topographical works were published in the eighteenth century, such as Vancouver's *Agriculture of Hampshire* and the same author's *Agriculture of Devonshire*, the two making a most interesting comparison, together with other volumes in the 'General View of Agriculture' series. Unfortunately all are extremely rare. A. Young's *Six Weeks' Tour through the Southern Counties* is rather easier to obtain. Arthur Bryant's *The England of Charles II* (Collins, reprinted 1955) and *The Age of Elegance, 1812-1822* (Collins, 1950) are both fascinating and easily read studies of critical periods in the history of the countryside. John Summerson's *Georgian London* (Pleiades Books, 1946) is the best historical-cum-architectural guide to the changing profile of the metropolis in the eighteenth and early nineteenth centuries. A full and detailed history of the part played by canals in changing the face of England will be found in *British Canals* by Charles Hadfield (Phoenix House, 1950).

Life in town and country in the Victorian era is best inferred from the works of contemporary novelists, especially Charles Dickens, as in *David Copperfield* and *The Pickwick Papers*. William Cowper's *Letters* have many references to the countryside of Olney and the Ouse Valley. Arthur Bryant's *English Saga 1840-1940* (Collins, 1940) is one of the best general surveys of the period, and like all this author's other works shows sympathetic insight into the development of the land as of every other facet of English life.

INDEX

Abbeys, 97, 115 et seq.
Afforestation, 33, 34, 36 et seq., 44. 87,
    88, 101 et seq., 131, 168, 180 et seq.,
    202
Aldeburgh, 17
Alfred, King, 96, 105
Alluvial land, 25, 27, 28
Ambersbury Banks, 103
Anderida (Roman fort), 79
Anderida, Forest of, 33, 44
Angles, 83, 84
Anglo-Saxon England, 78 et seq.
Archaeology, 45, 59, 74
Arden, Forest of, 44
Ashdown Forest, 20, 23, 32, 211, 212
Aston Hall, 147
Audley End, 147
Avebury, 51, 54

Barrows, 51, 52
Basalt, 15
Bath, 77, 167
Bayham Abbey, 214
Beachy Head, 18, 186
Beaulieu Heath, 101
Bedford, Earls of, 139 et seq.
Bedfordshire, 125, 194
Bere, Forest of, 104
Berkshire, 156
Berkshire Downs, 23, 44
Bignor (Roman villa), 72, 73
Birmingham, 133, 150, 165, 177
Black Country, 150, 165
Black Death, 105, 108
Blean, Forest of, 88, 104
Blenheim Palace, 148
Bodmin Moor, 15, 16, 44, 193
Bokerly Dyke, 91
Border Country, 74, 113
Boudicca, 69

Boulder clay, 35
Breckland, 32, 181
Brickfields, 193, 194
Bridges, 74, 164
Brindley, James, 164
Bristol, 150
Bronze Age, 45
Brown, Capability, 121, 148, 192
Buckinghamshire, 125, 172
Building materials, 53, 117, 121, 122,
    157, 175
Burgh Castle, 80
Burghley House, 119
Burial places, Anglo-Saxon, 85
    prehistoric, 51 et seq.

Caesar, Julius, 59, 62
Cambridge, 118
Cambridgeshire, 140, 191
Canals, 162 et seq., 187
Canterbury, 63, 64, 65, 70, 81, 97, 113,
    115, 166, 173, 199
Car Dyke, 76
Caratacus, 69
Castle Cary, 199
Castles, mediaeval, 79, 80, 99, 117,
    122, 147
Caves, 16, 28, 29
Celtic fields, 49
Chalk, 21, 30
Charles I, King, 138
Charnwood Forest, 16
Chedworth, 72
Cheshire, 121
Chester, 74, 77, 150
Chevy Chase, 188
Chichester, 50, 63, 70, 77, 99
Chiddingstone, 124, 199
Chiltern Hills, 23, 34, 44, 86, 133,
    176, 185

Churches, mediaeval, 97, 107, 113, 134
Chute Causeway, 67
Cistercian Order, 100
Claudius, Roman Emperor, 63
Clay, 20, 21, 31 et seq., 211
    boulder, 35
    London, 42
Climate, variations in, 37 et seq., 73, 144, 203
Club mosses, 36
Coal, 38
Coalmining, 165, 193 et seq.
Cobbett, William, 188
Colchester, 63, 64, 65, 69, 178
Compton Wynyates, 121
Cornwall, 88, 102, 113, 136
Cotswold Hills, 34, 35, 72, 107, 113, 114, 121, 133, 160, 175
Cowdray Castle, 120
Cromwell, Oliver, 147
Crowland, 138
Cumberland, 114
Cunobelinus (Cymbeline), 63

Dane John, 55
Danelaw, 96
Danish invasions, 90, 95 et seq.
Dartmoor, 16, 29, 40, 42, 44, 103, 189, 193
Dean, Forest of, 104, 180
Defoe, Daniel, 151
Derby, 96
Derbyshire, 26
Devil's Dyke, 90
Devonshire, 88, 102, 113, 126, 136, 144, 159, 176
Dogger Bank, 43
Domesday, 86, 98, 99
Dorchester, 50, 77
Dorset, 154
Dovedale, 19
Dover, 78, 186
Drilling, 145
Drove Road, 182
Druids, 54

Dunwich, 17
Durham, 99, 177

East Anglia, 35, 79, 85, 96, 105, 107, 113, 122, 125, 178
Ecology, 29 et seq., 35
Elizabeth I, Queen, 119, 138
Elizabethan England, 115 et seq.
Ely, 99, 102, 138
Enclosure, 94, 104 et seq., 110 et seq., 136, 153 et seq.
Enclosure Commissioners, 155
Epping Forrest, 103
Erosion, 17 et seq., 29, 203, 204
Essex, 24, 85, 102, 113, 143, 157, 169, 191, 193
    Forest of, 102 et seq.
Evesham, Vale of, 128
Exmoor, 44, 102, 161, 201

Farmhouses, 122, 136, 143, 157, 168
Fens, drainage of, 131, 137 et seq.
Feudal system, 97 et seq., 108
Fingal's Cave, 16
Flamborough Head, 30, 35
Fleam Dyke, 90
Flints, 30
Forest, mediaeval, 101 et seq.
Forestry: see Afforestation
Forestry Commission, 180
Fossils, 26, 36
Foss Way, 66
Frinton, 176
Furry Dance (Helston), 127

Gardens, 129 et seq., 146, 168
Giant's Causeway, 16
Glaciers, 19, 35, 49, 52
Gloucester, 77
Gloucestershire, 112, 180
Goodwood, 182
Granite, 15
Greenwich Hospital, 147
Grim's Dyke, 90

Haddon Hall, 120
Hadrian's Wall, 75, 80
Halifax, 150
Hampshire, 187
Hampton Court Palace, 117, 130, 147
Hardwick Hall, 119
Hartland Point, 22
Harvest Festival, 128
Haslemere, 176
Hatfield Forest, 104
Hatfield House, 144, 147
Hedges, 156 et seq., 184
Hedingham Castle, 99, 102
Herefordshire, 114, 144
Hereward the Wake, 102
Herstmonceux Castle, 117
Hertfordshire, 146
Hever Castle, 129
Holkham, 161
Holyhead Road, 65
Huntingdonshire, 146

Ice Age, 27, 35, 203
Icknield Way, 48, 66, 85, 86, 193
Iron Age, 41, 45 et seq., 103

James I, King, 138, 144
Jones, Inigo, 147
Jutes, 85

Kent, 77, 85, 88, 105, 107, 113, 124, 128, 143, 157, 169

Lacock, 199
Lake District, 44, 83, 89, 96, 172, 175, 183
Lancashire, 25, 26, 137, 143, 164, 177, 183
Land's End, 16
Latimer, Bishop, 113
Launceston, 102
Layer Marney Towers, 117

Leeds, 165
Leicester, 66, 77, 96, 173
Leicester, Earl of, 161 et seq.
Leicestershire, 125, 154, 159, 169, 179, 193
Letchworth, 176
Limestone, 21 et seq., 31 et seq., 42
Lincoln, 96, 99
Lincolnshire, 137, 140, 142, 191, 201
Liverpool, 150
London, 64, 65, 77, 86, 96, 99, 130, 143, 149, 150, 167, 177, 204 et seq.
Lullingstone, 144
Lulworth Cove, 22
Lyme Regis, 203
Lynchets, 49

Maiden Castle, 56, 57
Malvern Hills, 16, 42, 57
Manor Houses, 107, 109, 120
Marl, 31
Marlborough Downs, 23, 24, 30, 44, 74
Marram grass, 32
Martello towers, 186
Mayday celebrations, 127
Merton, Statute of, 105
Milton Abbas, 149
Monasteries, dissolution of, 115
Morton's Leam, 138

Nains, Richard, 129
Nash, John, 167
Needles, The, 18
New Forest, 32, 100, 103, 188
Newcastle, 74, 165
Newton Ferrers, 176
Norfolk, 85, 140, 145, 161
Norman England, 97 et seq.
North Downs, 23, 129, 182, 211
Northamptonshire, 113, 125, 154, 169
Northumberland, 143, 176, 177, 187, 189
Norwich, 99, 150

Offa's Dyke, 90
Open-field system, 109, 136
Otterburn, 187, 188
Oxford, 118, 174

Pakefield, 17
Palladio, 147
Parks, 130, 146, 168, 180, 192, 197
Parks, National, 172, 194, 198
Peacehaven, 175
Peak Forest, 102
Peat and peat bogs, 40
Pennant, Thomas, 164
Pennine Chain, 20, 24, 28, 34, 40, 51,
    114, 122, 150, 193
Penshurst Place, 107, 214
Pepys, Samuel, 151
Pevensey, 79
Pilgrims Way, 48
Place names, Anglo-Saxon, 85 et seq.
Place names, Celtic, 88, 89
Planning, Town and Country, 196 et
    seq.
Population, estimates of, 47, 75, 81,
    108, 135, 150, 153, 196 et seq.
Portchester, 79
Prehistoric man, 28, 30, 40, 43 et seq.,
    212
Puritan legislation, 127
Pylons (grid), 185

Quarries, 193 et seq.

Railways, 162 et seq., 174
Reclamation (fen and marsh), 131
Reformation, The, 114
Renaissance, 119
Revolution, Agricultural, 144 et seq.,
    153
Revolution, Industrial, 144, 152 et seq.
Richborough, 64, 76, 79
Rievaulx Abbey, 100
Roads, 157 et seq., 174 et seq., 193, 200
Roads, Roman 60–61 (map), 64, 80

Roads, Saxon, 65, 93, 94
Rochester, 64, 99
Rockingham Forest, 104
Rocks, igneous, 15 et seq.
    sedimentary, 20 et seq., 42, 211
Roman Britain, 58 et seq.
Romney Marsh, 76, 113
Rothbury Forest, 104, 189, 193
Royal Society, 145
Rutland, 154
Rye, 25

Saffron Walden, 128, 143
St Albans, 63, 69
St Bede the Venerable, 59
Salisbury Plain, 22, 23, 44, 51, 74,
    187
Sandstone, 21, 30 et seq., 211
Saxons, 83 et seq.
Saxon Shore, Forts of, 79 et seq.
Scott, Reginald, 129
Selborne, 104
Selsey peninsula, 86
Shap Fell, 185
Sheffield, 130, 173
Sheppey, Isle of, 76
Sherwood Forest, 44, 101, 103
Shropshire, 114
Silbury Hill, 55, 67
Silchester, 71
Soil formation, 29 et seq.
Somersetshire, 112, 128, 137
South Downs, 23, 33, 73, 172, 182,
    211
Special Areas, 177
Stamford, 96, 135
Stone Age, 28, 45 et seq.
Stone Circles, 53
Stonehenge, 24, 51, 53
Stowe Park, 148
Stratford on Avon, 144
Suffolk, 85, 113, 128, 157, 184
Surrey, 31, 104, 172, 176, 182
Surveying, Roman, 68
Sussex, 26, 86, 88, 119, 121, 131, 156,
    169, 172, 175

Tacitus, 59
Telford, Thomas, 65, 164
Tenterden, 113
Teynham, 129
Three-field system, 92, 98
Tonbridge, 213
Towns, mediaeval, 96, 166, 210
    Roman, 68 et seq.
Townshend, Viscount, 145
Trackways, ancient, 45, 48, 66
Trees: see Afforestation
Trust, National, 172, 173
Tudor England, 108 et seq.
Tunbridge Wells, 211, 214
Turnpike Acts, 82
Two-field system, 92, 98

Undertakers (in fenlands), 138 et
    seq.

Vanbrugh, Sir John, 148
Vermuyden, Cornelius, 139 et seq.
Verulamium, 64, 69
Vikings, 90
Villa, Roman, 72 et seq., 78
Village, development of, 123 et seq.,
    157, 168, 198
Volcano, 16

Wakehurst, 119
Wansdyke, 90
Warwickshire, 159, 175
Waterfalls, 18
Watling Street, 65, 70, 76
Welwyn Garden City, 176
Wensleydale, 19, 34, 114, 160
Wensum, river, 76, 78
Wentworth Woodhouse, 194
Wessex, 86, 88, 90, 96
Westminster Abbey, 97
Wharfedale, 34, 114, 160
Whinlatter Pass, 183
Whitley Bay, 176
Whittlesey, 141
Wight, Isle of, 85
Winchester, 77, 96
Windmills, 141 et seq.
Windsor Park, 192
Woburn Park, 192
Wolsey, Cardinal, 117, 118
Worle Head, 57
Wren, Sir Christopher, 118, 119, 147
Wychwood, 161
Wycombe, High, 176
Wycombe, West, 199

York, 65, 74, 77, 150
Yorkshire, 100, 114, 150, 164, 177, 198